D0877114

# SPIRITUAL ENCOUNTERS

Interactions between
Christianity and native
religions in colonial America

# SPIRITUAL ENCOUNTERS

## Interactions between Christianity and native religions in colonial America

Edited by
Nicholas Griffiths
and Fernando Cervantes

University of Nebraska Press
Lincoln

Copyright © University of Birmingham Press 1999

While copyright in the volume as a whole is vested in the University of Birmingham Press, copyright in individual chapters belongs to their respective authors, and no chapter may be reproduced wholly or in part without the express permission in writing of both author and publisher.

First published in the United States by the University of Nebraska Press.

First published in the United Kingdom by The University of Birmingham Press, Edgbaston, Birmingham, B15 2TT, UK.

ISBN 0-8032-7081-X

Library of Congress Catalog Card Number: 98-87297

Printed in Great Britain by Alden Press Limited

*In memory of Bob Scribner*

# Contents

# Notes on contributors

LOUISE BURKHART is an Associate Professor in the Departments of Anthropology and Latin American and Caribbean Studies, University at Albany, State University of New York, USA. Her publications include *The Slippery Earth: Nahua–Christian Moral Dialogue in Sixteenth-Century Mexico* (1989), *Holy Wednesday: A Nahua Drama from Early Colonial Mexico* (1996), and the forthcoming *Before Guadalupe: The Virgin Mary in Early Colonial Nahuatl Literature*.

FERNANDO CERVANTES is a Lecturer in Hispanic and Latin American Studies at the University of Bristol, UK. He is the author of *The Devil in the New World. The Impact of Diabolism in New Spain* (1994). He has also published articles on the intellectual, cultural and religious history of Spain and Spanish America.

IRIS GAREIS (MA, PhD, University of Munich, Germany) was awarded the 1997/98 Frobenius Prize, and is currently a Fellow of the Frobenius Institute in Frankfurt (Main), Germany. She also teaches in the department of anthropology, Institut für Historische Ethnologie, Johann Wolfgang Goethe Universität, Frankfurt.

LANCE GRAHN is Associate Professor in the Department of History at Marquette University, USA, and an Associate Member of the Center for Latin America at the University of Wisconsin-Milwaukee. He lectures on the history of Latin America, early modern Spain and the Caribbean, and his publications include *The Political Economy of Smuggling: Regional Informal Economies in Early Bourbon Colombia* (1997) and *La crisis centroamericana: un enfoque cristiano* (1991).

NICHOLAS GRIFFITHS is a Lecturer in Hispanic Studies at the University of Birmingham, UK. He is the author of *The Cross and the Serpent: Religious Repression and Resurgence in Colonial Peru* (1996). He has also published several articles on the interaction of Christianity and Andean religion, and the social history of religion in Spain.

WILLIAM B. HART is Assistant Professor of American History at Middlebury College, Vermont, USA. His research interests include ethnohistory, colonial America, and race and religion in early America. His most recent publication is 'Black "Go-Betweens" and the Mutability of "Race", Status, and Identity on New York's Pre-Revolutionary Frontier' in *Contact Points: American frontiers from the Mohawk Valley to the Mississippi, 1750–1830* (1998).

J. JORGE KLOR DE ALVA is President of the University of Phoenix, USA, and the former Class of 1940 Professor of Comparative Ethnic Studies and Anthropology at the University of California, Berkeley. His interests include historical ethnography, and the comparative study of culture conflict and accommodation; his geographical focus is Mexico, the United States and Europe. His most recent books are *The Americans: Reconstruction Through the Twentieth Century* (forthcoming, 1999) and *Across the Centuries: Middle Ages to Enlightenment* (forthcoming, 1999)

DAVID MURRAY is a Senior Lecturer in American Studies at the University of Nottingham, UK. His research interests include American Indian culture and writing, African-American music, Ezra Pound, Charles Olson, the New York Poets, and literary theory. He is the author of *Forked Tongues: Speech,Writing and Representation in North American Indian Texts*, and editor of *Literary Theory and Poetry: Extending the Canon* (1989) and *American Cultural Critics* (1996).

ALEJANDRA B. OSORIO is a doctoral candidate at the State University of New York at Stony Brook, USA. She is currently finishing her dissertation, 'Inventing Lima: the Making of an Early Modern Colonial Capital, c. 1540–1680'. She has published articles in *Historia y Cultura* and *Allpanchis*.

OSVALDO F. PARDO is Assistant Professor of Spanish at the Department of Modern and Classical Languages of the University of Connecticut, USA. His research interests include colonial Spanish American literature and intellectual history.

CYNTHIA RADDING is Assistant Professor of History at the University of Illinois at Urbana-Champaign, USA. Her current research interests include the ethnohistory of northwest Mexico, environmental history, and ecology and cultural persistence in northwest Mexico and eastern Bolivia during the transition from colonial to national rule. Her publications include *Wandering Peoples: Colonialism, Ethnic Spaces, and Ecological Frontiers in Northwestern Mexico, 1700–1850* (1997) and *Entre el desierto y la sierra. Las naciones O'odham y Tegüima de Sonora, 1530–1840* (1995).

# Introduction

NICHOLAS GRIFFITHS

It is now broadly recognized that the interaction of Christianity
with native American religions in the colonial era (and indeed
subsequently) was characterized by reciprocal, albeit asymmetrical, exchange rather than the unilateral imposition of an uncom-
promising, all-conquering and all-transforming monotheism.[1] Yet
despite the emergence in recent years of a thoughtful and sophisticated literature treating the varied manifestations of these reciprocal spiritual encounters, there has been little attempt to draw
comparisons between different regions of the New World.[2] This
book aims to begin to fill this gap. By adopting a cross-hemispheric approach, and by drawing on the experiences of religious
exchange in the colonial period, principally in hispanophone
America, but also in anglophone and francophone America, it
seeks to open up fresh perspectives and highlight fruitful avenues
for further research.[3] The articles in this volume address themes
that transcend cultural frontiers and illuminate the circumstances
and conditions which determined the form that spiritual encounters took across the hemisphere. What follows in this introduction seeks to outline these common themes and to attempt some
tentative comparisons. It should be stressed that, in a book of this
size, it would be impossible systematically to summarize or cover
all the potential fields of investigation, or indeed to include all
the regions of the hemisphere for which data is available. The
broad sweep of regions included here – Central Peruvian Highlands, New Granada, Central Mexico, Northwestern Mexico, New
France, New England – is not intended to be comprehensive,
but rather representative. Other regions (for example, Portuguese
America) which could have laid equal claim to inclusion, have
been omitted due to constraints on space. The extensive temporal range of the articles (from the sixteenth century through the
eighteenth century) derives in part from the delayed develop-

1

ment of English and French evangelization in comparison with Iberian efforts, but it also reflects a need to appreciate the differential chronological development of certain aspects of spiritual encounters (for example the rejection of Christianity, as late as the eighteenth century, by native groups who found no useful meaning in it). If the articles are characterized by geographical and chronological breadth, they also represent an ample spectrum of interpretations, exploring the full gamut of native responses, emphasizing both, on the one hand, resistance and continuity, and, on the other, accommodation and change. Such an approach reflects the current realization that in the past the loss and destruction involved in the contact between Europeans and natives has been prioritized, in the religious sphere as elsewhere, at the expense of understanding the manifold strategies of adaptation on the part of indigenous communities. These strategies could range from more or less complete acceptance (the rarest response) to resistant adaptation (perhaps the most frequent response) to passive resistance (the now familiar 'weapons of the weak'). (See Scott 1985; 1990.) This volume aims to examine these varied responses in cross-hemispheric perspective.

Recent scholarship has stressed that the concept of 'conversion', with which analyses of religious change in colonial America have traditionally been concerned, is highly problematic, not least because, in so far as it derives from the terminology (and hence the world view) of the original missionaries and clergy themselves, it perpetuates their understanding of the process of religious change as the total and unilateral displacement of native spiritual error by universal religious truth. In the context of Spanish America, but with implications relevant to the entire hemisphere, Nancy Farriss (1984: ch. 10) has highlighted the inadequacy of the old two-tiered model that saw Christianity and indigenous religion as mutually exclusive alternatives from which native peoples had to choose and between which they might switch back and forth. She stresses that the arrival of Christianity led not to a shift from one type of religion to another, nor to the superimposition of the new religion on a pagan base, but rather brought about a set of horizontal, mutual exchanges across three comparable levels. The first level was the macrocosmic, universal, or philosophical sphere, the level of 'official' religion on both sides; the second was the private sphere of 'magic', involving the manipulation of highly discrete and localized supernatural forces for the benefit of the individual and his or her family; and the third or 'middle' level was the corporate sphere of patron deities and saints (still microcosmic because local, but less particularistic than the magical). For Farriss, it was at this corporate or parochial level of religion that the Maya and Spanish systems competed and interacted most directly. This analysis has contributed considerably to replacing the old view of both Christianity and native religions as monolithic and fundamentally separate entities with a new perspective that acknowledges the commensurability of both religious systems and the differential degrees of interaction that occurred at various levels. Farriss's observations have become an important point of reference for scholars working subsequently on religious interaction in colonial Spanish America.

Another related problem with the concept of 'conversion' is that it has tended to encourage scholars to seek a recognizable end-point to religious interaction at which a stable synthesis is presumed to have occurred, often described in the language of 'syncretism'. William Taylor's thoughtful analysis suggests that scholars have hypothesized religious change in Mesoamerica in terms of one of three processes: Christian transformation, 'pagan' resistance, or syncretism. At one pole, exemplified by Robert Ricard's classic study of the 'Spiritual Conquest' (1966), Spaniards, as the active agents of history, are considered to have thoroughly imposed their religion on supine Indian masses; at the other pole, Indians are regarded as having maintained 'a triumphal, idols-behind-altars resistance, only pretending to "convert" to new beliefs'. Between these poles are to be found the multiple 'syncretic' interpretations which emphasize mutual influences and adaptations, generally sharing the view that 'colonial Indian communities independently achieved a more or less full and, by the mid-seventeenth century, stable synthesis, a synthesis in which Christian traits had been absorbed incrementally into native religion'. As a corrective, Taylor cautions against this tendency to seek a stable, 'syncretic' fusion and doubts whether the process of religious change reached an 'end state of completion and wholeness' at all, let alone in the first generations of colonization as some have suggested (Taylor 1996: 51, 52, 53, 59).[4]

Both Taylor's triptych of hypotheses and his caution regarding the search for end-points may also usefully be applied to interpretations of religious change elsewhere in Spanish America. According to Enrique Dussel, the Indian population in colonial Spanish America was in a state of progressive catechumenization, which had been initiated but not completed. The native adoption of Christianity was not superficial, nor in appearance only, but, on the contrary, authentic and substantial; however, the process remained at an intermediate stage. Individuals were to be found on a continuum between the pole of simple initiation and the pole of authentic and conscious faith, in a form of 'chiaroscuro' in which it is impossible to judge where one pole begins and another ends (Dussel 1974: 124-8).[5] The relative positions on this continuum are made easier to conceptualize by Meiklejohn's distinction between evangelization and Christianization. Whereas Christianization denotes the formal, exterior process whereby a non-Christian is brought into the fold (essentially by the instruction which follows baptism), evangelization refers to the internal process whereby a non-believer, or a believer who has only been baptized, becomes immersed in the meaning and values of the religion. For Meiklejohn, there is no doubt that by the end of the sixteenth century almost all Lupaqas in colonial Chucuito had been Christianized, but there is less cause for optimism about their successful evangelization. Consequently, he too counsels against looking for an end-point at which, if ever, the Lupaqas were converted. To the extent that conversion is not just a simple external sociocultural process, but also involves an interior change which affects the fundamental attitudes and behaviour of a person, it is doubtful, for Meiklejohn, that the majority of the Peruvian natives were converted by the early missionaries but rather they may have gradually assimilated and absorbed elements of the faith within the residue of their own religions (Meiklejohn 1988: 248-51). Despite differences in approach, then, much recent work on the issue of conversion in Spanish America shares a common emphasis on processes rather than end-points.

The issue of 'conversion', and above all how one may judge whether a 'genuine conversion' has taken place, has dominated the debate surrounding religious interaction in North America too. With regard to John Eliot's work in New England, Salisbury doubted that Indian neophytes genuinely understood Puritan theology, or that the missionaries expected their Indians' conversions to measure up to those of the English. Those few Indians who converted 'sought to invest the imposed religion with traditional meaning', but in the end were left suspended between two cultures, without a spiritual home or social identity (Salisbury 1974: 49-51).[6] Amongst the French missions in Canada, Jaenen identified less a process of sincere acculturation than the mere addition of Catholicism as a cultural overlay (Jaenen 1976: 66-77). Trigger attributed the apparent inability of the Jesuits to convey an accurate understanding of Christianity to the broader failure to subordinate native peoples to European power, without which Indians stood little chance of grasping the 'meaning and spirit' of Christianity (although it might be noted that the greater imposition of European power in the central regions of Spanish America has not led all observers to attribute greater success to their endeavours). He concluded that many, if not most, of the small number of Indian conversions in the northeast were not made in good faith (Trigger 1985: 294-6).[7] Adding his voice to those of the sceptics, Bitterli (1989: 104) felt that the genuineness of the occasional mass conversions among the Hurons after 1640 was 'a question better left unanswered'.

James Axtell, on the other hand, has challenged the scepticism of these historians and insisted that there were 'bona fide conversions' and that the vast majority of converts kept the new faith (Axtell 1988: 100-21). For him, the missionaries' success is to be attributed to the quality of their preparation for the task of evangelization, the high standards they set (both Puritan and Jesuit) for baptism and church admission, the continuous care with which they nourished their converts, and not least the 'shamanistic' powers which they adopted (for which, see the section on disease and healing below). The misleading suggestion that Indians in the northeast converted because they were forced to take on protective coloration by the harsh realities of imperial subjection simply 'confuses the social functions of conversion for groups with its emotional and intellectual meaning for individuals', and 'confuses the explanation of conversion with the validity or quality of the result' (Axtell 1988: 118-19). Axtell also shrewdly observes that analysis has been hampered by the lack of explicit criteria for judging the success or failure of a missionary programme and a common tendency to assess the mission effort from the perspective of the missionaries (Axtell 1982: 35-41). He suggests that a different, more meaningful, measure of success may be attained by asking whether the Indians from their point of view were successful or not in adopting or adapting Christianity. It is clear, for instance, that some Indians converted to Christianity because it provided a better answer to the urgent social and religious questions that they were facing at that particular juncture in their cultural history. Rather than achieving a nativistic revitalization at the hands of a charismatic prophet, the Indians of the praying towns of New England used the religion of Christ to the same end.[8] Even though it entailed wholesale cultural changes from the life they had known before, it preserved their ethnic identity as particular Indian groups on familiar pieces of land. Hence, for Axtell, the fact of ethnic survival is all-important in assessing the success or failure of mission efforts from the native perspective.[9]

Adopting similar criteria, others have agreed that individual Indians were capable of converting to Christianity in good faith. In his study of New France, John Webster Grant suggests that many Indians, though certainly not all, were receptive to the solutions offered by the new religion and were capable of taking the decisive step from their old religions to the new, without deceiving either themselves or the missionaries. He points out that since the Indians were under no direct compulsion to embrace Christianity (unlike in Spanish America), there could have been no native Christian communities unless they had voluntarily converted themselves. It is significant that some conversions took place in distinctively Indian ways. For example, it was through dreams that many became Christian. Native willingness to respond to Christianity was genuine but conducted on its own terms; conversion represented not so much a rejection of the old way as a conviction that Christianity offered more powerful *mana* (spiritual power) for a changed situation. Uniquely equipped to make sense of an unexpectedly expanding new cosmos, Christianity offered a means of reintegrating societies in which old standards had broken down. Thus, conversion was essentially 'a phenomenon of the moon of wintertime, when ancestral spirits had ceased to perform their expected functions satisfactorily and angel choirs promised to fill a spiritual vacuum' (Grant 1984: 44, 239–41, 244–5).[10]

Grant invites us to dwell on the many potential responses of native peoples to Christianity. Although many Indian Christians were clearly breaking with the past, it is also possible that others were not so much engaging in rebellion against their traditional ways as seeking in Christianity opportunities to supplement them. Then again, for many, perhaps most, the profession of Christianity may have been a subtle but effective way of rejecting it, or what Grant has termed 'a "yes" that means "no"'. Since apparent agreement may conceal fundamental differences of understanding, an Indian who sincerely accepted everything the missionaries said might also interpret what he heard in terms of presuppositions at odds with those of the missionaries.[11] Although such a response raises doubts once again about the quality of Indian conversions, Grant suggests that it may not be so incompatible with genuine adherence to Christianity as it appears, and prompts us to ask: 'Was it always Christianity itself to which their yes meant no, or could it sometimes have been the frame in which it was mounted?' (Grant 1984: 249–51). It might be argued, after all, that Christianity has not really taken root in a community until it has fused with its culture sufficiently to make possible its appropriation in distinctively indigenous ways and on terms consonant with native modes of thought and relevant to perceived needs (Grant 1984: 247, 263).

One of the principal purposes of the articles presented in this volume is to explore the manifold potential responses to Christianity indicated above, the complexity and variety of which has often been obscured in the past by the tendency (already noted) to conceptualize religious change according to the Christian rhetoric of 'conversion' and to accept its implicit assumption that the arrival of Christianity involved a one-way process whereby supine native religions were totally transformed by a more active, dynamic force. A salient theme of the research offered here is that spiritual encounters in colonial America were characterized by reciprocal interaction down a two-way street, in which there was less 'conversion' than 'conversation'.[12] David Murray demonstrates in this volume that the Christian ideal of the 'unilateral gift' which would 'replace or transform what was there before, in a one-way transmission' was, in fact, subverted by an actual process of reciprocity, conscious or unconscious, which asserted itself despite the professed intentions of churchmen and missionaries. In their endeavours to erect bridges between the two religions, Christians inadvertently compromised their message and – however inad-

missible and (consciously, at least) unthinkable such a phenomenon might be – allowed some adaptation to take place on their
side.

Such adaptation went beyond the mere recognition and exploitation of compatibilities between native spirituality and Christianity, or the benevolent tolerance of aspects of native culture
which did not directly contradict the faith. The search by Franciscan missionaries in sixteenth-century Central Mexico for points
of similarity between Mesoamerican religion and their own (for
example the association of Mesoamerican deities and Catholic
saints, or the parallels between certain Mesoamerican rituals and
the sacraments of baptism, confession and communion), or the
concessions to indigenous cultural values made by seventeenth-
century Jesuit priests among the Hurons (by allowing chants in
the native tongue or by turning a blind eye to certain burial customs) did not represent the limit, nor even the most significant
aspect, of Christian adaptation.[13] Indeed, the extent of adaptation in Central Mexico was such that scholars have spoken of the
'Nahuatlization' of Christianity.[14] Louise Burkhart's work on the
corpus of Christian doctrinal literature in Nahuatl and other
Mesoamerican languages has shown how, in their efforts to seek
the closest parallels for Christian concepts in order the more readily to slip them into the native spiritual consciousness, the Franciscan friars were obliged to accommodate their teachings to native thought categories to a greater degree than they or their
apologists dared to admit, and even greater than they may have
realized.[15] Developing the concept of the 'dialogical frontier' (a
term adopted from D. Tedlock) – that is to say, the liminal zone
where Nahua thought categories were synthesized with Christian
ideology – Burkhart demonstrates how, by allowing Christian
doctrine to be shaped by Nahuatl terminology, the friars inadvertently fostered the retention of much indigenous belief within
what was essentially a colonial Nahuatl interpretation of Christianity.[16] The most significant consequence was that Christian doctrine, as the friars presented it, contained many elements which
the Indians could easily interpret in their own terms and use to
reinforce their own beliefs. In this way, the friars ensured that
Christianity in some form would be adopted, but at the same
time they inadvertently aided their subjects' struggle for cultural
survival.

Certain genres of religious literature translated into the Na-huatl language acted both as vehicles for the transmission of Christian concepts and figures, and as a means whereby natives could reinterpret these figures in ways which were meaningful to them. In this volume, Burkhart explores how the Virgin Mary was represented to the Nahuas in late sixteenth-century miracle narratives (a brief account of a miraculous deed executed by Christ, or a saint, on behalf of a devotee), the extent to which the natives' understanding of Mary was conditioned by such texts, and the adaptations to which the narratives were subjected for indigenous purposes, in ways that both bolstered and subverted Christian authority. On the one hand, Mary was portrayed as far less capricious and far more indulgent than preconquest deities. The fact that marvels occurred in answer to prayers without the accompanying ritual offerings or penitential precautions which were so central to preconquest encounters with the deities indicated that the friars' goal of undermining kinship and community bonds in order to promote a more individualized and personalized identity had been advanced. On the other hand, by conveying the impression that Mary possessed personal power in her own right, over and above her appeals to God, and by not explicitly repudiating the belief that devotion to Mary could ensure salvation, these narratives encouraged Christian Nahuas to construct their own religious concepts which remained outside the control of the priesthood and church officials and continued to maintain a dialogue with ancient pre-Columbian forms of the supernatural.[17] Such a phenomenon is a fine illustration of Murray's observation in this volume that the missionaries could not control the meanings of what they gave or introduced; once religious concepts or entities entered into circulation, they could not from that point onwards be restricted or authorized only by their Christian origins.

The point is demonstrated in a different but comparable context by William Hart's article here, which shows that the indigenous reinterpretation of the significance of the Virgin Mary enabled her to play a special role as a bridge or gateway between Christianity and native religion for converts among the Hurons and Iroquois in seventeenth-century New France. The assimilation of the Virgin Mary to the Sky Woman's daughter (the mother of Huron and Iroquois humankind, who was mysteriously impregnated by a divine being and gave birth to twin sons while remaining a virgin) is a good illustration of how, as in Mexico, the 'blessed Virgin' was assigned new meanings and thereby accommodated within native traditions. Hart suggests that native converts were able to define Mary in both Catholic and Huron or Iroquois ways at the same time. For example, she was seen to act both as an intercessor, in the orthodox Christian manner, and also, in traditional native terms, as an *orenda*, or spirit, who could be supplicated and whose power was accessible to meet indigenous needs. Like Burkhart for Central Mexico, Hart finds among the Hurons and Iroquois new possibilities for redefining native religious identity or for reinforcing existing definitions by means of creative readings of a 'usable' Virgin Mary.

Moving beyond the comparisons that may be made between native appropriations of the Virgin Mary, there are two aspects of spiritual exchange between Christians and Nahuas which have direct relevance to encounters throughout America. The first is that priests and missionaries in other regions also adapted Christianity to indigenous religious concepts. In seeking to convert Algonquians in northeastern North America by attacking native beliefs, Jesuit missionaries, for tactical reasons, often themselves accepted native premises. For example, their ridicule of the *manitous* ('spiritually powerful men' or 'spiritual beings' capable of taking manifold physical forms) was overtly conceived in Algonquian terms. Missionaries often did not challenge the native logic of why fish or game appeared or failed to appear, but instead they denied credit to the *manitous* and gave it to Christ. Heads of animals once offered to the *manitous* at feasts were now offered to Christ, and public offerings were made to the cross and to the Christian god, dubbed the 'Great Manitou'. Adaptation was so considerable that, according to one scholar, 'Indians were not so much being converted to Christianity as Christ was being converted into a *manitou*' (White 1991: 26, 27). Another scholar has suggested that 'study of the Martha's Vineyard faithful reveals Christianity Indianized as well as Indians Christianized' (Ronda 1981: 371).[18] Although on a conceptually less sophisticated scale, this would appear to be comparable to the process of Nahuatlization noted for Mexico.

Closely related to the first, the second aspect of spiritual exchange in Central Mexico which is pertinent to experience elsewhere is that Christian teaching was effective only to the extent that it was compatible – or appeared in translation to be compatible – with pre-existing belief and practice.[19] It was invariably the case that the new religion could be made meaningful only if it continued to be experienced more within the continuum of the familiar than as a sharp break with it (Klor de Alva 1993: 175,180).[20] Christian concepts were generally accepted only in so far as they could be molded to fit indigenous ones. In her study here of mission communities in northwestern New Spain, Cynthia Radding explores how indigenous peoples appropriated Christian symbols – such as the cross, the rosary, and personalized saints – in order to give renewed expression to ancient understandings of the relationship between human and cosmic forces. Thus, piles of stones along roadways that invoked the protection of spiritual powers for travellers and pilgrims were often crowned with simple crosses; and young men who became disturbed after experiencing visions while out in the wilds were restored to sanity by wearing a rosary. Christian symbols served, in this context, to link individuals to pre-existing loci of spiritual power. (Radding stresses, it may be noted in passing, that this process was part of a duality of adaptation and defiance, since Christian symbols could be seized and overthrown as well as appropriated, and religious icons could themselves become the focal points of rebellion, both military and spiritual.) Elsewhere, the priority of the indigenous religious matrix was reaffirmed when the Christian sacrament of baptism was interpreted as a curing ritual. The natives of Martha's Vineyard accepted baptism as preventive medicine and many Hurons regarded the sacrament as a talismanic aid in order to ward off disease (Bowden 1981: 81, 89, 123; Trigger 1985: 201; Ronda 1977: 72). Similarly, the Jesuits' claim that baptized Hurons went to heaven rather than to the traditional villages of the dead fitted native belief in the separation of the souls of people who died at different stages of their life or in different ways (Trigger 1985: 252).

As Robert Hefner has noted, the doctrines and meanings formalized in religious canons may, in fact, have little to do with believers' motives for embracing them (Hefner 1993: 16). Indeed spiritual motives may have played less of a role in the apparent acceptance of Christianity than economic or political motives. The Jesuit Father Biard noted that the converts among the Acadian Micmac 'accepted baptism as a sort of sacred pledge of friendship and alliance with the French' but had no notion of its deeper theological meaning (Salisbury 1982: 73).[21] Similarly, the Hurons seem to have interpreted baptism as a token of alliance with the French rather than a commitment to abandon traditional religious practices (Trigger 1985: 201). It is also important not to underestimate the desire to gain access to European technology and trade as a motive for embracing Christianity. The special perquisites given to Christian traders persuaded many Hurons to adopt Christianity or tolerate the presence of missionaries for mercantile advantage (Bowden 1981: 88). Thus, Huron chiefs and leading traders consistently protected the Jesuits and prevented their communities from wreaking revenge for supposed witchcraft at least in part because the Hurons had no other source of European goods than from the French (Trigger 1985: 247).[22] The motives of the Tarahumaras (Chihuahua, Northern Mexico) for requesting the presence of Jesuit missionaries among them from the early seventeenth century were typical of many native peoples, in that religious teachings were far less important than three other motives: to gain access to the priests' supernatural power, especially for curing the Old World diseases; to seek protection against military conquest, enslavement and encroachment by non-Indian settlers; and to acquire European goods, either directly from the missionaries or indirectly through trading with or working for the non-Indian settlers, to whom the missions offered them greater access (Merrill 1993: 138).[23] In his article in this volume, Lance Grahn demonstrates that those Guajiro peoples of northern New Granada who adopted mission life did so for what they perceived to be its relatively greater economic security rather than for cosmological reasons. And David Murray investigates here how far the translation and propagation of the Christian message involved mixed messages, whether wittingly or unwittingly abetted by missionaries, about the material benefits that would accrue. The significance attributed to the prayer 'Give us today our food' might have owed as much to the strong spiritual connections of food and feasting in Huron culture as to faithful native understanding of the missionaries' message when they taught the prayer, suggesting once again how the most fundamental aspects of Christianity were interpreted according to the native world view.

The weighing of Christianity on native terms might lead to its rejection rather than its acceptance. Here Lance Grahn argues that, in many non-core regions of Hispanic America, despite

European economic, technological, political and even religious benefits, Christianity did not, in the main, displace native beliefs and mores and the main impact of missionization was to deepen native religion. He concludes that 'Indian values won; European religious values lost'. Thus, for example, the Tepehuan Indians in seventeenth-century Nueva Vizcaya rejected Jesuit teachings since they were incomprehensible and failed the test of practical utility. Similarly, the Pueblo Indians of New Mexico renounced the validity of Christianity when it became clear that the Christian world view could not guarantee good harvests and freedom from disease. Elsewhere, the Cuna Indians of Darién (northern New Granada) opted not to change their religious allegiance on account of Christianity's failure to furnish a better explanation of the world. Although a few leaders of the Guajiro saw in the missions potential economic gain and judged direct contact with Christianity to be a useful tool, the majority rejected the new religion because it threatened broader indigenous economic opportunities. Grahn suggests that religious motivation went only as far as economic and political self-interest dictated. Even the Guajiros' economic adaptations to European imperialism demonstrated their continuing control over their own lives in that they could fully incorporate commercial pastoralism into their culture and society even as they steadfastly refused to accept fully the religion of their trading partners. The refusal to incorporate Christianity within their religious lives shows that native peoples retained their persistent spiritual and religious agency and remained in charge of their own religious fate.[24]

This emphasis on native agency is echoed in research in other areas of Hispanic America. According to Merrill, the response of the Tarahumaras to the colonial Jesuit mission programme was not uniform but varied according to time, place and different components of the programme. The Indians responded most positively to mission formation and baptism during times of crises, when the advantages of the mission programme appeared to outweigh the disadvantages. Epidemics in the early 1600s and 1670s apparently motivated some Indians in the Lower and Upper Tarahumara areas respectively to request missionaries in the belief that they could cure the diseases. Similarly, encroaching Spanish settlement in the Lower Tarahumara region in the 1640s and fear of the Spanish military in the Upper Tarahumara region after the revolts of the 1690s seem to have encouraged Indians in these areas to seek the protection of the mission system. In the absence of such adverse conditions, the Indians were more reluctant to enter the mission system, leading Merrill to conclude that to a considerable extent the Tarahumaras controlled the conversion process (Merrill 1993: 131, 138, 141). The focus on Indian agents as the major determinant of religious change and conversion is also an important characteristic of the new mission history. Thus, the nature of the Indian society that came into contact with Europeans – whether sedentary, semi-sedentary, or non-sedentary, whether located in the temperate zones or the tropics, the relative accessibility to penetration by European settlers – and the circumstances in which that contact took place may be more significant than, for example, the methodology employed by different missionaries.[25] As Eric Van Young has stressed, it is important to remember that the successes of missionaries do not occur *ex nihilo* but within an already existing cultural matrix into which the missionary enterprise is injected (Eric Van Young 1989: 94).[26]

# Disease and healing

One crucial arena for negotiation and 'dialogue' between Christianity and indigenous religions was the interpretation of the spiritual significance of disease and the effectiveness of measures to counter it. In colonial Spanish America, Christians responded with considerable ambivalence to the direct challenge posed to their authority by the cures of native medical practitioners. On the one hand, in order to loosen the thrall in which they held indigenous communities, native healers were to be discredited and exposed as frauds and tricksters (see the articles by Griffiths and Pardo in this volume).[27] On the other hand, the genuine efficacy of much native medicine could not be denied and was attributed by Spanish churchmen and theologians either to natural causes (since they were aware of the superior knowledge of natives regarding the natural properties of herbs and plants) or to demonic intervention. However, ultimately, as Griffiths demonstrates in this volume, neither cause offered a satisfactory rationalization for native cures since both effectively conferred too much power on indigenous healers. This tension, never effectively resolved in the Hispanic world, appears to have arisen elsewhere in colonial America. In New France, Grant detects a similar quandary for priests in deciding whether shamans (specialists in direct confrontation with the supernatural world) were mere charlatans or had some access to demonic power (Grant 1984: 44). The recourse to judicial process in Spanish America in order to control recalcitrant offenders may create the impression of greater credulity in the Hispanic world than was in fact the case. Despite employing the accusation of a pact with the devil as a legal framework and justification for prosecution and punishment, in practice Spaniards were more inclined to regard native healers as fraudulent. To what degree were missionaries and theologians in New England and New France more credulous than their counterparts in the Hispanic world? How typical was Puritan Edward Winslow in his belief that the *pow-wows* often successfully cured their patients with the aid of the devil, and that the *pnieses* invoked Satan when they called upon and visualized Hobbamock (a spirit who cured wounds and diseases) (Salisbury 1982: 137)? A detailed comparison across America would shed interesting light on an important conceptual interaction in the spiritual realm.

Paradoxically, the determination to demonstrate the superior effectiveness of Christian healing and other magical techniques, common to priests and missionaries across the hemisphere, implicitly acknowledged the claim to genuine supernatural powers on the part of the very native specialists whom they wished to outwit, and illustrates once again that Europeans were prepared to move onto indigenous ground in order to make Christianity fit native expectations. Murray, in this volume, reminds us of the irony of the missionary who sought to play the role of the 'juggler' or shaman he was trying to discredit. The role of the Jesuit priest in Mexico in interpreting visions experienced by native neophytes and acting as the mediator between the Indian and the supernatural has led historian Serge Gruzinski to remark 'comme il y a le chaman, il y a le jésuite', and to suggest that, in so far as the Jesuit sought to demonstrate a greater competence than that of the native specialist, he implicitly conceded that the battle was to be fought on the latter's own territory and therefore had to some extent become incorporated (or acculturated) into the native conceptual system (Gruzinski 1974: 465, 473). The Jesuits in North America seem not only to have passively tolerated native

15

perception of them as equivalents of traditional shamans but to have actively encouraged the association as a means of supplanting their rivals for the Indians' allegiance by defeating them in their own domain.[28] They conformed to native expectations of spiritually powerful men, not only as purveyors of European technological superiority in tools and weapons, but also as bearers of new knowledge such as the ability to predict eclipses, explain the action of the moon upon the tides, and 'read minds at a distance' from the pages of a book (Axtell 1992: 160; 1985: 101; Richter 1992: 112–13). They were not above conducting rain ceremonies in order to prove that the true God would answer their prayers for rain; Father Jean de Brébeuf's success as a rain-maker played no small part in the reputation he gained among the Hurons for his shamanistic skills (Bowden 1981: 80; Trigger 1985: 202, 252). The Indians also ascribed to the missionaries powers to which they did not lay claim but which had been the preserve of traditional shamans, such as the ability to prophesy the whereabouts and number of game (Conkling 1974: 15). Furthermore, the Jesuits were understood to possess double-edged spiritual power which could be malevolent as well as benevolent; their 'talking papers' and rites of baptism were often blamed for epidemics (Axtell 1988: 91; Trigger 1985: 246; Bowden 1981: 77; Richter 1985: 5, 6; 1992: 107; Dennis 1993: 92; Morrison 1990: 419–20; Ronda 1977: 72). It is well known that the demonstration of extraordinary supernatural power on the part of Christian priests led them to be assimilated to the concept of *manitou* throughout the Algonquian-speaking world of central and eastern North America (Axtell 1985: 10, 17, 77; Salisbury 1982: 37, 39; White 1991: 25). The danger of such a strategy, as Pardo stresses in this volume, was that, for Indians accustomed to the concept of the spiritual force of healers, the attempt by the Christian priest to outshine his native equivalent might not prove the invincible power of Christianity but rather a more personal feature of the priest.[29] Consequently, as Axtell has suggested, the latter would be regarded not as a mere intermediary whose only strength lay in supplication and explanation, but, in the way of a native shaman, as the possessor of a personal supernatural power that allowed him to manipulate the spiritual world (Axtell 1985: 17 and 77).[30]

Although the donning of the mantle of shaman compromised the integrity of Christian teachings on the function of the priest, it may also have been one of the most potent factors in drawing the Indians to the new faith. Robert Conkling has argued that the *legitimation* of Christian beliefs (as opposed merely to their *imposition*) among the northeastern Algonquian in Maine and the Maritime provinces in the seventeenth and eighteenth centuries may be attributed to the acquisition by French priests of the charismatic status of the shaman in contests with him (Conkling 1974: 1-24). The missionaries, in their efforts to discredit the Indian shamans, took on the special 'strange and extraordinary cast' of a typical charismatic leader; on the basis of this newly acquired authority, they were able to usurp the positions of the shaman-*sagamores* and persuade at least some of the Indians to transfer their allegiance from the latter to themselves. As a result, they were the major instigators of a genuine charismatic Christian movement which, at the same time, incarnated an authentic regeneration of the aboriginal religious system. The power of the missionaries was conceded by the Indians because the priests met the native idea of charismatic qualification for an authoritative role in indigenous society. It is this, according to Conkling, which explains the profound conversions of many of these Indians, who remain steadfast Catholics today. In this way, the mantle of shaman, precisely because it conceded so much to native spiritual realities, may have helped to produce genuine conversions. Similarly, Axtell attributes the great successes of the Jesuits of New France (measured by the thousands of *bona fide* converts they were able to bring into the fold before 1763 in comparison with their English Protestant rivals and their Catholic rivals in Canada and Louisiana) in large part to their ability to become accepted as the social and spiritual equivalent of the shamans they were trying to supplant. As Murray observes in this volume, the greater use of ritual and ritual objects on the part of Catholics made them seem more like shamans than their Protestant counterparts. The Puritans, for example, made little use of the compatibilities that existed between the native religion and their own. Rather than emphasizing common ideas or encouraging Indians to use them as bridges for crossing over to Christianity, they chose rather to heighten the contrast between Indian religiosity and their own by denouncing all pre-contact activity as devil worship (Bowden 1981: 122). Axtell observes that Puritan missionaries were also more 'culturally inflexible' and were incapable of assuming the role of shaman for purposes of infiltrating native society; instead they sought to destroy it (Axtell 1988: 84, 95, 98). [31]

Although native shamans among Indians of francophone and anglophone America were not rendered utterly impotent by their Christian rivals, they were generally not strong enough to resist the missionaries in the long run.[32] Hispanic America seems to offer a marked contrast, since here native healers played a central role in the accommodation of Christianity to native religions. As Griffiths, Pardo and Osorio show in this volume, one principal function of native healers was to forge a meaningful relationship between indigenous and Christian supernatural power. Pardo highlights the 'urgent preoccupation' of native healers with 'the need to build authority and legitimacy in a context in which both Nahua and Christian beliefs and practices were still redefining their boundaries'. Similarly, Griffiths demonstrates for the Andean region how one healer sought to legitimize his healing skills by means of the sanction of Christian authority and thereby 'articulate a new hierarchy which set the two religious traditions in a logical relationship to each other, not as antagonistic and contradictory systems but as complementary and mutually sustaining parts of a greater supernatural whole'. In this way, healers maintained dialogue with the native supernatural world, a dialogue, furthermore, which they continued to interpret according to indigenous criteria. Thus, they not only functioned as a bridge between elements of two healing traditions, aiding the slippage of Christian elements into the native repertoire, in what Osorio calls 'an irrepressible process of transculturation', but they also served as synthesizers of those elements into a coherent new system.

## The role of coercion

Coercion played a much more central role in the evangelization of Hispanic America than it did in North America. To some extent, the explanation is to be found in the diverse chronologies of expansion and in the different relationship that prevailed between church and state. In Spanish (and Portuguese) America, missionary policy was to a greater extent determined by the needs of state. Here the crown favoured rapid evangelization and forced conversion if need be, whereas the church adhered – in principle, if not always in practice, as will be explained below – to the idea that baptism must be voluntary. The rapidity of the Iberian military conquest was followed by the equally swift establishment of an official church hierarchy. By papal authority, the kings of Castile had been granted sole responsibility for the evangelization of the Indies; the *patronato real* (royal patronage) of 1508 also gave the crown control over ecclesiastical appointments and financial matters relating to the church in America. Consequently, the Spanish monarchy maintained a deep commitment to rapid evangelization of the indigenous population since it constituted an important justification for Spanish rule in America. The Portuguese crown exercised similar privileges to those of the Spanish crown by means of the *padroado* of 1514, although Portuguese kings were slower to assert their authority in America, largely because of Brazil's limited wealth and smaller indigenous populations. By contrast with Iberian America, in what would become French and British America, evangelization was not conducted principally as a state-backed enterprise through patronage conferred by the Pope; in areas evangelized by Catholics, native populations remained under the direct spiritual jurisdiction of the papacy, and responsibility for conversion and Christian instruction fell on missionary orders acting independently of the state. Furthermore, no systematic attempts to convert the Indians were implemented before the early seventeenth century nor was any action taken to impose institutional authority or establish an official church hierarchy until the mid-seventeenth century in either New France or British America. In the absence of any significant intervention on the part of the French crown, the Jesuits carried out the colonization of New France almost by themselves. And at least by the end of the 1660s, the spiritual well-being of the Indians had ceased to be the focus of religious interest in the New World for the church authorities. Thus, whereas in Iberian America, evangelization was, from the beginning, an integral part of the process of conquest and settlement, in French and British America, on the other hand, the crown regarded the process of conversion as an ancillary part of its presence. The contrast between the uniformity of Iberian

Catholicism and the diversity of Protestant British America was also stark (McAlister 1984: 194-6, 285; Codignola 1994: 35-7; 1995: 199-203, 208, 211; Burkholder & Johnson 1990: 83-96).[33]

Even so, the use of coercion in Spanish America cannot be attributed solely to the role of the state; its origins must also be sought within the church and the religious orders themselves. The early ideal of conversion by the power of the word and the infectiousness of example, so characteristic of the first Franciscan missionaries who arrived in New Spain in the 1520s, was soon displaced by the reality of the necessity of physical coercion (Clendinnen1982; 1987a). Submission to baptism might remain strictly speaking a voluntary act, but Indians could be compelled to abide by their faith once it had been avowed. Confidence in the effectiveness of violent compulsion and strict punishment originated in what historian Inga Clendinnen has called the 'paternalist metaphor of authority', whereby Indians were perceived as children entrusted to the care of benevolent fathers for instruction but also chastisement when necessary (Clendinnen 1982: 41). The most famous advocate of this approach, Franciscan Provincial Diego de Landa, presided over the indiscriminate application of torture to more than 4500 Indians and the deaths of more than 150 victims under interrogation, during the course of idolatry trials in the Yucatan in the 1560s (Clendinnen 1982: 46; 1987a: 83). In the absence of permanent ecclesiastical and lay authority, inquisitorial powers were invested in the Provincial, but the willingness and determination to use them in such a brutal way derived from the Franciscan understanding of their role, not simply from the force of the state. Despite the fierce controversy that Landa's actions provoked, the use of force was not repudiated but, on the contrary, became integrated into the standard repertoire of missionary strategies used by the Franciscans, by members of other orders and by secular clerics (Clendinnen 1982: 29-30). Missionaries in the field were henceforth entitled to call on the secular arm in order to compel the Indians to attend to their message. Nor did Franciscan excesses lead to a rejection of the recourse to judicial process as a means of rooting out 'idolatries' (as Spaniards labelled manifestations of native religion). It is true that the inquisitorial model which Landa had employed was repudiated in so far as it related to the Indians. As is well known, the Landa trials were crucial in the decision of the crown to exclude the native population from the jurisdiction of the Inquisition when the tribunal was established in Mexico and Lima in 1571 (Clendinnen 1987a: 109).[34] However, idolatries remained a judicial offence. The obligation to investigate, try and punish offenders was transferred to episcopal jurisdiction through the office of the *provisor* (vicar general) which was by no means inactive in this field in the sixteenth and seventeenth centuries.[35] Even if the ultimate sanction – the death penalty – was not to be countenanced, strict punishment remained an appropriate response (Clendinnen 1982: 29, 33, 34).

In the Andes too, the initial model of conversion by persuasion implemented by missionaries such as Domingo de Santo Tomás in the early decades of evangelization was supplanted by an ever-increasing insistence on authority and religious coercion. Sabine MacCormack has stressed that most missionary campaigns began with acts of violence, even if, overtly, coercion was employed only to bring about abandonment of old beliefs and not the adoption of Christianity. The native acceptance of baptism was anchored in the exercise of authority and force and thus precluded real inner assent (MacCormack 1985: 446, 451, 454, 455).[36] But, whereas in Mexico the greatest use of force was expended in the first forty years or so after the conquest and subsided in the second half of the sixteenth century and the seventeenth century, in the Andes, by contrast, the destruction of the material representations of native religions and the punishment of offenders proceeded intermittently throughout the sixteenth century and only gathered ever-accelerating momentum in the seventeenth century.[37] In the early and mid-seventeenth century, successive Archbishops of Lima unleashed the quasi-inquisitorial judicial process traditionally termed the Extirpation of Idolatry, which became the most systematic and sustained attempt to obliterate colonial Indian religious deviance ever seen in Peru or any other part of colonial Spanish America.[38] As Gareis demonstrates in this volume, the eradication of native religions was considered a necessary pre-condition for the successful Christianization of the Andeans. Although the Extirpation professed a didactic as much as a corrective or punitive purpose and incorporated programmes of instruction in Christian doctrine, these were consistently overshadowed by coercive actions (Mills 1997: 267). The use of violence to repress native religions echoed the employment of punitive strategies by Dominican friars in the initial evangelization of Peru which had itself been more superficial and cursory than in Central Mexico (Meiklejohn 1988: 44).[39] The conviction that violence on Indian bodies was justified by the need to preserve Indian souls remained a controversial but enduring facet of the debate about the best means to correct persisting native religious deviance in colonial Spanish America.

Such systematic, organized campaigns of violence in pursuit of religious objectives were not found in North America, nor were coercion and punishment such ready weapons in the armoury of missionaries. The acute vulnerability of almost all missionaries in North America, who were greatly outnumbered and who generally worked without the ability to call upon the secular arm, obliged them to rely less upon compulsion and more upon the natives' perception of their own self-interest, especially their growing dependence on trade with Europeans and military assistance against enemies (Axtell 1985: 71; Trigger 1985: 202; Bitterli 1989: 99).[40] Too stark a contrast should not, however, be drawn between the Hispanic world, on the one hand, and French and British America, on the other. Force was not a universal element within the Spanish mission programme.[41] In most environments outside the core regions of Central Mexico (and the Yucatan in the early years) and the Central Andes, missionaries found themselves as vulnerable as their North American counterparts and equally reliant on more subtle strategies of conversion. Conversely, the relative absence of state-backed overt coercion by missionaries in French and British America may ultimately have been of less significance in determining the trajectory of religious change than the wider context of the vast imbalance of power between Europeans and natives, the ravages of disease, the rapid changes in technology, and the considerable loss of land which followed upon contact in some areas, factors which have led some scholars to question the appropriateness of the anodyne word 'encounter', as opposed to more traditional terms such as 'invasion' or 'conquest'.

Violent coercion had distinct limits as an effective technique for conversion or evangelization, as opposed to a means of attacking native religions. Gareis stresses in this volume that the ruthless iconoclasm and persistent hounding of native religious leaders which were the hallmark of the institutionalized Extirpation of Idolatry certainly had profound effects in their purely destructive aspect and, in addition, brought about fundamental changes in Andean practices and beliefs (at least in the minority of regions exposed to this form of judicial process). But it is highly doubtful whether coercive methods had anything other than a negative impact on the Christianization of native peoples. Furthermore, they may have led, at best, only to a modification of the fundamentals of Andean religions and may not ultimately have been one of the major factors of cultural change in the Andes.[42]

By contrast, in Central Mexico the use of force gave way to more subtle means of securing the Indians' allegiance to the new faith. As early as the first half of the sixteenth century, a shift took place from inquisitorial techniques of random investigation and selective punishment (a poor mechanism for effectively regulating masses of unacculturated Indians) to a technique of penitential discipline that acted as both an external mechanism of social control, subjecting personal behaviour and subjective ideas to the public scrutiny of non-Indians, and as an internal mechanism of self-control, which resulted from successful attempts to inculcate guilt, fear or devotion upon the minds of the penitents (Klor de Alva 1991: 12; 1992: 91). Since the new discipline was to be exerted over the soul rather than the body, it ultimately served as 'a mechanism of control far more pervasive, efficient, economical and subtle than torture or punishment'. In this volume Klor de Alva demonstrates that the penitential system strove through sacramental confession to impose a new regime of self-decipherment and autobiographical discourse, whereby native 'self-forming practices' would be superseded and replaced by Christian ones, and a complete reconfiguration of the Nahua sense of self would be accomplished. The outcome of this struggle between two contrasting ways of making up and representing the self was ambivalent. On the one hand, since the new regime of self-formation was only imperfectly accepted, the Indian self was not reconstructed enough to recite a convincing Christian autobiography. On the other hand, to the extent that Indians internalized the need to recount the story of a moral self which was not theirs, their ability to conceive possible redefinitions of the truth of the Europeans was seriously constrained. The significance of this for an assessment of whether the Nahuas were 'converted' is suggested by Hefner's observation that the most necessary feature of religious conversion is:

not a deeply systematic reorganization of personal meanings but an adjustment in self-identification through the at least nominal acceptance of religious actions or beliefs deemed more fitting, useful or true.... [A]t the very least, conversion implies the acceptance of a new locus of self-definition, a new, though not necessarily exclusive, reference point for one's identity. (Hefner 1993: 17)

By such a definition, sacramental confession in Central Mexico may have achieved far more in the way of Christianization than other methods. The fact that Puritan missionary John Eliot used the confessions of his neophytes as a measure of the sincerity of conversions suggests interesting possibilities for comparative research on the use of the sacrament as a means of conversion across the hemisphere (Axtell 1988: 114).[43]

These considerations focus attention once again on the theme with which this introduction began: is 'conversion' a useful concept to describe the interaction of Christianity and native religions or does it obscure more than it reveals? How is one to define, in any case, criteria by which it may be judged whether and at what point 'conversion' has been achieved? The articles included here demonstrate that the manifold responses to the new religion which coexisted across the hemisphere make it impossible to find one single universally applicable definition of conversion.[44] As Merrill has observed, 'the status of convert can be withheld, refused or contested as well as bestowed and accepted; people can appropriate the beliefs and practices of a religion at the same time that they reject formal affiliation with it' (Merrill 1993:154).[45] Clearly, if the boundaries to the interaction of religions were set as much by native protagonists as by European ones, then it follows that the success of 'conversion' across the hemisphere needs to be judged principally by native criteria if it is to be meaningful. The same criteria must equally apply for all aspects of the interaction of religions in colonial America. If such an approach simply provokes new questions rather than resolving old ones, then the articles in this volume will have served their principal purpose.

# Bibliographical note

It is only possible to mention here some of the most significant works chosen from a large and growing bibliography on spiritual encounters in the New World. For North America, a pioneer in the new approaches to the interaction of Christianity and native religions has been James Axtell (1982; 1985; 1988; 1992). Also significant for anglophone America are Kupperman (1980), Ronda (1977), Salisbury (1982; 1974), and Simmons (1986). For francophone North America, see Grant (1984), Moore (1982), Richter (1985), Trigger (1985), White (1991), and Bonvillain (1985). A useful review of work which attempts to trace the process of change within native belief systems in North America is Brightman (1988).

For Mexico, see especially Burkhart (1989), Clendinnen (1982; 1987a; 1987b; 1990), Farriss (1984), Gruzinski (1993; 1989), and Klor de Alva (1982). Also useful are Cervantes (1993; 1994), Cline (1993), Gutiérrez (1991), Lockhart (1992: ch. 6), Nutini (1976), and Taylor (1996).

For Peru, see especially Griffiths (1996), MacCormack (1985; 1991), Marzal (1983), Meiklejohn (1988), Mills (1997), Salomon (1990), Salomon and Urioste (1991), Spalding (1984), Stern (1982), and Wachtel (1977).

For hispanophone America in general, see Gossen et al. (1992), Langer and Jackson (1995), and Ramirez (1989). For works on the founding, establishment and function of the colonial church in Spanish America, and the role of regular and secular clergy in evangelization, see Armas Medina (1953), Bayle (1950) Borges (1977; 1940), Gómez Canedo (1977), Espinosa (1988), Murray (1965), Phelan (1956), Porras Muñoz (1990), Ricard (1966), Sylvest (1975), Tibesar (1953), and Vargas Ugarte (1953–62).

# Notes

1    I am grateful to Fernando Cervantes and David Murray for their comments on earlier drafts of this introduction.
2    See the bibliographical note above.
3    Such a hemispheric-wide perspective has already been adopted in recent work on mission history. See the important collection of essays in Langer and Jackson (1995). For an earlier study which, although not hemispheric in approach, does cross the border between English, French and Spanish missions in North America, see Bowden (1981).

4    Lockhart also questions the utility of the concept of 'conversion', pointing out that Spanish ecclesiastics spoke mainly in terms of instruction
or indoctrination rather than conversion. See Lockhart (1992: 203–6)
for discussion of this and other issues also treated by Taylor. Theories
of syncretism are not discussed in this introduction partly because a
summary that does justice to a vast literature would require more space
than is available here and partly because the analytical precision of the
term has been called into question. Baird (1971) has argued that borrowing and blending towards a new synthesis is so present in religions
that the term 'syncretism' is superfluous because it does not add to our
understanding. Ringgren (1969: 7) has questioned whether syncretism
is so homogenous as to be capable of exact definition. It has, for
example, been employed by scholars to denote two entirely different
phenomena: on the one hand, any mixture where elements from different religions are merged and influence each other mutually, and on
the other hand cases when elements from one religion are accepted
into another without basically changing the character of the receiving
religion (because of the relatively small quantity of adopted elements).
Others have doubted that the term is a useful characterization of the
interaction of religions. Burkhart has insisted that the dialogical frontier is not the locus of syncretism, since syncretism implies a resolution
of contradictions, a half-way meeting between complementary elements.
In Central Mexico, Christian surface was combined with Nahua structure and the result was syncretic in the sense that it combined elements
of both cultures, but not in the sense of a simple sum of parts or of
attaining a true synthesis (Burkhart 1989: 190). Sabine MacCormack
considers that it would be wrong to see religious change in the Andes
as a process of syncretism whereby elements of Christianity and Hispanic culture came to coexist with an Andean substratum (MacCormack 1988: 960).

5    Dussel classifies scholars of the evangelization of the Andes in a tripar-
tite system: those who believe that Indians only accepted Christianity
externally ('idols-behind-altars' tradition, for example, George Kubler);
those who believe that Indians are essentially Christians although with
deficiencies (for example, C. Bayle and F. Armas Medina); and those
who believe in a juxtaposition of two different religions, whereby the
Indians tried to combine Christianity with paganism (for example, P.
Borges and N. Wachtel). He rejects the concept of a mixed religion in
the Andes on the grounds that a truly mixed religion should express its
mixtures through dogma (for example, Brazilian spiritism, one of the
few cases which has managed to express a theoretically mixed religion).

6    For the counter-argument that the Martha's Vineyard Indian faithful
     displayed a genuine understanding of Christian fundamentals, see
     Ronda (1981: 393).

7    I draw here on Axtell's critique of Salisbury, Jaenen and Trigger (Ax-
     tell 1988: 102–4).

8    It is worth remembering that the adaptation of Christianity to meet
     native needs and the use of the new religion as a vehicle for revitaliza-
     tion may be more effective than so-called nativist movements. Steve J.
     Stern has drawn attention to the ambivalence of Taki Onqoy, the nativ-
     ist revivalist movement which flourished in the Central Andes in the
     1560s. Although the movement preached that a pan-Andean alliance
     of deities would defeat the Christian god and kill Spanish colonizers
     with disease, the assimilation of some *taquiongos* (adherents of the
     movement) to Christian saints rather than Andean *huacas* (spiritual
     entities) betrayed a desire to ally with some elements of the Hispanic
     supernatural world and expressed an underlying crisis of confidence
     in the capacity of Andean gods by themselves. Thus traditional sources
     of spiritual power may no longer be sufficient in the face of new super-
     natural realities (Stern 1982). See also Wachtel (1977) on Taki Onqoy.

9    See also Axtell (1985: 283–6) for elaboration of the same points. Cod-
     ignola agrees that some Indians consciously chose a new faith, tried to
     understand it and made it coincide with their own traditional beliefs,
     values and behaviour (Codignola 1994: 43). Richter argues that the
     Jesuits made many sincere converts but 'on the basis of diplomatic,
     political and religious considerations that were essentially Indian and
     traditional rather than European and Christian' (Richter 1992: 111).
     Ronda insisted some time ago that the possibility of genuine conver-
     sion on the part of Indians searching for spiritual meaning should not
     be overlooked (Ronda 1981: 370).

10   For a similar function of Christianity as a means of reconstructing
     native societies in the wake of the material and spiritual dislocation of
     the Spanish conquest, see Wachtel (1977) and Farriss(1984).

11   In this context, it is pertinent to bear in mind Brightman's reference to
     the 'Janus-faced' orientation of many Indian responses to religious
     change – the simultaneous and ambivalent valuation and disparage-
     ment of both the traditional and the innovative (Brightman 1988: 241).
     The notion of 'Janus-faced orientation' is borrowed from Worsley
     (1968). An example of a 'yes that means no' in the Hispanic context
     might be the stance of the indigenous priests referred to in Bernardino
     de Sahagún's *Libro de los coloquios* who allowed themselves to be
     baptized because their gods had been defeated by the Christian god, a
     good illustration of how aspects of Christianity may be accepted but

not the world view implied by them. See Klor de Alva (1982). For discussion of native misappropriations and misinterpretations in general, see Todorov (1985) and León-Portilla (1975: 11–36). Something akin to a 'yes that means no' may also be detected in Taylor's observation that colonial Indians could operate comfortably in more than one religious tradition at a time, resisting some of the priests' ways of being 'truly' Christian and adding others to fill out their understanding of the divine and sense of well-being without rejecting Christianity (Taylor 1996: 66). Sweet considers the fundamental differences in the ways missionaries and Indians understood the latter's relationship to the new faith, differences which 'gave the praying Indians of every frontier a certain comparatively safe space within which to maneuver culturally and ideologically. Inside that safe space they could hold on to whatever traditional beliefs were still persuasive to them' while 'adapting and developing their practices as Christians' (Sweet 1995: 39).

12　A phrase used by Vincent Diaz, cited in Sweet (1995: 9).

13　On the Franciscan missionaries, see Clendinnen (1987b) and Madsen (1967). For the Jesuits, see Grant (1984: 35).

14　See Dibble (1974), Burkhart (1989), Klor de Alva (1993), and Duverger 1993: 132, 145–62). Interesting parallels may be found in Steven Kaplan's study of the role of Western missionaries in the 'Africanization' of Christianity (Kaplan 1986).

15　The summary of Burkhart's work offered here is based on Burkhart (1988: 252–3) and Burkhart (1989: 16, 28, 31, 44, 185–92). A good example of the accommodation of Christian teachings to native thought categories is the substitution of the Nahuatl term *tlatlacolli* for sin, which profoundly altered the concept since the literal meaning of *tlatlacolli* was 'something damaged' and could describe any sort of error or misdeed, from moral transgressions to judicially defined crimes to accidental or unintentional damage. Furthermore, *tlatlacolli* assumed intervention of supernatural entities to impose sanctions in this life but not in the afterlife.

16　In large measure, the dilemma was one of language: to favour the use of Spanish terms in attempting to explain Christian concepts to Indians would make Christian teachings superficial, unintelligible and unassimilated in native mentality; but to use Nahuatl equivalents (in the end, the preferred option) risked carrying native concepts over into the most fundamental aspects of Christian moral teaching (Dibble 1974; Burkhart 1989).

17　See also Clendinnen (1990) on the appropriation of the Virgin Mary in sacred art by the Indians of Central Mexico.

18　Considering religious beliefs and practices among the contemporary

Oglalas of the Pine Ridge Indian Reservation in South Dakota, William K. Powers' observation that the Indians 'were not so much to become Christianized as Christianity was to become nativized' furnishes an interesting echo in the modern era of both Ronda's study of Martha's Vineyard and Dibble's 'Nahuatlization' of Christianity. This suggests that interesting parallels with other epochs and regions of America may be drawn (Powers 1987: 102, 107).

19  So, for example, among the Nahuas, the idea that Christian confession 'cures' the heart or soul was easy to accept; that it worked on an immaterial spiritual level was incompatible with traditional thought and was not accepted. The idea that one should do penance on Christian holy days was compatible; that such penance functioned to prevent suffering after death was not (Burkhart 1989: 190).

20  For a comparable observation regarding Christian identity among the Indians of Martha's Vineyard, see Ronda (1981: 391).

21  For similar perceptions of baptism as a pact of friendship and alliance, see Conkling (1974: 11).

22  See also Grant (1984: 42) on the relation between conversion and commercial relations.

23  Also on native motives for requesting missions, see Saeger (1985). Saeger makes interesting comparisons with the Yaqui missions in seventeenth-century Mexico, drawing on Hu-DeHart (1981).

24  See similar conclusions reached in Grahn (1995). For an interesting comparison with the Guaraní of the late colonial period, see Whigham (1995). Both articles emphasize the indigenous ability to adapt in order to maintain continuity and retain a measure of autonomy.

25  On this, see Sweet (1995). This new approach is a useful corrective to the view of more traditional historians like, for example, Edward Spicer, who attributed the varying degrees of acculturation among Indian groups exposed to Jesuit and Franciscan evangelization in northwest New Spain to differences in missionary methodology (Spicer 1961). For a critique of Spicer, see Polzer (1976: 54–6).

26  It is worth noting that Horton has emphasized that acceptance of a new religion is due as much to the development of traditional cosmology in response to other features of the modern situation as it is to the activities of missionaries (Horton 1971: 103, quoted in Hefner 1993: 22).

27  See also Griffiths (1996). For the same technique used by the Jesuits in North America, see Axtell (1985: 93).

28  See Axtell (1985: 93) for the techniques used to supplant shamans.

29  Richter agrees that it was the Jesuit's personal shamanistic power, not the message he preached, that initially impressed his audience (Richter 1985: 5–6).

30  Grant stresses that the priest might be regarded not merely as a dispenser of sacraments over which he had no proprietary right but as a shaman giving and withholding blessings at will (Grant 1984: 247).

31  Catholic Christianity has generally been held to be more effective at replacing native ceremonies, images, processions and symbols than Protestantism was. See Ronda (1981: 393) and Ronda and Axtell (1978).

32  See, for example, Salisbury (1974: 40). However, attempts to supplant native shamans by moving onto their ground also meant that, in the right circumstances, the tables could be turned and traditionalist shamans might win back disciples in many of the same ways that priests had first lured them away. Better fortunes in raids and in war in the 1670s, for example, increased Iroquois perceptions of their own spiritual strength (Richter 1985: 11).

33  Van Young (1989: 95–6) differentiates the case of colonial Latin America from missionary fields elsewhere in the world on account of the role of the state as one of the major 'instrumentalities' in the process of Christianization, observing that in Latin America colonial conquest was underwritten by military authority.

34  For the issue of inquisitorial jurisdiction over the Indians in Mexico, see Greenleaf (1965; 1991) and Moreno de los Arcos (1991). Also useful are Greenleaf (1962; 1977–78; 1992).

35  After 1571, the Holy Office acted primarily as a fact-finding agency in uncovering and disciplining Indian transgressions against orthodoxy. Jurisdiction for trial and punishment was reserved to the *provisors* who used a bureaucracy of officials and appointed delegates and commissaries in provincial areas. Confusion arose because these officials often called themselves 'inquisitors ordinary', following the tradition established during the episcopal inquisition. Disputes over competence of the tribunal and the *provisorato* continued in the seventeenth and eighteenth centuries (Greenleaf 1991: 261). On anti-idolatry activities and extirpators of native religion in colonial Mexico, see Bernand and Gruzinski (1988), and the editors' introduction to Ruiz de Alarcón (1984).

36  On religious coercion, also see Mills (1994) and Harrison (1994).

37  For a consideration of some of the factors that might explain this contrast, including the swift completion of military subjection, the relative lack of overt widespread military resistance to Christianity, and more extensive iconoclasm in New Spain by comparison with the Andes, see Klor de Alva (1982).

38  On the Extirpation of Idolatry in the Andes, see Burga (1988), Duviols (1986; 1971), García Cabrera (1994), Gareis (1989), Griffiths (1996; 1994), MacCormack (1991), Millones (1987) (among several other works

by this distinguished historian); Mills (1997), Salomon and Urioste (1991), Sánchez (1991), and Silverblatt (1987).

39 There is a surprising dearth of modern studies of the evangelization of Peru and the missionary methods adopted by different orders. The main points of reference are Armas Medina (1953), Borges (1977; 1940), and Tibesar (1953).

40 Sweet argues that persuasion played a greater role than force in the process of conversion among the Jesuits of Canada than among the Jesuits of the Amazon (Sweet 1992: 277). On occasion, force was employed in New France both to win converts and to keep new Catholics in the observance of their duties, but resort to the secular arm was not frequent (Jaenen 1976: 70–1).

41 In Northern New Spain, for example, among the Tarahumaras and the Yaquis, mission work proceeded, at least in the early stages, without compulsion or forcible military conquest (Merrill 1993: 137; Spicer 1961: 19).

42 See Griffiths (1996) and Mills (1997; 1996). In the latter article, Mills makes the point that the Extirpation made Andeans more distrustful and dismissive of official religion (201). One of the methodological problems inherent in the use of documents from idolatry trials and Spanish accounts of Indian idolatry in the seventeenth century as measures of the process of religious acculturation is their overwhelming preoccupation with practices that deviated from Christian doctrine and general neglect of those that conformed to it (Taylor 1996: 64).

43 For the Andes, see Barnes (1992) and Harrison (1994).

44 In order to demonstrate the complexity of these manifold responses, Brightman has proposed a typography which includes responses as diverse as sincere and 'literal' conversion, nominal conversion, categorical rejection, indigenous Christian movements, self-consciously syncretic movements, unconsciously syncretic movements, compartmentalization, and exclusivism. The point is well made, though it is worth maintaining a certain scepticism about the usefulness of some of these categories, as we have seen, since the lived reality may be more fluid (Brightman 1988: 241). A similar exercise was undertaken by Klor de Alva for Mesoamerica (Klor de Alva 1982). For a study of the range of responses in Spanish America, see Deeds (1995). The many different and conflicting motives for accepting Christianity have been considered by Eric Van Young, who contrasts three basic models employed by scholars to explain why non-Christians embrace Christianity. First, there is the ideational/symbolic mode, in which a genuine educational and communication process takes place between missionary and convert. Second, there is the sociological model, in which social or peer

pressures, sociopolitical crisis etc., would induce large numbers of individuals to embrace an alien system of belief (the initial conquest years of Latin America provide a case of this). Third, there is the rational choice model, in which individuals embrace Christianity because it is an optimizing strategy for themselves, usually in economic terms. These models are not mutually exclusive but may coexist at the same time (Van Young 1989: 96). What Van Young characterizes as the Indian 'smorgasbord' approach to acculturation (94) is highlighted in the work of other scholars. For example, Saeger's study of the Mbayás shows how they adopted the Christian religion as they took other aspects of Spanish culture, accepting what they wanted when they wanted it (Saeger 1989: 66).

45    The distinction between beliefs and practices is crucial in determining criteria for whether 'conversion' has taken place. Both Taylor and Clendinnen stress that the issue of conversion has inappropriately centred attention on religion as belief rather than religion as performance and hence failed to catch the quality of a lived faith. See Taylor (1996: 52) and Clendinnen (1990: 110). See also Morrison (1990: 425). Merrill points out that converts and missionaries can agree, on the basis of religious practices alone, that conversion has taken place even though a major transformation in belief has not occurred

# Bibliography

Armas Medina, Fernando de (1953), *Cristianización del Perú (1532-1600)*, Seville: Escuela de Estudios Hispanoamericanos.

Axtell, James (1982) 'Some Thoughts on the Ethnohistory of Missions', *Ethnohistory* 29: 35-41.

    (1985), *The Invasion Within: The Contest of Cultures in Colonial North America*, New York and Oxford: Oxford University Press.

    (1988), *After Columbus: Essays in the Ethnohistory of Colonial North America*, New York and Oxford: Oxford University Press.

    (1992) *Beyond 1492: Encounters in Colonial North America*, New York and Oxford: Oxford University Press.

Baird, Robert D. (1971), *Category Formation and the History of Religion*, The Hague/Paris: Mouton.

Barnes, Monica (1992) 'Catechisms and Confessionarios: Distorting Mirrors of Andean Societies'. In Robert V. H. Dover,

Katherine E. Seibold and John H. McDowell (eds), *Andean Cosmologies through Time: Persistence and Emergence*, Bloomington: Indiana University Press.

Bayle, C. (1950), *El clero secular y la evangelización de América*, Missionalia Hispanica no. 6, Madrid: CSIC.

Bernand, Carmen and Serge Gruzinski (1988), *De l'idolâtrie: Une archéologie des sciences religieuses*, Paris: Seuil.

Bitterli, Urs (1989), *Cultures in Conflict: Encounters between European and non-European Cultures 1492-1800*, trans. Ritchie Robertson, Cambridge: Polity.

Bonvillain, Nancy (1985) 'Missionary Rule in French Colonial Expansion: An Examination of the Jesuit Relations', *Man in the Northeast* 29: 1-14.

Borges, Pedro (1940) *Métodos misionales de la cristianización de América, siglo XVI*, Madrid: Consejo Superior de Investigaciones Científicas.

——— (1977), *El envío de misioneros a América durante la época española*, Salamanca: Universidad Pontificia de Salamanca.

Bowden, Henry Warner (1981), *American Indians and Christian Missions: Studies in Cultural Conflict*, Chicago History of American Religion, Chicago and London: University of Chicago Press.

Brightman, Robert A. (1988), 'Toward a History of Indian Religion: Religious Changes in Native Societies'. In C. G. Calloway (ed.), *New Directions in American Indian History*, Norman: University of Oklahoma Press.

Burga, Manuel (1988), *Nacimiento de una utopía: Muerte y resurrección de los incas*, Lima: Instituto de Apoyo Agrario.

Burkhart, Louise M. (1988), 'The Solar Christ in Nahuatl Doctrinal Texts of Early Colonial Mexico', *Ethnohistory* 35: 234-56.

——— (1989), *The Slippery Earth: Nahua-Christian Moral Dialogue in Sixteenth-Century Mexico*, Tucson: University of Arizona Press.

Burkholder, M. A. and L. L. Johnson (1990), *Colonial Latin America*, Oxford: Oxford University Press.

Cervantes, Fernando (1993), 'Christianity and the Indians in Early Modern Mexico: The Native Response to the Devil', *Historical Research* 66: 177-96.

——— (1994), *The Devil in the New World. The Impact of Diabo-*

*lism in New Spain*, New Haven: Yale University Press.

Clendinnen, Inga (1982), 'Disciplining the Indians: Franciscan Ideology and Missionary Violence in Sixteenth-Century Yucatan', *Past and Present* 94: 27–48.

(1987a), *Ambivalent Conquests: Maya and Spaniard in Yucatán, 1517-1570*, Cambridge: Cambridge University Press.

(1987b), 'Franciscan Missionaries in Sixteenth-Century Mexico'. In J. Obelkevich, L. Roper, and R. Samuel (eds), *Disciplines of Faith: Studies in Religion, Politics and Patriarchy*, London and New York: Routledge and Kegan Paul.

(1990), 'Ways to the Sacred: Reconstructing Religion in Sixteenth-Century Mexico', *History and Anthropology* 5: 105–41.

Cline, Sarah L. (1993), 'The Spiritual Conquest Reexamined: Baptism and Christian Marriage in Early Sixteenth-Century Mexico', *Hispanic American Historical Review* 73: 453–80.

Codignola, Luca (1994), 'The French in Early America: Religion and Reality'. In Deborah L. Madsen (ed.), *Visions of America Since 1492*, London: Leicester University Press.

(1995), 'The Holy See and the Conversion of the Indians in French and British North America 1486–1760'. In Karen Ordahl Kupperman (ed.), *America in the European Consciousness 1493-1750*, Chapel Hill and London: University of North Carolina Press.

Conkling, Robert (1974), 'Legitimacy and Conversion in Social Change: The Case of French Missionaries and the Northeastern Algonkian', *Ethnohistory* 21: 1–24.

Deeds, Susan M. (1995), 'Indigenous Responses to Mission Settlement in Nueva Vizcaya'. In Langer and Jackson (eds), *The New Latin American Mission History*, Lincoln and London: University of Nebraska Press.

Dennis, Matthew (1993), *Cultivating a Landscape of Peace: Iroquois-European Encounters in Seventeenth-Century America*, Ithaca and London: Cornell University Press.

Dibble, Charles E. (1974), 'The Nahuatlization of Christianity'. In Munro S. Edmonson (ed.), *Sixteenth-Century Mexico: The Work of Sahagún*, Albuquerque: University Of New Mexico Press.

Dussel, Enrique D. (1974), *Historia de la iglesia en américa latina: coloniaje y liberación (1492-1973)*, 3rd edn, Barcelona:

Editorial Nova Terra.

Duverger, Christian (1993), *La Conversión de los indios de Nueva España*, Mexico: Fondo de Cultura Económica.

Duviols, Pierre (1971), *La Lutte contre les réligions autochtones dans le Pérou colonial*, Lima: Institut Français d'Etudes Andines.

(1986), *Cultura andina y represión. Proccsos y visitas de idolatrías y hechicerías, Cajatambo, siglo XVII*, Cusco: Centro de Estudios Rurales Andinos 'Bartolomé de Las Casas'.

Espinosa, José Manuel (1988), *The Pueblo Indian Revolt of 1696 and Franciscan Missions in New Mexico*, Norman: University of Oklahoma Press.

Farriss, Nancy M.( 1984), *Maya Society under Colonial Rule: The Collective Enterprise of Survival*, Princeton: Princeton University Press.

García Cabrera, Juan Carlos (1994), *Ofensas a Dios. Pleitos e injurias: causas de idolatrías y hechicerías, Cajatambo, siglos XVII-XIX*, Cusco: Centro de Estudios Rurales Andinos 'Bartolomé de Las Casas'.

Gareis, Iris (1989), 'Extirpación de idolatrías e inquisición en el virreinato del Perú', *Boletín del instituto Riva-Agüero* 16: 55-74.

Gómez Canedo, Lino (1977), *Evangelización y conquista: experiencia franciscana en Hispano-América*, Mexico: Porrúa.

Gossen, Gary G., Miguel León-Portilla, Manuel Gutiérrez Estévez and J. Jorge Klor de Alva (eds) (1992), *De palabra y obra en el nuevo mundo*, 3 vols., Madrid and Mexico: Siglo XXI.

Grahn, Lance R. (1995), 'Guajiro Culture and Capuchin Evangelization: Missionary Failure on the Riohacha Frontier'. In Langer and Jackson (eds), *New Latin American Mission History*, Lincoln and London: University of Nebraska Press.

Grant, John Webster (1984), *Moon of Wintertime: Missionaries and the Indians of Canada in Encounter since 1534*, Toronto: University of Toronto Press.

Greenleaf, Richard E. (1962), *Zumárraga and the Mexican Inquisition 1536-43*, Washington: Academy of American Franciscan History.

(1965), 'The Inquisition and the Indians of New Spain: A Study in Jurisdictional Confusion', *The Americas* 22: 138-66.

(1977-78), 'The Mexican Inquisition and the Indians: Sources for the Ethnohistorian' *The Americas* 34: 315-44.

(1991), 'Historiography of the Mexican Inquisition: Evolution of Interpretations and Methodologies'. In Mary Elizabeth Perry and Anne J. Cruz (eds), *Cultural Encounters: the Impact of the Inquisition in Spain and the New World*, Los Angeles: University of California Press.

(1992), *La Inquisición en Nueva España siglo XVI*, Mexico: Fondo de Cultura Económica.

Griffiths, Nicholas (1994), 'Inquisition of the Indians? The Inquisitorial Model and the Repression of Andean Religion in Seventeenth-Century Peru', *Colonial Latin American Historical Review* 3(1): 19-38.

(1996), *The Cross and the Serpent: Religious Repression and Resurgence in Colonial Peru*, Norman: University of Oklahoma Press.

Gruzinski, Serge (1974), 'Délires et visions chez les Indiens de Méxique', *Mélanges de L'Ecole Française de Rome: Moyen Age - Temps Modernes* 86: 445-80.

(1989), *Man-Gods in the Mexican Highlands: Indian Power and Colonial Society, 1520-1800*, trans. Eileen Corrigan, Stanford: Stanford University Press.

(1993), *The Conquest of Mexico: The Incorporation of Indian Societies into the Western World, 16th-18th Centuries*, trans. Eileen Corrigan, Cambridge and Oxford: Polity Press.

Gutiérrez, Ramón (1991), *When Jesus Came, the Corn Mothers Went Away: Marriage, Sexuality, and Power in New Mexico, 1500-1846*, Stanford: Stanford University Press.

Harrison, Regina (1994), 'The Theology of Concupiscence: Spanish-Quechua Confessional Manuals in the Andes'. In F. J. Cevallos-Candau, Jeffrey A. Cole, Nina M. Scott and Nicomedes Suárez-Araúz (eds), *Coded Encounters: Writing, Gender and Ethnicity in Colonial Latin America*, Amherst: University of Massachusetts Press.

Hefner, Robert W. (ed.) (1993), *Conversion to Christianity: Historical and Anthropological Perspectives on a Great Transformation*, Berkeley: University of California Press.

Horton, Robin (1971), 'African Conversion', *Africa* 41: 85-108.

Hu-DeHart, Evelyn (1981), *Missionaries, Miners, and Indians: Spanish Contact with the Yaqui Nation of Northwestern New*

*Spain, 1533-1820*, Tucson: University of Arizona Press.

Jaenen, Cornelius J. (1976), *Friend and Foe: Aspects of French-Amerindian Cultural Contact in the Sixteenth and Seventeenth Centuries*, New York: Columbia University Press.

Kaplan, Steven (1986), 'The Africanization of Missionary Christianity: History and Typology', *Journal of Religion in Africa* 16(3): 166–86.

Klor de Alva, J. Jorge (1982), 'Spiritual Conflict and Accommodation in New Spain: Toward a Typology of Aztec Responses to Christianity'. In George A. Collier, Renato I. Rosaldo and John D. Wirth (eds), *The Inca and Aztec States, 1400–1800: Anthropology and History*, New York: Academic Press.

—— (1991), 'Colonizing Souls: the Failure of the Indian Inquisition and the Rise of Penitential Discipline'. In Mary Elizabeth Perry and Anne J. Cruz (eds), *Cultural Encounters: the Impact of the Inquisition in Spain and the New World*, Los Angeles: University of California Press.

—— (1992), 'Sin and Confession Among the Colonial Nahuas: The Confessional as a Tool for Domination'. In Ricardo A. Sánchez Flores, Eric Van Young and Gisela von Wobeser (eds), *Ciudad y campo en la historia de Mexico: Memoria de la VII Reunión de Historiadores Mexicanos y Norteamericanos*, 2 vols., Mexico: UNAM, vol. 1.

—— (1993), 'Aztec Spirituality and Nahuatized Christianity'. In Gary H. Gossen and Miguel León-Portilla (eds), *South and Mesoamerican Native Spirituality: From the Cult of the Feathered Serpent to the Theology of Liberation*, New York and London: SCM Press Ltd.

Kupperman, Karen Ordahl (1980), *Settling with Indians: the Meeting of English and Indian Cultures in America 1580–1640*, London: Dent.

Langer, Erick, and Robert H. Jackson (eds) (1995), *The New Latin American Mission History*, Lincoln and London: University of Nebraska Press.

León-Portilla, Miguel (1975), 'Testimonios nahuas sobre la conquista espiritual', *Estudios de cultura Nahua* 11: 11–36.

Lockhart, James (1992), *The Nahuas after the Conquest: A Social and Cultural History of the Indians of Central Mexico, Sixteenth through Eighteenth Centuries*, Stanford: Stanford University Press.

MacCormack, Sabine (1985), '"The Heart has its Reasons": Predicaments of Missionary Christianity in Early Colonial Peru', *Hispanic American Historical Review* 65: 443-66.

(1988), 'Pachacuti: Miracles, Punishments, and Last Judgment: Visionary Past and Prophetic Future in Early Colonial Peru' *American Historical Review* 93: 960-1006.

(1991), *Religion in the Andes: Vision and Imagination in Early Colonial Peru*, Princeton: Princeton University Press.

Madsen, William (1967), 'Religious Syncretism'. In *Handbook of Middle American Indians*, vol. 6, R. Wauchope (general ed.) Austin: University of Texas Press.

Marzal, Manuel M. (1983), *La transformación religiosa peruana*, Lima: Pontificia Universidad Católica del Perú.

McAlister, Lyle N. (1984), *Spain and Portugal in the New World 1492-1700*, Europe and The World in the Age of Expansion, no. 3, Minneapolis: University of Minnesota Press.

Meiklejohn, N. (1988), *La iglesia y los lupaqas durante la colonia*, Cusco: Centro de Estudios Rurales Andinos 'Bartolomé de Las Casas'.

Merrill, William L. (1993), 'Conversion and Colonialism in Northern Mexico: the Tarahumara Response to the Jesuit Mission Programme, 1601-1767'. In Hefner, Robert W. (ed.), *Conversion to Christianity: Historical and Anthropological Perspectives on a Great Transformation*, Berkeley: University of California Press.

Millones, Luis (1987), *Historia y poder en los Andes centrales: desde los orígenes al siglo XVII*, Madrid: Alianza.

Mills, Kenneth (1994), 'The Limits of Religious Coercion in Mid-Colonial Peru', *Past and Present* 145: 84-121.

(1996), 'Bad Christians in Colonial Peru', *Colonial Latin American Review* 5: 183-218.

(1997), *Idolatry and its Enemies: Colonial Andean Religion and Extirpation, 1640-1750*, Princeton: Princeton University Press.

Moore, James T. (1982), *Indian and Jesuit: A Seventeenth Century Encounter*, Chicago: University of Chicago Press.

Moreno de los Arcos, Roberto (1991), 'New Spain's Inquisition for Indians from the Sixteenth to the Nineteenth Century'. In Mary Elizabeth Perry and Anne J. Cruz (eds), *Cultural Encounters: the Impact of the Inquisition in Spain and the*

*New World*, Los Angeles: University of California Press.

Morrison, Kenneth M. (1990), 'Baptism and Alliance: The Symbolic Meditations of Religious Syncretism', *Ethnohistory* 37(4): 416–37.

Murray, Paul V. (1965), *The Catholic Church in Mexico*, Mexico D.F.

Nutini, Hugo G. (1976), 'Syncretism and Acculturation: The Historical Development of the Patron Saint in Tlaxcala, Mexico (1519–1670)', *Ethnology* 15: 301–21.

Phelan, John Leddy (1956), *The Millennial Kingdom of the Franciscans in the New World. A Study of the Writings of Gerónimo de Mendieta (1525–1604)*, Berkeley and Los Angeles: University of California Press.

Polzer, Charles W. (1976), *Rules and Precepts of Jesuit Missions of Northwestern New Spain*, Tucson: University of Arizona Press.

Porras Muñoz, G. (1990), *El clero secular y la evangelización de Nueva España*, Mexico: UNAM.

Powers, William K. (1987), *Beyond the Vision: Essays on American Indian Culture*, Norman: University of Oklahoma Press.

Ramírez, Susan E. (ed.) (1989), *Indian-Religious Relations in Colonial Spanish America*, Foreign and Comparative Studies/Latin American Series 9, Maxwell School of Citizenship and Public Affairs: Syracuse University.

Ricard, Robert (1966), *The Spiritual Conquest of Mexico. An Essay on the Apostolate and the Evangelizing Methods of the Mendicant Orders in New Spain: 1523–1572*, trans. Lesley Byrd Simpson, Berkeley and Los Angeles: University of California Press.

Richter, Daniel K. (1985), 'Iroquois versus Iroquois: Jesuit missions and Christianity in Village Politics 1642–1686', *Ethnohistory*, 32: 1–16.

—— (1992), *The Ordeal of the Longhouse: The Peoples of the Iroquois League in the Era of European Colonization*, Chapel Hill and London: University of North Carolina Press.

Ringgren, Helmer (1969), 'The Problems of Syncretism'. In Sven S. Hartman (ed.) *Syncretism: Based on papers read at the symposium on cultural contact, meeting of religions, syncretism, held at Abo on 8–10 Sept 1966*, 3 vols., Scripta Instituti Donneriani Aboensis, Stockholm: Almqvist and Wiksell.

Ronda, James P. (1981), 'Generations of Faith: The Christian Indians of Martha's Vineyard', *William and Mary Quarterly* 38: 369–94.

— (1977), '"We Are Well As We Are": An Indian Critique of Seventeenth-Century Christian Missions', *William and Mary Quarterly* 34: 66–82.

Ronda, James P. and Axtell, James (1978), *Indian Missions: A Critical Bibliography*, Bloomington: University of Indiana Press.

Ruiz de Alarcón, Hernando (1984), *Treatise on the Heathen Superstitions*, trans. and ed. J. Richard Andrews and Ross Hassig, Norman: University of Oklahoma Press.

Saeger, James S. (1985), 'Another View of the Mission as a Frontier Institution: The Guaycuruan Reductions of Santa Fe, 1743–1810', *Hispanic American Historical Review* 65: 493–517.

— (1989), 'Eighteenth-Century Guaycuruan Missions in Paraguay'. In Ramirez (ed.), *Indian-Religious Relations in Colonial Spanish America*, Foreign and Comparative Studies/Latin American Series 9, Maxwell School of Citizenship and Public Affairs: Syracuse University.

Salisbury, Neal (1974), 'Red Puritans: The 'Praying Indians' of Massachusetts Bay and John Eliot', *William and Mary Quarterly* 31: 27–54.

— (1982), *Manitou and Providence: Indians, Europeans and the Making of New England 1500–1643*, New York and Oxford: Oxford University Press.

Salomon, Frank (1990), 'Nightmare Victory: The Meanings of Conversion among Peruvian Indians (Huarochirí, 1608?)', Working Papers no. 7, Maryland: Department of Spanish and Portuguese, University of Maryland.

Salomon, Frank, and Urioste, George L. (trans. and eds) (1991), *The Huarochirí Manuscript. A Testament of Ancient and Colonial Andean Religion*, Austin: University of Texas Press.

Sánchez, Ana (1991), *Amancebados, hechiceros y rebeldes (Chancay, siglo XVII)*, Cusco: Centro de Estudios Rurales Andinos 'Bartolomé de Las Casas'.

Scott, J. C. (1985), *Weapons of the Weak*, New Haven: Yale University Press.

— (1990), *Domination and Arts of Resistance: Hidden Transcripts,*

New Haven: Yale University Press.

Silverblatt, Irene (1987), *Moon, Sun and Witches: Gender Ideologies and Class in Inca and Colonial Peru*, Princeton: Princeton University Press.

Simmons, William S. (1986), *Spirit of the New England Tribes: Indian History and Folklore, 1620–1984*, Hanover: University Press of New England.

Spalding, Karen (1984), *Huarochirí: An Andean Society under Inca and Spanish rule*, Stanford: Stanford University Press.

Spicer, Edward H. (1961), *Perspectives in American Indian Culture Change*, Chicago: University of Chicago Press.

Stern, Steve J. (1982), *Peru's Indian Peoples and the Challenge of Spanish Conquest: Huamanga to 1640*, Madison: University of Wisconsin Press.

Sweet, David (1992), 'Misioneros Jesuitas e Indios "Recalcitrantes" en la Amazonia Colonial' in Gossen, Gary G., et al. (eds), *De palabra y obra en el nuevo mundo*, 3 vols., Madrid and Mexico: Siglo XXI, vol. 1.

—— (1995), 'The Ibero-American Frontier Mission in Native American History'. In Langer and Jackson (eds), *The New Latin American Mission History*, Lincoln and London: University of Nebraska Press.

Sylvest, Edwin Edward (1975), *Motifs of Franciscan Mission Theory in Sixteenth-Century New Spain*, Washington D.C.: Academy of American Franciscan History.

Taylor, William B. (1996), *Magistrates of the Sacred: Priests and Parishioners in Eighteenth-Century Mexico*, Stanford: Stanford University Press.

Tibesar, Antonine (1953), *Franciscan Beginnings in Colonial Peru*, Washington: Academy of American Franciscan History.

Todorov, Tzvetan (1985), *The Conquest of America*, New York: Harper and Row.

Trigger, Bruce G. (1985), *Natives and Newcomers: Canada's 'Heroic Age' Reconsidered*, Montreal: McGill-Queen's University Press.

Van Young, Eric (1989), 'Conclusions'. In Ramirez, Susan E. (ed.) (1989), *Indian-Religious Relations in Colonial Spanish America*, Foreign and Comparative Studies/Latin American Series 9, Maxwell School of Citizenship and Public Affairs: Syracuse University.

Vargas Ugarte, Rubén (1953-62), *Historia de la Iglesia en el Perú*, 5 vols., vol. 1, Lima: Imprenta Santa María, 1953; vols. 2-5, Burgos: Imprenta de Aldecoa, 1959-62.

Wachtel, Nathan (1977), *The Vision of the Vanquished: The Spanish Conquest of Peru through Indian Eyes, 1530-1570*, trans. Ben and Sian Reynolds, Hassocks: Harvester Press.

Whigham, Thomas (1995), 'Paraguay's *Pueblos de Indios:* Echoes of a Missionary Past'. In Langer and Jackson (eds), *The New Latin American Mission History*, Lincoln and London: University of Nebraska Press.

White, Richard (1991), *The Middle Ground: Indians, Empires and Republics in the Great Lakes Region 1650-1815*, Cambridge: Cambridge University Press.

Worsley, Peter (1968), *The Trumpet Shall Sound*, New York: Schocken Books.

# 1
# Spreading the Word: missionaries, conversion and circulation in the northeast

DAVID MURRAY

During the seventeenth century the native peoples of northeast America were the subject of a series of missionary enterprises, which combined with varying degrees of contact with traders and settlers and the devastating effect of European diseases to create a profound challenge to their beliefs and social patterns. While the loss and destruction have been evident enough, the remarkable strategies of adaptation and change on the part of the Indian communities have only more recently been fully acknowledged, and it is in this context that the missionary encounter, and conversion itself, need to be seen. Conversion implies, at its simplest, changing something which is already present, and while the absolutist and exclusive rhetoric of a monotheistic Christianity may invoke total transformation, it is reasonable to ask of any conversion, as opposed to an *ex nihilo* creation, what exactly, and how much, is actually being changed.[1] Connected with this is the question of how far change might involve *ex*change, a two-way process, an altogether more problematic idea for Christian missionaries. Their enterprise entailed the dissemination of new ideas which were intended to replace or transform what was there before, in a one-way transmission, but I want to show how, since they were involved in a complex network of exchanges, cultural, economic and linguistic, the missionaries could not control the meanings of what they gave or introduced. What entered into circulation, whether a word, an idea, or a religious object, then took on a value given by its circulation within that particular material and discursive economy, and it could not from that point onwards be restricted or authorized only by its Christian origins.

The native peoples of the northeast ranged from subarctic hunters to largely sedentary farmers. They were mostly Algonquian-speaking, but the Jesuits were also deeply involved with Iroquoian-speaking peoples. The Puritans of New England encountered a patchwork of small Algonquian groups, prominent among whom, in missionary accounts, are the Massachusett, and the Narragansett of Rhode Island. Throughout, the missionaries encountered cultures which, for all their diversity, were alike in giving profound importance to redistribution, reciprocity and circulation, with well-established networks in which exchange was not merely a means to an economic end, but was in itself an enactment and reinforcement of a mutual relationship. By concentrating on some of the *range* of the cultural exchanges involved in the missionary encounter, I hope to show both some of the diversity of native responses, and the anxieties and crises of authority this could create for the missionaries. In its most extreme form this anxiety could take the form of a fear that the initial unilateral impulse behind conversion was falling foul of a reciprocity which might itself demand some converting, or at least adaptation, of the missionaries' own beliefs. Clearly this could not easily be even contemplated – but what, after all, was the translating or converting of Christian terms into native terms? And what about the adaptation and re-use of religious objects like rosary beads? In short, how was it possible to control the meaning of what was being introduced? Such questions involved the missionaries in a series of reciprocal and potentially relativizing and unsettling encounters.

In drawing my examples from the Jesuit missionaries of New France and the Puritans of New England both the similarities and the differences are important.[2] The Jesuits, unlike their predecessors the Recollects,[3] believed that the best way to effect conversion was to keep the Indians in isolation from civilizing influences, which would corrupt rather than advance their understanding.[4] Christian doctrine and terms would be translated into native terms, and traditional Indian patterns of life and behaviour would be changed only as and when necessary. While this policy did create some friction with traders, who felt they were being excluded from contact, it could coexist with broader economic policy in that the success of the fur trade required Indians to remain relatively isolated and intact in their traditional lifestyle. By contrast, the Puritans of New England were settlers, living in close proximity to farming Indians and in competition for their land. Largely committed to the idea of the depravity of the original Indians, Puritan divines – of whom the most publicized was John Eliot, the 'Apostle to the Indians' – insisted on civilization as a precondition of full conversion to Christianity. Crucial to Eliot's enterprise, as well as his translations of the Bible into Massachusett, was the setting up of what came to be known as 'Praying Towns', reflecting the Puritan belief that conversion of Indians required both full understanding of the tenets of religious faith and a way of life likely to embody and encourage those tenets. The self had to be reconstructed along Puritan lines, and this involved all aspects of life, including the secular (Morrison 1974; Holstun 1983; Kellaway 1961).

On the basis of this comparison it would be tempting to see the Jesuits as either more open to Indian ideas, less culturally aggressive and absolutist than the Puritans, or, put negatively, more superficial, settling for the show rather than the substance of conversion. Certainly this latter was the Puritan view, which also served to justify their own slow progress.

If wee would force them to baptisme (as the Spaniards do about Cusco, Peru, and Mexico, having learnt them a short answer or two to some Popish questions) .... we could have gathered many hundreds, yea thousands it may bee by this time, into the name of the Churches; but wee have not learnt as yet that art of coyning Christians, or putting Christs name and image upon copper mettle. (John Eliot, quoted in Holstun 1983: 134)

Eliot's resort to a metaphor of currency is very appropriate here in its invocation of a circulation of signs, but signs whose value is ultimately based on something – here it is gold – which guarantees and authorizes them. Conversion raises the prospect of counterfeiting, of false values masquerading as true, a prospect profoundly threatening to a Puritan community concerned to protect its claim to the true faith, but prey to powerful internal dissensions as well as the threat from outside, whether Catholic or Indian. For the Puritans, the Catholic use of religious paraphernalia chimed only too well with pagan superstition and magic as a threat to the purity of the Word.

45

Catholics too, though, were exercised by how to judge a true conversion. Although the Jesuits in particular gave a very high priority to baptism (Trigger 1976: 503), they were, contrary to Protestant propaganda, reluctant to baptize prematurely. Father Biard, for instance, stressed the particular difficulty of dealing with nomadic and savage people. Even in South America where 'the people are not Savage but civilised; not wandering but stationary; not abandoned but under the watchful care of Pastors, namely in Peru and Mexico' – even there, premature baptisms had led to 'a Synagogue of Samaritans rather than a Church of the faithful. For these who were too soon Baptised willingly came to Church but it was to mutter there their ancient idolatries. They observed the appointed saints' days but it was while carrying on their sacrifices, dances, and superstition' (Thwaites 1896–1901: vol. 3, 145).

The Indians Biard first encountered in the north had been inadequately catechized and had no understanding of what was required of them. They had 'accepted baptism solely as a sign of friendship', and were unpleasantly surprised to discover that it entailed obligations like monogamy. Biard insisted that it needed to be seen like a contract, and his legal metaphor is revealing. Just as one cannot hold a person to an oath he does not understand, so one cannot expect 'a rational being of competent age to make a solemn profession of the law of God (which is done through Baptism)' when he has never been taught 'the rules and duties of the profession' (Thwaites 1896–1901: vol. 3, 147). The convert, then, must be already a rational being *before* he can become a Christian. On the other hand, this idea of the rational contract misrepresents the full Christian message in ignoring the emphasis on the overwhelming power of grace, the free and unconditional gift of Christ's sacrifice. This absolute sovereignty, expressed in the gift of grace, is not to be accessed by contracts and rationality but by the irrationality of spiritual and emotional surrender, as the preachers of the Great Awakening were later so influentially to demonstrate.[5] Contract, then, may be too narrow a term to describe either side's understanding of conversion adequately, but what Biard dismisses here as a 'sign of friendship' may point to an indigenous idea of reciprocal obligations based on giving, exchange and sacrifice which offers a more fundamental link. According to Morrison, for instance, the Montagnais believed that 'human beings and other-than-human persons were bound by webs of ritual exchange' (Morrison 1990: 418). These webs of obligation were based on the existence of an overall donor power whose actions transcended any contractual sense of fairness or obligation, and, as Morrison has shown, there was a close enough resemblance between the way the Jesuits conceived grace and the Montagnais idea of power for the conversion of ideas, if not souls, to take place.

As well as benevolence, though, the Christians introduced the crucial element of fear and judgement, based on the idea of fundamental human sinfulness. The efficacy of fear was not lost on the missionaries, and from the Indian point of view the message of a retributive and angry God seemed to be backed up in drastic terms by the devastating effects of illness and cultural change. Where originally, then, the congruence of ideas made it possible for Indian groups to accept a Christian power that could be seen as a new manifestation of traditional categories, material afflictions, combined with the Christian message of personal sin and guilt, had a cumulative impact. According to Morrison, 'At the end of the 1630s the Montagnais had internalized the Jesuit theory of sin to such an extent that continuing crisis over which they had no control implied their overwhelming guilt' (Morrison 1990: 432). In trying to make a distinction between the assimilation of Christian elements within a native religious framework and the replacement of that fundamental framework itself – which is what the missionaries would presumably require to register it as authentic conversion – the recognition of sin might well be a key moment, the point at which an alien element becomes fundamental, and a spiritual dependency is created. Between the original religious beliefs and complete conversion, though, there is a huge and complex range of beliefs and activities on the part of the Indians which deserves attention.

Though the assimilation and conversion of ideas by the Indians themselves into native categories was crucial, the missionaries had a great deal invested in minimizing this. Given their lack of interest in cultural dialogue or accommodation, the missionaries' ideal conversion would be a unilateral gift, a benevolent imposition without the complications of negotiation or exchange – the introduction of new ideas into an empty space. This filling of an empty space is altogether less messy than conversion of existing ideas (and is as seductive as the myth of the virgin land which has operated for so long at the political level in North America)[6] and it appears as early as 1555 in Richard Eden's preface to the first English edition of Peter Martyr's *De Orbe Novo, The Decades of the New World of West India.* Eden saw the influence of civility as an inevitable effect of contact with Christians, just as 'they that goo much in the soonne, are coloured therewith although they go not with such purpose'. Unlike the Jews, who were already confirmed in a false set of beliefs, 'these simple gentiles lyvinge only after the lawe of nature, may well bee lykened to a smoothe and bare table unpainted, or a white paper unwritten, upon the which yow may at the fyrst painte or wryte what yow lyste, as yow can not uppon tables alredy paynted, unlesse yow rase or blot owt the fyrste formes' (Eden 1885: 57).

This is repeated in both Puritan and Jesuit thinking, where it is linked to the common ethnocentric characterization of the Indians in terms of what they lacked, whether writing, government, or religion. In New England, John Eliot's ambition was 'to write and imprint no nother but Scripture principles in the *abrasa tabula s[c]raped board* of these naked people, that so they may be in all their principles a choice people unto the Lord' (Eliot 1660: 27). In New France, too, the Jesuits felt that the conversion of the Indians 'would be all the easier; because – as upon a bare tablet, from which there was nothing to erase – we might without opposition impress on them the ideas of a true God' (Ronda 1972: 388). It is worth noting here that the scraped board and the bare tablet represent different states, and Eliot's notion is in fact more accurate in its underlying implication that something has to be removed before the message can be applied. This relates to the issue of nakedness, whereby the absence of Christian belief or of European clothes represents not an alternative but an absence, in a binary system in which difference simply equals absence. The brute force underlying the idea of stamping or writing the Christian message, of shaping the raw material, is brought out by Richard Hakluyt: 'If gentle polishing will not serve then we shall not want hammers and rough masons enough, I mean our old soldiers trained up in the Netherlands, to square and prepare them to our Preachers hands' (Cave 1985: 12).

The realities of daily communication gave the lie to this idea of a sort of spiritual *vacuum domicilium*, but one way of recog-

nizing the existence, while dismissing the validity, of Indian religious belief, was to characterize it as worship of the devil, and we
can see some of the complexities of this operation in one of the
most perceptive of Puritan commentators, Roger Williams. At
times Williams was able to recognize the plurality of gods in the
Indian pantheon without needing to reduce them to a Christian
dualism. As Neal Salisbury puts it, he was able to see the Indians
as 'polytheists not crypto-monotheists' (Salisbury 1982: 136). This
is an important distinction when seen in the context of the metaphors of true and counterfeit coins and of the *tabula rasa*, since it
recognizes that there is something there to be changed, but this
does not in any way make Williams more tolerant or relativist
about such beliefs. His belief in the efficacy and reality of the evil
they express is so complete that it prevents him from even observing ceremonies, 'for after once being in their Houses and
beholding what their Worship was, I durst never bee an eye wit-
nesse, Spectatour, or looker on, least I should have been partak-
er of Sathans Inventions' (Williams 1643: 127–8).

Ironically, this belief in the efficacy of Indian ceremonies and
beliefs, for all its reductiveness to Christian categories, did actually allow native American gods to preserve a real existence and
efficacy, denied by later sceptical or rationalist observers who, as
a corollary to their more relativist and value-free position could,
at best, deal with them only in terms of belief rather than reality.
The main effect of this perception of Indian ceremonies and beliefs
was a blinkered approach not only to ideas but also to practitioners, and this was at the cost of a consistent blindness to the full
role of what we would now recognize as shamans, who were partly equated with witches. There is a distinct lack of evidence, even
at the level of hearsay, for shamans as practitioners of witchcraft in
the sense of *maleficium*, or malign acts against others, whereas
there is strong evidence, even from Puritans themselves, that these
figures were healers in a longstanding and widespread shamanic
tradition. The fact that these 'Witches or Sorcerers' could 'cure
by help of the devill' (Thomas Shepard, quoted in Cave 1992:
251) did not make them any less of a threat to the Puritan enterprise. 'The shamans' crime in Puritan eyes was not that they did
evil, but rather that they used their presumed alliance with the
Devil to do good.' (Cave 1992: 252)[7] Chrétien LeClercq, too, in
his account of the Micmac, is quite clear about his preconcep-

tions. 'It is true that I have never been able to discover any pact, explicit or implicit, between the jugglers and the Devil; but I cannot persuade myself on that account that the devil is not predominant in their nonsense and their impostures' (LeClercq 1910: 216).

It is in the accounts of shamans and the determination to present them as malign that we see perhaps most clearly the limitations which Christian ideology imposed, in that difference must be asserted even in the face of massive similarities. The contest for legitimacy between missionaries and shamans as upholders of traditional values is regularly presented in Christian accounts as evidence of the defeat of superstition, but it is worth looking more closely at some of the issues raised. Robert Conkling argues that the legitimation of Christian beliefs as opposed merely to their imposition was due to the taking on by the priests of the charismatic status of the shaman in contests with him, (Conkling 1974; see also Morrison 1979), but a closer look at the terms of these contests is necessary.

Accounts of the defeat of shamans actually involve an appeal to several different sorts of superiority on the part of the whites. In their own minds they may have been able to distinguish the power of new technology (such as the impressive effect of gunpowder) and scientific knowledge (such as the ability to predict an eclipse or treat illness) from the power of prayer, but their demonstrations of God's power to bring rain or cure sickness would certainly have compounded the confusion of magical and technological efficacy experienced by the Indians. This overlapping area of magic, technology and prayer raises some interesting questions about missionary belief and practice. Stanley Tambiah has usefully summarized the distinctions to be drawn between Christianity, particularly Protestant Christianity, and what the Christians would describe as pagan practices. Primitive religions saw the gods at work in nature as an integral part of it, and therefore saw them as capable of being induced to make things happen. In contrast, the Judeo-Christian God was seen as absolute, sovereign and outside of, and prior to, nature. Apart from the problematic instance of miracles, the rule was that God was not to be influenced directly, but that his will was sovereign and independent. While a spell would claim to effect a change in nature, a prayer was altogether more indirect. Tambiah also underlines the specifically Protestant associations of this, and the connection with the more general desacralization of the world described by Weber.

> It was inevitable and logical given this formulation of God's sovereignty that Protestant theologians would hammer out the distinction between religious acts as primarily intercessionary in character, and magical acts as being coercive rituals ambitiously attempting to manipulate the divine.... [For them] there was a fundamental distinction between prayer and spell, the former belonging to true religion, the latter to false religion. (Tambiah 1990: 17)

Certainly for the Jesuits of New France, according to Trigger, their belief in God's intercessionary power was barely distinguishable from magic in Tambiah's description. They believed themselves to be

> serving a god who could intervene in human affairs at any moment.... Moreover, while the Jesuits did not believe in magic in the strict sense of thinking that Roman Catholic rituals gave them the power to control nature automatically, they were convinced that their god would answer prayers for rain or good harvests, if this would convince the Indians of his glory and help to undermine the Indians' respect for their own shamans. (Trigger 1976: 503)

This is backed up by Conkling's description of the similarity of Jesuit and Indian attitudes. Whether seen negatively or positively, the elements of Christian ritual were seen to have an efficacy close to that of magic. As Conkling puts it, 'The same Christian paraphernalia – baptismal water, crosses, images, rosaries – to which some Indians attributed evil power, others, like the missionaries themselves, attributed the power to cure' (Conkling 1974: 13).

While Protestants were officially rigorous about avoiding such 'superstitious' beliefs, they were not always above exploiting Indian confusion about the efficacy of their religious powers. Edward Winslow describes an Indian accusation that the English 'had the plague buried in our store-house; which, at our pleasure, we could send forth to what place or people we would, and destroy them therewith'. In response to the accusations, the ground under the storehouse was dug up and barrels of powder were found. The Puritans therefore denied the Indian accusations, but one of them added 'but the God of the English had it in store, and could send it at his pleasure to the destruction of his and our enemies' (Winslow in Young 1971: 292). In this scene lethal technological power (gunpowder), disease and supernatural power are intriguingly, and for the Puritans fruitfully, confused.

Overall, though, the greater use of ritual and ritual objects on the part of the Catholics made them seem more like shamans than their Protestant counterparts, confirming the latter's suspicions about Catholic superstition. Protestant scrupulousness was no less characteristic of later missionaries, as in David Brainerd's careful explanation of the covenant of grace and of the sacrament as a seal or sign of that covenant. He insists that the Indians 'were likewise thoroughly sensible that 'twas no more than a seal or a sign, and not the real body and blood of Christ; that 'twas designed for the refreshment and edification of the soul, and not for the feasting of the body' (Pettit 1985: 388). The Catholic missionaries encountering the Hurons and Iroquois were posed an additional problem by the central role of torture and the ritual eating of prisoners in these cultures. While they had to accept the presence of these practices, the missionaries had an unexpected difficulty in preventing the Indians from equating the tortures of hell, as the missionaries described them, with their own ritual tortures which conferred respect and honour on those who withstood them bravely, and therefore carried too many positive connotations (see Steckley 1972: 489–92).

The most important and visible religious activity which was likely to be seen as shamanistic was baptism. For a long time this was assumed by Indians to be a curing ceremony, at least partly because priests, although reluctant to baptize healthy Indians until they were sure they were genuinely converted, made a point of administering the sacrament to those they thought on the point of death. Many of the baptized died, which did nothing for the priests' reputation as healers, but did reinforce the idea that they had power of some description. This, combined with the regular appearance of disease wherever they had been, gave strong evidence to the Indians that the priests were witches. Interestingly, though, a fair number of those baptized and assumed to be dying did in fact recover, which might suggest that their ceremony worked regardless of their intentions because of Indian belief in its efficacy. Also, as Kenneth Morrison explains, 'thinking in terms of the vital symbols of traditional power, the Montagnais concluded that if baptism could kill, it might also cure' (Morrison 1990: 420).

The refusal of Christian missionaries to recognize Indian religion as a system of beliefs and practices comparable to their own was often sustained by a working assumption that Indians simply lacked a spiritual dimension. As befitted their primitive state, they were chained to the material and animal levels. The response of one Indian when asked for his favourite prayer, 'Give us today our food, give us something to eat. This is an excellent Prayer', produces a resigned response from Le Jeune. 'I am not surprised at this Philosophy: Animalis homo, non percipit ea quae sunt Spiritus Dei. He who has never been at any school but that of the flesh, cannot speak the language of the Spirit' (Thwaites 1896–1901: vol. 8, 35). As Michael Pomedi has demonstrated, though, the Huron saw food and feasting as having strong and specific spiritual connections, and their translation of food terms makes this explicit, as he shows in the translation of the above passage from the Lord's Prayer (Pomedi 1991: 52–3). Furthermore, Le Jeune's description of the very clear message given to the Indians about the material benefits to be gained from God raised the question of how the missionaries should communicate the spiritual message, and of how far the translation and propagation of the Christian message involved mixed messages about material benefits. After all, in addition to the traditional exchanges of gifts, missionaries found it necessary to give presents as inducements to attend to the Gospel, and there must have been an awareness on the Indian side of the importance given by the French – missionaries as well as traders – to the purely economic advantages of the fur trade. There is no shortage in missionary accounts of Indian statements about blunt materialism; and the missionaries were perhaps as irritated by the accuracy of such statements as by their intellectual naivety.[8]

A fundamental issue was how the terms of Christianity were to be translated into Indian terms, and vice versa. This involved not just the word but the belief system in which it operated. As long as the missionaries refused to recognize an equivalent spiritual content in Indian beliefs, they could not invoke any for comparison. Later in the same year that Le Jeune made the above comment, there is a revealing account of an exchange following from the Indian expression of wonder at European mechanical products, particularly a chiming clock.

> But they have said all when they have said they are *ondaki*, that is *Demons*; And indeed we make profitable use of the word when we talk to them.... 'You think you are right when you see something extraordinary, in saying *ondaki*, to declare that those who make so many marvels must be Demons. And what is there so wonderful as the beauty of the Sky and the Sun?' (Thwaites 1896–1901: vol. 8, 109)

In this picture of a Jesuit reproving the Indians for not seeing 'some beneficent *oki* and some supereminent intelligence' in nature we might find a great deal of irony given the prevailing modern view of Christian exploitative views of nature versus Indian holism and ecological awareness, until we remember that Le Jeune is working his way toward God, rather than remaining at a celebration of nature, and he has already dismissed the relevance or validity of native beliefs. Rather than try to examine the full meanings of the various native terms, missionaries more usually made them fit the Procrustean bed of their own religious terminology.[9]

The limitations of the way in which native terms are used and then restricted by translation into European cultural as well as linguistic terms is well demonstrated in the description by Roger Williams of a similar concept to that described by Le Jeune (above) among the Indians of New England.

> There is a generall Custome amongst them, at the apprehension of any Excellency in Men, Women, Birds, Beasts, Fish &c. to cry out *Manittoo*, that is, it is a God, as thus if they see one man excell others in Wisdome, Valour, strength, Activity &c. they cry out *Manittoo* A God: and therefore when they talk amongst themselves of the *English* ships, and great buildings, of the plowing of their Fields, and especially of Bookes and Letters, they will end thus: *Manittowock* They are Gods: *Cummanittoo* you are a God &c. (Williams 1643: 126)

What is initially being admired here (rather than worshipped) is the 'Excellency' of technology and strangeness, but the translation of the term as 'it is a God' means that Williams is then able to make an immediate transition in order to transpose this term into general religious feeling and then Christianity. 'A strong Conviction naturall in the soule of man, that God is; filling all things, and places, and that all Excellencies dwell in God, and proceed from him, and that they only are blessed who have that Jehovah their portion.' Elsewhere Williams confirms the general use of the term ('*Manittooes*, that is, Gods, Spirits or Divine powers, as they say of every thing which they cannot comprehend' (Williams 1643: 103)) but once he has used a term from his own religion ('god') then he cannot allow such a term to float about. The sacred must be defined and clearly located. In general, Puritan cultural isolationism meant that even towards the Praying Indians there was little sense of the possibility of a reciprocal relation. The ruthless exercise of linguistic and interpretative as well as political authority is thrown into relief in the following account of John Eliot's reaction when a famous 'powah' or shaman told people:

> that a certain little hummingbird did come and peck at him when he did aught that was wrong, and sing sweetly to him when he did a good thing or spake the right words; which coming to Mr Eliot's ear he made him confess, in the presence of the congregation, that he did only mean, by the figure of the bird, the sense he had of right and wrong in his own mind. (Simmons 1986: 42)

So Eliot stringently controls who has the proper interpretation ('he did only mean').

What we have seen so far is that, though there was clear evidence of an Indian spirituality, the missionaries' preconceptions about the material limitations of primitive mentality meant that they could dismiss it as a superstitious and fetishistic attitude to objects conceived as magical. It is worth giving some more attention, though, to the role of particular objects in cultural and spiritual exchanges. While the missionaries may have conceived of their aim and activities as fundamentally spiritual they did introduce a tangible set of ritual objects to which they seemed to ascribe magical properties, and which then entered the discursive and spiritual economy of the Indian cultures. For Catholic and Protestant missionaries, the Bible, together with the cross, would have been the most potent symbol not just of the technology of writing, like other books, but of the Word of God. The extent to which non-literate cultures conceived of writing as magic or powerful has been much debated,[10] and there are clear instances in North America of the association of the Book with other dangerous powers, as in the report of the Huron dream in which 'they had seen black gowns in a dream ... who were unfolding certain books, whence issued sparks of fire which spread everywhere, and no doubt caused the pestilential disease' (Thwaites 1896–1901: vol. 20, 31–3).

In addition to these objects the Catholics also distributed images and used incense, vestments and the rosary, which already had a close resemblance to the native uses of religious and ceremonial objects. We have, for instance, a record of a sick man applying to his body 'some Images, Rosaries and Crosses; for they make great account of these, using them against the molestations of the Demons'. (Thwaites 1896–1901: vol. 45, 63; and see Conkling 1974: 13 for further instances.) Whether this is a proper use of Christian symbols is not clear, and the missionaries themselves are sometimes hesitant about ascribing power to objects.[11]

This sort of instance was close enough to native practice to scandalize the Puritans, but the Catholic missionaries were also often disturbed by the uncontrolled and unauthorized uses to which Christian objects were put once they entered the circulation of cultural signs among Indians responding to these new items. This can be seen in Chrétien LeClercq's account of the Micmac. As a result of seeing the respect accorded to missionaries,

> some of these barbarians have often been seen meddling with, and affecting to perform, the office and functions of missionary, even to hearing confession, like us, from their fellow-countrymen. So therefore, when persons of this kind wish to give authority to that which they say, and to set themselves up as patriarchs, they make our Gaspesians believe they have received some particular gift from heaven. (LeClercq 1910: 229)

One man, who claimed to have received 'an image from heaven', had in fact 'only a picture which had been given him when he was trading with our French'. The claim to have received a gift from supernatural donor powers here chimes with the pre-established native religion, rather than Christianity, but the fact that the picture is a trade object is also significant. A few pages later LeClercq describes a woman (he describes her as 'a famous one', suggesting a pre-established shamanic status perhaps) who 'had as the basis for all her ridiculous and superstitious devotions some beads of jet, which were the remains of an unthreaded rosary'. She gives these to people claiming that they are from heaven. Another woman has five mysterious rosary beads and wants LeClercq to believe that they are 'a present which Heaven had made to this pretended *religieuse*' (LeClercq 1910: 231), but LeClercq disabuses her of this idea by an act of conjuring, palming one of them and making it disappear and reappear, thus demystifying the beads but also, ironically, playing the role of the 'juggler' or shaman he is trying to discredit.

His approach to the woman is one of ridicule, and he tells us that, as well as the beads, she has 'a King of Hearts, the foot of a glass, and a kind of medal' before which she prostrates herself 'as before her divinities'. She is from 'the Crossbearer nation' and has decorated her cross with 'beadwork, wampum, painting and porcupine quills'. We have a glimpse here of a really thoroughgoing syncretism, which is recognized by LeClercq even if his word 'pleasing' is used ironically.

> The pleasing mixture thereof represented several and separate figures of everything which was in her devotions. She placed it [the cross] usually between her and the French, obliging them to make their prayers before her cross, whilst from her side she made her own prayers, according to her custom, before her King of Hearts and her other Divinities. (LeClercq 1910: 232–3)

From being the credulous butt of LeClercq's ridicule, she is now revealed as a skilled intermediary, concretely embodying the ambivalent and Janus-faced aspects of spiritual power in a situation of crisis and change. Her cross that faces two ways, encrusted with different symbols of value, offers us a powerful image of cultural adaptation, and would connect her with the extensive recent debates over the role of Native American women as mediators and cultural brokers.[12] What LeClercq saw as a misuse of Christian symbols we can more usefully see as their assimilation into a complex mixture of trade goods and objects traditionally valued for their exotic origins or associations. It is not surprising that rosary beads are in this case being redistributed and recycled, given the well-established role of wampum and other forms of beads in overlapping value-systems, ranging from the monetary to the religious (Miller and Hamell 1986).

We have seen the ways in which what the missionaries introduced – whether words, ideas or objects – circulated within a set of economies, changing their nature in the process or, like the Micmac woman's cross, facing both ways. Although part of the missionaries' rhetoric may have been that of dissemination, of spreading the Word and the seed, they were also concerned to control and to limit the interpretation, to authorize and to define the proper interpretation of their cultural property. For both Puritan and Jesuit, the gift of God to the Indians was a one-way not a reciprocal process. Such isolationism, of course, went against Indian practice at all levels, and there is evidence that accusations of witchcraft against missionaries were largely the result of their violation of norms of cooperation and reciprocity (Trigger 1976: 67). This was not just because of the missionaries' need for privacy, or their selfishness. They were aware of the need to be seen to be generous, and were careful to provide presents to fit in with native customs. They were, too, convinced that they were giving the inestimable gift of God's Word, but they were incapable of understanding the need also to take, and to accord some respect for what the Indians believed. A particularly clear instance with which to conclude is their reaction to the ceremony known as the Feast of the Dead, one of the most important ceremonies among the Huron, which also spread to some Algonquian groups.

Harold Hickerson's account of the Algonquian forms sees the rise and fall of the feast as reflecting a growing influx of goods and a communal response to this which stressed redistribution and exchange at a practical and a spiritual level (Hickerson 1960). Nicolas Denys, for instance, describes the throwing into the grave of 'bows, arrows, snow-shoes, spears, robes of Moose, Otter, and Beaver' but also 'when they were not yet disabused of their errors, I have seen them give to the dead man, guns, axes, iron arrow-heads, and kettles' (Denys 1908: 439). His explanation is that 'they held all these to be much more convenient for their use than would have been their kettles of wood' but other sources suggest a more complex valuation of the kettle.

Laurier Turgeon, demonstrating how the European-made kettle became invested with a complex of values that went well beyond its utility, shows how, though it did fit in with pre-existing belief systems (such as the colour symbolism explored by Hamell), it also actively gained power by its provenance from outside. Turgeon argues that the kettles seemed to be reserved for ceremonial and ritual use, as in feasts (including cannibal activities), and was associated with group cohesion and identity. Of particular interest is the kettles' relation to the Feast of the Dead, the central activities of which are described in metaphors of cooking and the kettle. Kettles were systematically destroyed, or rather made non-functional in terms of their original purpose, so that they could function in a different way. As Turgeon puts it, 'The copper kettle served as a catalyst for identity formation *because* [my italics] it was an appropriated object. The act of appropriation, more than the object itself, produced the creative tension involved in identity formation (Turgeon 1997: 21).

In the feast of the Dead those who had died since the last ceremony were disinterred and their bones all buried together in one place, representing and reinforcing the unity and friendship of their descendants, who marked this with feasts and the exchange of gifts (Tooker 1991: 139). The many items buried with the dead, as elsewhere (see Simmons 1970), included a notable number of trade goods, as well as other items of value like wampum, and the ceremony had a crucial role in the redistribution of goods, to which the mingling of bones was a symbolic corollary. As Bruce Trigger has argued, the fact that following the increase in trade and in material wealth the Huron chose to elaborate the Feast of the Dead, 'a ritual that depended so heavily on redistribution and making offerings to the dead', is evidence of the ways in which they were incorporating new items and new wealth into the traditional patterns. Not only did the Jesuits oppose the obvious waste of burying goods with the dead, but neither could they allow the mingling of Christian and pagan bones. Even in death, the Christian could not be assimilated into the processes of inclusion and circulation which were as fundamental to the Indians as they were threatening to the purity of the Gospel.

## Notes

1     The process was often described as 'reducing' the Indians to Christianity, which has misleading modern connotations, and meant then 'turning towards'. It also, of course, echoes the Spanish policy of *reducción* in Paraguay and elsewhere.

2     For a useful survey of missionary activity in North America see Bowden (1981). For a brief overview of Catholic missions in the northeast see Campeau (1988) and for Protestant activity in the northeast see Beaver (1988).

3     A reformist branch of the Franciscan Observants started in France at the end of the sixteenth century.

4     For Jesuit policy see Healy (1958). For a summary of Recollect policy see Trigger (1976: 376–81). The North American ventures were influenced by accounts of successes in Paraguay (see Trigger 1976: 577). For a summary in English of recent approaches to Latin American missions, see Langer and Jackson (1995: 1–48).

5     See Murray (1996) and Heimert and Miller (1967). It is interesting that the Indians themselves seem to have developed a highly charged style of preaching which anticipated the emotional intensities of the preachers of the Great Awakening (Bragdon 1996: 585).

6     The ideological implications of the cluster of gendered images of virgin land, *vacuum domicilium*, and nakedness which persist from the earliest accounts have been much discussed. See, for example, Rabasa (1993: 23–48).

7     The Puritan blindness seems also to have blinded them to the true status of two of their most important intermediaries, who were clearly shamans and whose names seemed to indicate this, one of them even being called Hobomok (Shuffleton 1976). Edward Winslow's account of the Indians of New England as encountered by the Pilgrims shows the actual movement away from the idea of an absolute absence to an uneasy parallel with Christian dualities of God and devil. Having identified Kiehtan as a positive deity, Winslow then seems to have to present the other major figure, Hobbamock, negatively: 'this, as far as we can conceive, is the devil'. This is in spite of the fact that he describes in some detail how Hobbamock is called upon 'to cure their wounds and

diseases and that those who communicate with him, through visions and observances, the powahs and pnieses are clearly men of superior personal qualities, of great courage and wisdom' (Young 1971: 359). The problem for the modern reader is in finding where exactly this evil is supposed to reside which makes the distinction so absolute, but for Winslow the distinction between good and evil deities was a given.

8    I have concentrated in this essay on some of the magical properties assigned to European goods, but from the Indian perspective the (over)valuation of fur by the Europeans was equally remarkable. Where further south gold was the lure and the focus of fetishism, in the north it was beaver skins. One much-quoted comment reveals a keen awareness of what we might now see as the fetishism of the commodity.

> The savages say that it [the beaver] is the animal well-beloved by the French, English and Basques – in a word, by the Europeans. I heard my host [a Montagnais chief] say one day jokingly, *Missi picoutau amiscou*, 'The beaver does everything perfectly well, it makes kettles, hatchets, swords, knives, bread; and in short it makes everything.' He was making sport of us Europeans who have such a fondness for the skin of the animal and who fight to see who will give the most to these Barbarians, to get it. (Thwaites 1896–91: vol. 6, 298–9)

(Cf Taussig 1980 for a fuller discussion in the context of South America.)

9    Thus 'demon' is used (and in the original French) and 'esprit' serves for soul and all similar Indian concepts. See Pomedi (1991) for fuller discussion of *oki*, and the Jesuit use of it, and Steckley (1972) on Iroquoian terms. See also Hamell (1986–87: 92).

10   See Wogan (1994) for a useful and sceptical survey of this theme.

11   See Biard's cautious explanation for the cure of the son of the influential Membertou after Biard had applied a holy relic to him (Thwaites 1896–1901: vol. 2, 19).

12   For a useful critical survey of recent work, see Strong (1996).

# Works cited

Beaver, R. Pierce (1988), 'Protestant Churches and the Indians'. In Wilcomb Washburn (ed.), *History of Indian–White Relations, Handbook of North American Indians*, Washington: Smithsonian Institution, vol. 4.

Bowden, Henry Warner (1981), *American Indians and Christian Missions: Studies in Cultural Conflict*, Chicago and London: Chicago University Press.

Bragdon, Kathleen (1996), 'Gender as a Social Category in Native Southern New England' *Ethnohistory* 43: 573–92.

Campeau, Lucien (1988), 'Roman Catholic Missions in New France'. In Wilcomb Washburn (ed.) *History of Indian-White Relations, Handbook of North American Indians*, Washington: Smithsonian Institution, vol. 4.

Cave, Alfred A. (1985) 'Richard Hakluyt's Savages: The Influence of 16th Century Travel Narratives on English Indian Policy in North America', *International Social Science Review* 60(1): 3–24

—— (1992), 'Indian Shamans and English Witches in Seventeenth Century New England', *Essex Institute Historical Collections*, 128: 239–54.

Conkling, Robert (1974), 'Legitimacy and Conversion in Social Change: The Case of French Missionaries and the Northeastern Algonkian', *Ethnohistory* 21: 1–24.

Denys, Nicolas ([1672] 1908), *The Description and Natural History of the Coasts of North America*, ed. W. F. Ganong, Toronto: The Champlain Society.

Eden, Richard (1885), *The Decades of the New World of West India*, repr. in Edward Arber (ed.), *The First Three English Books on America*, Birmingham.

Eliot, John (1660), 'The Learned Conjectures of Reverend Mr. John Eliot Touching the Americans, of New and Notable Consideration, Written to Mr. Thorowgood', in Thomas Thorowgood, *Jewes in America*, London.

Hamell, George R. (1986–87), 'Strawberries, Floating Islands, and Rabbit Captains: Mythical Realities and European Contact in the Northeast during the Sixteenth and Seventeenth Centuries', *Journal of Canadian Studies* 21: 72–94.

Healy, George R. (1958), 'The French Jesuits and the Idea of the Noble Savage' *William and Mary Quarterly* 15: 143–67.

Heimert, A. and P. Miller (eds) (1967), *The Great Awakening*, Indianapolis: Bobbs Merrill.

Hickerson, Harold (1960), 'The Feast of the Dead Among the Seventeenth Century Algonkians of the Upper Great Lakes', *American Anthropologist* 62: 81–107.

Holstun, James (1983), 'John Eliot's Empirical Millenarianism', *Representations* 4 (Fall): 128-53.

Kellaway, William (1961), *The New England Company, 1649-1776: Missionary Society to the American Indians*, London: Longman.

Langer, Erick and Robert H. Jackson (eds) (1995), *The New Latin American Mission History*, Lincoln and London: University of Nebraska Press.

LeClercq, Chrétien ([1691] 1910), *New Relations of Gaspesia, with the Customs and Religion of the Gaspesian Indians*, ed. W. F. Ganong, Toronto: The Champlain Society.

Miller, Christopher and George R. Hamell (1986), 'A New Perspective on Indian-White Contact: Cultural Symbols and Colonial Trade', *Journal of American History* 73: 311-28.

Morrison, Kenneth M. (1974) '"That Art of Coyning Christians": John Eliot and the Praying Indians of Massachusetts', *Ethnohistory* 21: 77-92.

— (1979), 'Towards A History of Intimate Encounters: Algonkian Folklore, Jesuit Missionaries, and Kiwakwe, the Cannibal Giant', *American Indian Culture and Research Journal* 3(4): 51-80.

— (1990), 'Baptism and Alliance: Symbolic Mediations of Religious Syncretism', *Ethnohistory* 37: 416-37.

Murray, David (1996), 'David Brainerd and the Gift of Christianity', *European Review of Native American Studies* 10(2): 23-9.

Pettit, N. (ed.)(1985) *Jonathan Edwards, The Life of David Brainerd*, vol. 7 in *Works of Jonathan Edwards*, New Haven: Yale University Press.

Pomedi, Michael M. (1991), *Ethnophilosophical and Ethnolinguistic Perspectives on the Huron Indian Soul*, Lewiston, Queenston, Lampeter: Edwin Mellen Press.

Rabasa, José (1993), *Inventing America: Spanish Historiography and the Formation of Eurocentrism*, Norman and London: University of Oklahoma Press.

Ronda, James P. (1972) 'The European Indian: Jesuit Civilisation Planning in New France', *Church History* 41: 385-95.

Salisbury, Neal (1982), *Manitou and Providence: Indians, Europeans and the Making of New England, 1500-1643*, New York and Oxford: Oxford University Press.

Shuffleton, Frank (1976), 'Indian Devils and Pilgrim Fathers: Squanto, Hobomok, and the English Conception of Indian Religion', *New England Quarterly* 49(1): 108–16.

Simmons, W. (1970), *Cautantowwit's House: An Indian Burial Ground on the Island of Conanicut in Narragansett Bay*, Providence: Brown University Press.

—— (1986), *Spirit of the New England Tribes: Indian History and Folklore, 1620–1984*, Hanover and London: University Press of New England.

Steckley, John (1972), 'The Warrior and the Lineage: Jesuit Use of Iroquoian Images to Communicate Christianity', *Ethnohistory* 39: 479–509.

Strong, Pauline Turner (1996), 'Feminist Theory and the "Invasion of the Heart" in North America', *Ethnohistory* 43: 683–712.

Tambiah, Stanley J. (1990), *Magic, Science, Religion and the Scope of Rationality*, Cambridge: Cambridge University Press.

Taussig, Michael (1980), *The Devil and Commodity Fetishism in South America*, Chapel Hill: North Carolina University Press.

Thwaites, Reuben G. (1896–1901), *The Jesuit Relations and Allied Documents*, 73 vols., Cleveland: Burrows Brothers Press.

Tooker, Elisabeth (1991), *An Ethnography of the Huron Indians, 1615–1649*, Syracuse NY: Syracuse University Press.

Trigger, Bruce G. (1976), *The Children of Aataentsic: A History of the Huron People to 1660*, Kingston and Montreal: McGill-Queens University Press.

Turgeon, Laurier (1997), 'The Tale of the Kettle: Odyssey of an Intercultural Object' *Ethnohistory* 22: 1–29.

Williams, Roger ([1643] 1971), *A Key into the Language of America, or An Help to the Language of the Natives in that part of America called New England*, Ann Arbor, Michigan: Gryphon Books.

Winslow, Edward ([1841] 1971), 'Good News From New England'. In Alexander Young (ed.), *Chronicles of the Pilgrim Fathers of the Colony of Plymouth, 1602–1625*, New York: Da Capo Press.

Wogan, Peter (1994), 'Perceptions of European Literacy in Early Contact Situations' *Ethnohistory* 41: 407–27.

Young, A. ([1841] 1971), *Chronicles of the Pilgrim Fathers of the Colony of Plymouth, 1602–1625*, New York: Da Capo Press.

# 2

# 'The kindness of the blessed Virgin': faith, succour, and the cult of Mary among Christian Hurons and Iroquois in seventeenth-century New France

WILLIAM B. HART

Paul Ragueneau, the Jesuit missionary at Saint-Marie, the Huron mission, noted in the early 1650s shortly after the mission's demise that some of the Christian Huron refugees held 'God as present in their minds, from morning to night, as if they saw him with their eyes', and 'lived in constant desire of belonging wholly to him'. 'Others,' Ragueneau observed, 'have a devotion for the most blessed Virgin'. One of the male Indian converts, 'a good Christian', according to Ragueneau, recently informed him that 'although he had been asking, for over ten years, for many favors and many things difficult to obtain, he did not remember having ever been refused' by the Virgin Mary. Ragueneau's informant added:

> She it is ... who delivered me from the hands of the Iroquois when they held me captive with Father Isaac Jogues, who finally died there [at Gandaouague]; she it is who had given back to me as many children as death had ravished from me; she it is who, ever since misfortunes have assailed us, has preserved all the members of my family, as regards both the health

of their bodies and that of their souls. She it is who gives me patience in the sufferings that I constantly endure; she it is who obtains for me grace to pay little heed to the good things of this life, and to fear not its evils; she has cured all those on whose behalf I have invoked her aid; and she does all that I wish, as I desire to do nothing and to wish for nothing except what she wishes. (Thwaites 1959: vol. 36, 209)

Here, Ragueneau constructs an image of a pious Huron Christian man for whom the Virgin Mary was, in the words of one scholar, 'the Woman for All Seasons – And All Reasons' (Pelikan 1996: 215). As with Christians through the centuries, the blessed Virgin stood for many things to this Huron informant: she was redeemer, mother-provider of life and good health, intercessor, counsellor, staff of support, healer, and personal *orenda*, or guardian spirit.

From our vantage point of relativism in the late twentieth century, Ragueneau's claims may appear to be spurious, for we know that the *Jesuit Relations* contain embellished accounts, invented speeches, and inflated claims (Trigger 1987: 17). Nevertheless, it is not useful to assume that all that appears in the *Jesuit Relations* is hyperbole and fabrication; historian Bruce Trigger has noted that most Jesuits were careful reporters who were mindful to 'record and evaluate their sources of information' (Trigger 1987: 469). Some historians believe that the Jesuits in New France were quite tolerant of Indian culture and have read (mistakenly, Trigger believes) in their reports in the *Relations* 'a brand of cultural relativism' (Axtell 1985: 279; Trigger 1987: 469–70). The aim of the Jesuits, most historians have agreed, was to stamp out the 'traditional' religion of the Indians and replace it with Roman Catholicism through coercion, threats, cajoling, and instruction (Trigger 1987: 468–70). Ragueneau, whom Trigger suggests is reasonably trustworthy because he was more accepting than many of his peers of Huron sacred practices and sometimes questioned the oppressive consequences of some of the teachings of his Jesuit brethren, offers a credible Huron reading of a usable Virgin Mary (Trigger 1985: 265–6; Trigger 1987: 738; Axtell 1985: 80–1). It is a reading that reveals myriad native perceptions of the Virgin Mary.

Historians and anthropologists who have studied religious change among Indians have noted that, in some instances, native converts to Christianity reinterpreted sacred Christian personages, objects, places, and principles, often assigning them native meanings. During the early stages of evangelization, Catholic missionaries frequently pointed out parallels between Christian precepts and Indian-belief concepts so that their native catechumens might more quickly and easily grasp Christianity. This process often resulted, however, in the unintended indigenization of Christianity. Many converts came to understand God or Jesus as the Great Creator, the Garden of Eden as a native paradise, baptism as a ritual that offered a measure of protection or symbolized adoption, and the burning of incense as a ritual of purification akin to the burning of tobacco (see Grant 1984; Burkhart 1989; 1992; Axtell 1985: 110–12; Peers 1996: 284–302; Shoemaker 1995: 49–71; Blanchard 1982: 77–102). One question that has not been fully addressed by historians and anthropologists is: What did the Virgin Mary mean to Christian Indians during the contact period in northeastern North America? More specifically, how did Huron and Iroquois converts in seventeenth-century New France under the tutelage of such Jesuit missionaries as Paul Ragueneau conceive of the Virgin Mary? Did they assign native meanings to the blessed Virgin, or did they regard her in the same way as their Catholic catechists? Did Christian Iroquois and Huron men and women conceive of her in the same way? The evidence suggests that while many devout Indians shared the Jesuits' image of the blessed Virgin as the holy mother of Christ, many converts viewed Mary as a usable *orenda*, or spirit, whose power was accessible to meet native needs. For many converts to Catholicism, the blessed Virgin stood as a gateway to Christianity, a 'bridge builder', as one historian has put it, 'to other traditions, other cultures, and other religions' (Pelikan 1996: 67).[1]

## Early modern Europe and the cult of the Virgin Mary

France boasts twenty-two major shrines dedicated to the Virgin Mary. These shrines, built before and after the Reformation, attest to the long and profound history of the cult of the Virgin Mary in France (Carroll 1986: 11–12). French Jesuits in seventeenth-century New France drew upon this history as they strove to make new Huron, Iroquois, and Algonquian converts, and to solidify piety among the converted. Their teachings of the Virgin Mary, their use of icons and rituals, and their encouragement of cults and societies dedicated to the Virgin Mary, reflected the state of Marianism in seventeenth-century Europe.[2]

During the Reformation, many Protestant reformers pointed to the seeming idolatry of the Virgin Mary as just one of the many faults of the church. They denounced the church for promoting the use of relics, pilgrimages, and rituals dedicated to Mary as a means to redemption. Many Protestants harshly criticized the church for having bestowed the power of intercession upon Mary which they considered a power held only by God. Such idolatrous worship of Mary contradicted the Protestant belief that inner faith, moral rectitude, and purity of heart were essential for redemption. To Protestants, the Catholic church came dangerously close to violating the Christian world view of monotheism, which held that God and his powers alone were supreme (Warner 1976: 296).

The Catholic Counter-Reformation responded to its critics by defending the intercessionary power of the Virgin Mary and other saints, and by reinvigorating the reliance on externals, such as images and relics, to effect grace. The Catholic church has long accorded Mary the power of intercession, that is, of acting as a mediator between God and mankind. As Marina Warner has noted, Catholics have prayed to Mary to ask her to 'pray for us', rather than to answer our prayers directly. Mary takes our prayers to God, who in turn answers them, as only He can, for she does not have the power to grant our prayers. Yet the church has considered her power of mediation efficacious, for Jesus Christ, her son, the Lord God, cannot refuse her petitions. Hence, prayers of repentance and resolve, Warner points out, are 'wonder-working', and petitioners make little distinction between Mary's indirect power and the direct power of God. (Warner 1976: 286, 288, 296-7; Pelikan 1996: 131-4).

Many theologians viewed Mary's intercessionary role as particular to women. One fourteenth-century Franciscan *exemplum* held that

> When we have offended Christ we should first go to the Queen of heaven and offer her, instead of a present, prayers, fasting,

vigils and alms; then she, like a mother, will come between thee and Christ, the father who wishes to beat us, and she will throw the cloak of her mercy between the rod of punishment and us and soften the king's anger against us. (Warner 1976: 285, 388 n. 1)

This *exemplum* depicts Mary as the 'handmaid of the Lord' (Pelikan 1996: 83). The church of the early modern era represented Mary, the handmaid, as a woman of patience, of quietude, and of passivity, who was dutiful, obedient, contemplative, and submissive. She preferred the privacy and quiet of her home over the hubbub of the male public sphere, and she knew her place in the hierarchy of family and society. Clergymen painted a picture of Mary as the perfect woman for women (Pelikan 1996: 83-4; Ellington 1995: 247-59). All women - wives, mothers, daughters, sisters - were to be like Mary: gentle, forgiving, indulgent, merciful, humble, chaste, obedient, and brimming 'with a mother's love'. The second sentence of the *Ave Maria*, the prayer that begins 'Hail Mary, full of grace', underscores the prescriptive relationship of women to Mary; here the prayer deems Mary as 'blessed ... among all women' (Warner 1976: 286; Peers 1996: 288; Pelikan 1996: 14).

This effort to uphold Mary as the role model for all women was more an ideal than a reality, for as Marina Warner has pointed out, to emulate a perfect woman, who was both a virgin and a mother, was utterly impossible (Warner 1976: 336-9; Ellington 1995: 257-9). In reality, how could a woman be both a mother *and* a virgin, and, like Mary, continue to produce children *and* maintain her virginity? She was a virgin when she was delivered of Jesus, having been mysteriously impregnated by the Holy Spirit, and, according to Catholic tradition, remained a virgin throughout her life.

The Virgin Mary stood as a role model to men as well as women, for the church assigned to her the most critical role of 'mother of mercy'. As Ragueneau's male informant shows, Mary did not favour one gender over the other; she acted upon the Huron's petitions and saved him from certain death, ensured the health and welfare of his family and friends, and gave him strength and patience when he suffered. Mary took the side of the fallen, regardless of age or sex, and, in seeking salvation for sinners after

death, pleaded their cases before God. Mary continues to inter-
cede on behalf of repentant believers, who seek to have their sins
washed away in purgatory before ascending to heaven (Warner
1976: 315–18, 326).[3] Her chief function, then, is to listen to sup-
plications and ease the pain and suffering of sinners with the promise of 'heavenly medicine'. The last few words of the *Ave Maria*,
labelled 'the best-loved prayer of the Catholic world' by Marina
Warner, articulates this theory; reciters of the prayer ask Mary for
forgiveness in life and in death: 'pray for us sinners, now and at
the hour of our death' (Warner 1976: 331, 285; Pelikan 1995:
14).

In order to initiate and sustain prayer, worship, and the con-
templation of the powers of Mary, God, and the saints, the church
has relied historically upon external stimuli. The mass, sacred
music and rituals, the identification of holy places, and the use of
holy relics and pictures constitute just a few of the material ways
that the church has tried to bring its parishioners closer to God
and thus to Roman Catholicism (Warner 1976: 290). Paintings
and sculptures of Mary from different periods in history abound.
The significance of these icons lay not simply in their representation of the Virgin, but, as Warner has noted, how they possess
reality itself. For believers, the 'beneficent forces' imbedded in
such representations actually bring life to the icons. Eye-witness-
es have reported that smashed icons of the Virgin Mary have bled,
and that in some paintings the Virgin Mary has wept and her
breasts have excreted oil (Warner 1976: 292–3).[4]

The Virgin Mary of early modern Europe was a woman for all
seasons for various reasons. When the Jesuits brought the concept of the Virgin Mary to seventeenth-century New France, some
of their Indian catechumens understood Mary as a usable force.
She was to some the blessed Virgin, the mother of God; to others a powerful *orenda*.

## The blessed Virgin in New France

In the seventeenth century, the French Jesuits faced the formida-
ble task of converting the Indians of New France to Christianity.
Jesuit evangelization followed that of the Recollects, who failed
to reap a harvest of souls. The Jesuits enjoyed more success among
some Indian nations, particularly the Hurons. Most historians
trace their success to a modification of methodology: rather than

follow the Recollect model of settling French émigrés among the non-Christian Indians to act as role models for transforming Indians into French men and women, the Jesuits opted to isolate their Indian neophytes from what they viewed as the deleterious influences of the French in order to have complete control over the conversion process. In this way, the Jesuits kept together whole villages, which they then tried to convert. The Jesuits believed that the Hurons and other native converts did not have to become French in order to become Christians, just so long as they abandoned their sacred 'superstitions' (Trigger 1987: 468, 687, 702-3, 709, 711; Axtell 1985: 71-2).

According to Trigger, the Jesuits found it easier to make converts than to keep them. To ensure the latter, the Jesuits relied upon material rewards, such as food and weapons; ceremonies and rituals, such as prayers and processions; and the segregation of converts from traditionalists, with converts set apart and above their 'heathen' brethren through their enrollment in confraternities and sodalities. (Trigger 1987: 699-714). Above all, the Jesuits used the powerful tool of the Virgin Mary to secure and sustain converts. They helped their own cause by appointing Mary the patron saint of the church and of the province of Quebec. In 1637, Father Le Jeune remarked that 'we have taken for patroness of the church of Kebec the holy Virgin under the title of her Conception, which we believe to be immaculate, so we have celebrated this Festival with solemnity and rejoicing'. Two years later, the Jesuits declared that 'New France, with its King, acknowledged the Blessed Virgin as the Lady and Protectress of his Crown and of all his Estates'. Moreover, Montreal, founded 17 May 1642, was at one point named 'Ville-Marie, in honor of the Virgin Mary, to whom it was especially dedicated' (Thwaites 1959: vol. 11, 67; vol. 15, 223; vol. 21, 311-12, n. 4). As the protector of the province of Quebec, Mary, according to Jesuit thinking, also extended her protection and love to the Indians in the region.[5]

In order to keep the veneration of the Virgin Mary alive among their Indian converts, officials of the church in Quebec arranged to receive an icon of Mary from a small community in France. François-Joseph Le Mercier acknowledged in his relation that Quebec had received a 'statue of the most blessed Virgin, made from the oak in which, many years before, was found a miraculous Image of Our Lady of the Faith' in the town of 'Foye in the province of Liège, one league from the Town of Dinant'. The icon was sent to Quebec in order to be 'placed in some Chapel where the Savages ordinarily perform their exercises of piety'. The Reverend Father superior decided to make the icon a 'gift for a little Church that had just been completed in a Village of the Hurons, a league and a half distant from Quebec ... dedicated to Our Lady, under title of the Annunciation'. Indians were not the only ones who worshipped at the chapel; 'On Sundays and Feasts,' Le Mercier noted, 'there come hither from all parts so many Pilgrims, even from the French settlements that are farthest distant, that often they cannot all find entrance.' They came for various reasons, 'either to find relief there in their ailments, both bodily and spiritual; or to leave there, after being cured, signal evidence of their gratitude'. Some pilgrims remained at the chapel for nine consecutive days to observe their entire novenas (Thwaites 1959: vol. 53, 131-3; vol. 54, 287-9, 297; vol. 60, 71).

At least one Jesuit missionary, Jacques Bruyas, carried the icon southward into Mohawk country, where he hoped the image of the blessed Virgin would soften the hearts and souls of Christians and non-Christians alike. Bruyas's gesture coincided with Jesuit efforts to draw Mohawks and other Iroquois off to the Catholic mission at Kahnawake near Montreal. There, in 1679 in Iroquoia, Bruyas attributed the rise in Christian piety among the Mohawks at Gandaouague

> to the kindness of the blessed virgin, of whom there was sent to us a miraculous image from nostre dame de foy. I can say that since we were in possession of this precious trust, a complete Transformation has taken place in the church of agnie [Mohawks]; old Christians have regained their former fervor, and the number of the freshly-converted goes on increasing from Day to Day. (Thwaites 1959: vol. 61, 213-15)

Bruyas went on to describe how he and his Jesuit brethren 'unveiled that precious statue on the Day of the Conception of the Immaculate Virgin, with all the Ceremony in our power, and while chanting her litanies in the Iroquois language'. They established a ritual around the icon, unveiling it each Saturday 'during the Singing of the same litanies' and every Sunday, when the Indians assembled at the chapel three times during the course of

*Figure 1*    Native family shown praying syncretically. Detail from *Novae Franciae Accurata Delineatio.* Photo: Bibliothèque nationale de France.

the day to 'recite the Beads before their good mother and protectress' (Thwaites 1959: vol. 61, 213–15).

Bruyas probably overstated the degree of Christian fervour among Mohawks as a consequence of the icon of the Virgin Mary. Their familiarity with Christianity was probably similar to that of Hurons, which, according to Bruce Trigger, was minimal during the early years of Jesuit proselytization. Most Hurons had no true grasp of Christianity, but rather tried to replicate what they thought the Jesuits wanted (Trigger 1987: 710). Given that the Hurons had much more continuous contact with Jesuits than the Iroquois of New York, it is difficult to believe that 'a complete Transformation' took place at Gandaouague. Nevertheless, the Mohawks at Gandaouague probably supplicated the totem of Mary in the same way that they entreated their charms and totems, which were physical representations of *orendas*, or spirits. One propitiated these physical objects, even made sacrifices to them and held feasts in their honour, in order to ensure luck in hunting, favour in war, and success in everyday life (Gerhing & Starna 1988: 12; Trigger 1987: 78–9). As one early Jesuit put it, their 'devotion toward the Virgin does not end merely in reciting some prayers in her honor; it goes even to actual deeds. There is hardly one of the Inhabitants of that region, however poor he may be, who has not exerted himself to present something to her' (Thwaites 1959: vol. 13, 131–3).

For many Huron converts, Mary bridged Christianity and the Huron religion through parallel myths of virgin birth, or at least birth by mysterious means. Both Mary and the daughter of Sky Woman in the Huron and Iroquois creation myths were mysteriously impregnated by sacred beings, and, therefore, were virgins when they gave birth to divine sons. In the various versions of the Iroquois and Huron creation myths, a woman identified as 'the daughter' or 'the child' of Sky Woman – the goddess who plunged to earth from the Sky World above, and who, thus, represents the catalyst for Indian life on earth – gave birth to twin sons, the first divine humans to occupy the earth. Like Mary, the twins' mother was a virgin, having been miraculously impregnated by a mysterious suitor who placed two arrows across her body after she had fainted. Devotees to the Iroquois religion identified her good son, Teharonghyawago, as the Creator, who, like Christ, taught mankind ethical (as well as practical) ways of living. Shortly after being born, the evil twin, Tawiskaron, killed his mother, thereby conveniently preserving her virginity.[6]

Historians have noted that the Virgin Mary has long stood as a surrogate for female deities of existing female cults. However, the linkage breaks down in most cases, Michael Carroll has argued, over the Virgin Mary's virginity. Most female deities of goddess cults express their identities through their fertility, which, of course, they manifest through sexual activity (Carroll 1986: 32–5, 58). Not so with the Virgin Mary, nor with the daughter of Sky Woman. So conveniently did Mary and the mother of the twin Iroquois sons match each other that some converts regarded them as interchangeable. John Norton, the early nineteenth-century Scot-Cherokee writer, teacher, and culture broker who identified ethnically as Mohawk, explained in his *Journal* that many of the Christian Iroquois throughout southern Canada did not discredit the Iroquois creation myth that featured Sky Woman and her daughter. Rather, they 'endeavour[ed] to accommodate it [the myth] to the Scriptural account of our Blessed Lord'. Norton one day 'asked one of these old men, who in his youth had had much conversation with the Roman Catholic Priests, if he remembered the name of the Mother of Teharonghyawago'. His informant answered 'not in our language, but in that of the Europeans, she is called Maria' (Norton 1970 [1816]: 91).

Believers in both the daughter of Sky Woman and in the Virgin Mary disassociated the two women from sexuality. As far back as the early medieval period, devotees to the Virgin called her 'royal mother'; 'queen of the angels'; 'joy of saints'; 'consolation of the unhappy'; and 'refuge of all sinners'. The picture created by these images is of a regal yet compassionate, tender yet powerful, accessible yet lofty, divine Mother of Jesus (see Carroll 1986: 5–6, 21; Bynum 1982: 213, 225–6, 229 n. 203, 244; Peers 1996: 288). The Jesuits cast her as the fount of the Holy Family, which the missionaries promoted as the ideal family embodying ideal gender roles. The missionaries presented Mary as the model Catholic woman: loving, nurturing, humble, pious, and chaste (Peers 1996: 288). In 1653, Jesuit missionaries founded a congregation dedicated to the Virgin Mary in an effort to keep the Christian faith alive among Indian neophytes. The effect of the confraternity was to segregate Huron converts from their non-Christian families and friends through membership in the select sodality. Le Mercier explained that he and his colleagues admitted only those Huron men and women 'who [led] exemplary lives, and who, by their virtue, render[ed] themselves worthy of this grace'. Le Mercier went on to claim that each of the dozen or so converts selected for the first confraternity to the Virgin Mary in Huron country 'redoubled' his or her fervour and felt obliged to support the dignity of the exalted title, 'SERVANT OF THE VIRGIN' (Thwaites 1959: vol. 41, 147; vol. 58, 87–9).[7]

Membership in these organizations raises a number of questions about the relationship that native converts constructed with the Virgin Mary. Whom did the members actually serve? How did members conceive of the blessed Virgin? How did they define their relationship with the Virgin? Conceiving of Mary as a usable intercessor suggests that some converts constructed Mary in Iroquois ways while others strove to frame her in Jesuit terms.

# Huron and Iroquois converts, confraternities, and the usable blessed Virgin

While some Iroquois and Huron converts perceived some overlap between the daughter of Sky Woman and the Virgin Mary, many others noted similarities between Catholic confraternities and Huron medicine societies. In 1636, Paul Le Jeune wrote of a confraternity among the Hurons known as 'the Brotherhood of lunatics'. Members of this Huron medicine society danced the *Otakrendoiae*, which Le Jeune described as a frenzied dance that surpassed the 'Bacchantes of bygone times', who themselves were 'furious in their orgies'. Members of the Brotherhood of lunatics, a healing society, visited sick people. The dancers danced to cure the sick, using 'charms which they throw at each other, and which are composed of Bears' claws, Wolves' teeth, Eagles' talons, certain stones, and Dogs' sinews' (Thwaites 1959: vol. 10, 207-9; vol. 63, 306 n. 29).[8]

Not everyone was admitted to the 'Brotherhood of lunatics' society. Only select men and women were chosen to dance, which, according to Ragueneau, was 'the most celebrated in the country, because it is believed the most powerful over the Demons to procure, by their means, the healing of certain diseases'. Dancer-healers were inducted into the society with an elaborate ceremony, 'with great gifts, and after a declaration which they made the grand masters of this Brotherhood, to keep secret the mysteries that are instructed to them, as things holy and sacred' (Thwaites 1959: vol. 30, 23).

Le Mercier unknowingly made the connection between Huron medicine societies and the early pre-cult sodalities of early Huron and Iroquois converts. In writing about the Huron mission in 1653-54 which had been transplanted to the Island of Orleans located about two leagues below Quebec, Le Mercier noted that 'in former times there was a form of superstition which gave us much trouble to combat – singing in the presence of the sick in order to assuage their sufferings, with invocations to the demons of the illness. Now,' he was delighted to say, 'that custom has been turned into true devotion, the girl singers being called to the cabins of the sick, in order to sing the praises to God' (Thwaites 1959: vol. 41, 141). These singers visited the sick and sang to them in an effort to cure them in the same tradition as – if not as a substitute for – the Brotherhood of lunatics. The new and improved performances attracted the attention of the Jesuits, who, from their perspective, viewed the new expression as not only a change in the medium but also in the message: a holy choir offering hymns of the angels, rather than a raucous chorus wailing ditties to the devil to rescue the patient from illness and danger.

While pious Huron and Iroquois converts may have brought native meanings to the Virgin Mary and to Catholic sodalities, many regarded Mary in Catholic ways. Many said 'their prayers, morning or evening', and coerced others in the village to attend church. 'Not to attend and offer one's prayers to God, or not to hear Mass even on a workday when one is in the Village,' one missionary observed, 'passes with them for a serious offense' (Thwaites 1959: vol. 56, 21–3). As missionary Claud Dablon noted in 1670–71, some converts displayed their piety in myriad ways: 'in observing his holy commandments; [by showing] their zeal for his honor and glory, and for the conversion of the infidel Strangers who visit them or repair to their neighborhood; [by] their charity to the poor, even when the latter are French; [and in] their patience and their constancy in affliction' (Thwaites 1959: vol. 54, 287–9).

Many Huron and Iroquois Christian women in particular defined Mary in both Catholic and Huron or Iroquois ways. She was the intercessor, who, according to Jesuit teachings, provided motherly comfort and granted a miracle or two. The Virgin Mary, when properly supplicated, could restore one's health, ease one's panic over death, and bring loved ones back from the brink of death. One might offer salutary prayers to the Virgin Mary, knowing that she would carry the petitions to God, and at the same time supplicate Mary, the *orenda*, or powerful spirit, in order to receive special favours or consideration. One devout woman, for example, who, according to one missionary, was a 'member of [the holy family] association, bore her only son, who was on the verge of death, to the chapel. Laying him at the feet of the Virgin Mary, she prayed:

> "My dear Mistress, my All after God, here is my son, or rather yours, who is dying. If you choose to take him, he is yours; if you choose to restore him to me, I will be grateful to you all my life. Until now I have tried all remedies to snatch him from death, but in vain. I will no longer have recourse to them. All the glory must, after God, be yours, and you yourself must cure him.'" (Thwaites 1959: vol. 58, 89)

Afterwards, the mother carried her son back to her cabin. The following day, when everyone 'expected to find him [the boy] lifeless, they saw that he was much better. Two days afterward, he was out of danger', his health fully restored (Thwaites 1959: vol. 58, 89).

On the surface, this mother's actions might appear no different from those of thousands of mothers in early modern France who offered repentant prayers to God through Mary. However, this Huron Catholic mother in New France viewed Mary's function and usefulness differently, I would argue. She begged Mary to hear her prayers and to carry them to God, but she also viewed Mary as capable of intervening directly. Her words 'I have tried all remedies ... but in vain' suggest that this woman, who belonged to the local sodality and, therefore, was pious, nevertheless still clung to traditional Huron medicine practices. She implies that she had tried administering herbs and other potions, and consulted a shaman, who would have performed rituals of exorcism over her son. Traditional medicine had failed her. Now, in a last-ditch effort to save her son, she called upon what she hoped was a more powerful *orenda*, the Virgin Mary. To her relief, Mary's powers of intercession proved effective and edifying.[9]

Father Fremin at Saint Xavier des Prez witnessed a similar occurrence when a devout Christian Iroquois woman brought her sick son to him. She, too, had tried 'every conceivable remedy, but in vain'. At last, the devout women demonstrated 'her faith and her trust in the blessed Virgin'. She reminded Fremin that some time ago, she had brought her sick mother, then an infidel, to him and to the church. Masses were said for her mother, and eventually the Virgin Mary granted the woman her petition, thereby leading to the mother's full recovery and her subsequent conversion to Christianity. The daughter now hoped for the same intervention for her son; she gave Fremin a porcelain collar [wampum], 'which [she] offer[ed] to her [Mary].' The nine Masses said for the boy led to his complete recovery (Thwaites 1959: vol. 56, 23-25). No doubt, the mother was not certain about which petition spoke louder to Mary: the porcelain collar or the repentant prayers.

Faith in the Virgin Mary lowered one's anxiety over illness and death, and especially over what was to befall one after death.

'To be a Christian', one missionary argued, meant having 'defense against disease'. Perhaps some converts concurred with the missionary's assessment that all 'traditional' remedies were either 'veritable sorceries, or [we]re so full of forbidden superstitions that they can hardly become cured without committing a crime' (Thwaites 1959: vol. 23, 185). In life, Christians strove to become detached from worldly objects and personal relationships in order to make the transition from life to death easier. When the husband of Catherine Gandeacteua, a devout convert, was reported killed, Catherine replied, 'Now that I am free, I make the resolution to give half of all that I possess to the poor, and the other half to the church of the blessed virgin'. The report of her husband's death, however, proved to be premature. When he returned and found that she owned but 'a Girdle and bracelets of porcelain', she declared defensively that 'one ought not to wait for death to detach oneself from creatures' (Thwaites 1959: vol. 61, 203–5).

One of Mary's features that Huron and Iroquois women had to reconcile was her virginity. A number of historians have offered various explanations for why women like Kateri Tekakwitha, who was single, sickly, and adopted into Mohawk society, and her spiritual instructor, Catherine Gandeacteua, a married Erie woman who was a founding member of the Holy Family confraternity in 1664 at Kahnawake, were attracted to the Virgin Mary. Some scholars have argued that such marginalized women found meaning in identifying with the blessed Virgin, and that self-inflicting physically extreme *mea culpas* upon the body signified for young women membership in the confraternity of the Holy Family (Richter 1991: 126–8 Shoemaker 1995: 60–1). Others have used psychoanalytical arguments to posit that those in the cults of Mary were repressing sexual desires (Carroll 1986: 55–71). Both explanations carry some validity, but we must not lose sight of the fact that to belong to the cult of Mary and to be physically fervently devout, as was Kateri Tekakwitha, was to take on the sins of the world. To acknowledge and take responsibility for the sins of the world reflects a world view that differs from the native world view, in which sin did not exist, and outside agents rather than the individual were responsible for transgressions.

Moreover, for a woman to remain a virgin in seventeenth-century Huron or Iroquois society was to jettison her responsibility as a mother, sister, wife, and matron. One did not cast off this role lightly in a society constructed matrilineally and matrilocally. Women held significant political, economic, and social power and authority in Iroquois and Huron societies (Spittal 1990: 9–68, 149–59, 199–216). Some devout Iroquois and Huron women rejected their traditional roles and embraced instead the model of womanhood offered by the Virgin Mary. However, they did not simply declare their virginity, but rather took steps to show physically that they were 'off limits' to anyone but the Virgin Mary and Jesus Christ. According to one observer, the most devout women

> covered themselves with blood by disciplinary stripes with iron, with rods, with thorns, with nettles ... they put glowing coals between their toes, where the fire burned a hole in the flesh; they went bare-legged to make a long procession in the snows; they all disfigured themselves by cutting off their hair, in order not to be sought in marriage. These things, and all the harm that they could do to the body, which they call their greatest enemy, reduced them so low that it was not possible for ill-fed men to persevere further. (Thwaites 1959: vol. 63, 217–19)[10]

Jesuit missionaries taught their catechumens that 'true' Christians had to be suspicious of their bodies, had to distrust and deny sexual urgings, which could only lead them to temptation and to sin. One way of dealing with these feelings was to physically and psychologically repress them. Some of the most fanatically pious Catholic women in Europe practised making themselves less attractive to men and to themselves in order to suppress their sexual appetites and those of others. Their goal was to bring their bodies under control in order to elevate the spirit (Pelikan 1996: 114–19). Historian David Blanchard, however, has suggested that the kind of self-abuse practised by some of the devout Huron and Iroquois women at Kahnawake actually signified an effort to get in touch with the Iroquois spirit world 'on the other side of the sky', where Sky Woman once lived (Blanchard 1982). This interpretation holds some validity for those who adhered both to the Christian and to the Iroquois or Huron religions. The Huron and Iroquois religions, while specific about observing rites and rituals, were flexible and malleable, and adherents of these religions borrowed traditions from other cultures' belief systems to meet their needs (Trigger 1987: 75-7, 103-4; Axtell 1981: 183-6).

Because none of the Indians who claimed membership in the confraternity or cult to Mary left written records explaining their beliefs and actions, it is difficult to make claims for them beyond perhaps the most obvious: that most of its members, especially those who self-administered extreme *mea culpas*, sought to find a community of like-minded believers that would support and understand their new identities. Some, like Kateri Tekakwitha, who in Iroquoia was sickly and socially marginal, found a new identity and a new purpose in the confraternity at Kahnawake. Her new-found place bestowed power and prestige upon her, perhaps similarly to those keepers of the faith appointed in some Huron villages. One Jesuit observer noted that in one Huron village the men appointed two leaders, as did the women, who were 'two of the most exemplary and zealous of their number'. They were given 'ample power and authority' to give others 'occasional advice ... to prevent disorders ... remedy abuses, – and, in a word, enforce order throughout the whole village' (Thwaites 1959: vol. 54, 291).

For some young women, the confraternities and societies dedicated to the Virgin Mary stood as a kind of sisterhood. One missionary, Chauchetière, noted in the 1670s that 'confraternities [we]re being founded among them [at Kahnawake], and especially among the young girls, with the object of mutually assisting one another to live as Christian, and to prepare themselves for the most heroic actions'. Chauchetière did not define what he meant by 'most heroic actions', but he quite likely was alluding to the physically extreme *mea culpas* that some young Christian women either inflicted upon themselves or suffered at the hands of others because they were Christian. Chauchetière offered an account of two young Kahnawake women, one a widow, the other a young bride, that illustrate his point about 'heroic actions'. In 1692 while gathering nuts, these two young women were kidnapped, allegedly 'by the iroqouis, and burned by the hands of their own kindred, out of hatred for christianity, as well as hatred for the Sault'. They suffered tortures similar to those endured by Christ, and they responded to their torturers, according to Chauchetière, with

Christ-like stoicism. The younger woman, whose skin was pierced innumerable times with knives, received 'a shower of blows from clubs', which she accepted 'with such patience and resignation that all the people were touched'. Moreover, her torturers loaded her down 'with their packs and clothes', forcing her to carry the heavy burden, symbolic of Christ weighed down by his cross. Blood flowed freely from her wounds as she sat in her relatives' cabin, until her captors tossed her into the fire, where 'she died, a true martyr'. The older widow likewise suffered similar tortures, and was burned with hot irons. At length, she 'knelt on the glowing coals' and was consumed by the fire (Thwaites 1959: vol. 64, 125-9).[11]

The acceptance of the bodily depredations suffered by these two women mirrored the extreme acts of penance engaged in by the disciples of Catherine Gandeacteua and Kateri Tekakwitha, except that, as prisoners, their torture led to their deaths. A fine line separated extreme acts of penance as expressions of deep devotion and piety from behaviour that, from Chauchetière's perspective, was inspired by 'the demon', who 'transfiguring himself as an angel of light, urged on the devotion of some persons who wished to imitate Catherine [Gandeacteua], or to do severe penance for their sins', and drove such persons to excess in order 'to render christianity hateful even at the start; or in order to impose upon the girls and women of this mission, whose discretion has never equaled that of catherine, whom they tried to imitate'. (Thwaites 1959: vol. 64, 125-7; vol. 63, 215).

The 'heroic actions' of these two young women symbolized many things at once, including their membership in the Holy Family confraternity, their bravery as Christians, their worthiness as followers of Kateri Tekakwitha and Catherine Gandeacteua, and their love for and emulation of the Virgin Mary. They strove to follow the example of Catherine Gandeacteua, a founding member of the Holy Family confraternity at Kahnawake, who stood as an exemplar for most members of the order. One Jesuit described her as having 'an extraordinary devotion to the blessed virgin, and the devotion that she bore to her amounted to Incredible tenderness'. So humble and circumspect was she in her devotion to Jesus Christ and to the blessed Virgin that the 'loving mother of God did not fail to recompense this by the signal favors that she granted to her, for it was enough that Catherine should ask her for Anything, to obtain it, as she often experienced' (Thwaites 1959: vol. 61, 203). If only the other Indian converts followed the example of Catherine Gandeacteua, the Jesuit seems to imply here, then they, too, would achieve happiness ever-lasting.

## Conclusion

When Catherine Gandeacteua fell seriously ill and it became clear that she would not recover, her husband threw a 'feast to his friends, at which he made them this address:

> "Formerly," he said to them, "before we were christians, we made use of superstitions in order to cure our sick people; and their maladies threw us into the utmost distress. Now that we pray, we Invoke the name of Jesus Christ for their cure; if they die, we Comfort ourselves in the hope of seeing them again in Heaven. Let us say, then, our Beads for her who is agony, before beginning our feast'" (Thwaites 1959: vol. 61, 207).

Here, Catherine's husband, also a member of the Holy Family confraternity, suggests that he and new Christians like himself found succour in the Christian faith. Belief in Jesus Christ brought re-lief to those in pain and lessened one's anxiety over death. In claiming his new identity as a Christian, Catherine's husband re-jected his old belief system and healing practices, which he char-acterized as rooted in superstition, and replaced them with what some non-Christian Indians might have called another supersti-tion: the veneration and supplication of the Lord Jesus Christ. He believed – or at least wanted the missionaries to believe – that 'saying their beads' proved more effective than offering tobacco to the appropriate *orenda* for ensuring a satisfactory life after death.

Deep irony, however, colours Catherine's husband's position. He implies that prior to becoming Christian, he had no effective way of dealing with death. On the contrary, Eastern Woodland Indian religions accounted for death in very clear ways that were not that different from how Christianity managed death. Indian religions believed in the immortality of the soul, and in life after death. The soul, once separated from the body, lived on in a distant land beyond the setting sun, often called the Land of

Ancestors or the Land of Souls. It was a 'great and beautiful country in the midst of which is a large house one part of which is inhabited by the God, Tharonhiaouagon [the good son], and the other by Aataentsic [Sky Woman], his grandmother'. Upon arriving at this distant land, the soul of the deceased person was greeted by 'ravishing music', a 'sweet melody' played by 'the drum' and 'the turtle shell rattle'. There, the soul lived nearly the same lifestyle that its body once lived, and even had the same desires and needs, hence the necessity of burying grave goods with the dead body (Lafitau [1724] 1974: vol. 1, 253, 257; Axtell 1981: 186-7; Morgan 1962: 168-9). To say that Catherine's husband found a way of handling death through Christianity is to deny that he had a religion prior to coming to Christianity, or suggests that he abandoned altogether his 'traditional' sacred world. On the contrary, Christianity seems to have augmented his 'traditional' belief system, as evidenced by his insistence upon a mourning feast.

Catherine's husband retained the ancient custom of holding a feast during a sick person's final days. These feasts were sometimes held in order to cure the sick, but also properly to begin the journey to the next life after death (Trigger 1987: 85; Thwaites 1959: vol. 10, 267; Axtell 1981: 202). One Jesuit missionary noted that these feasts, which consisted of petitionary songs and dances to benevolent spirits, were often given before the sick person expired. The sick person made his or her 'farewell feast to their [sic] friends, at which they sometimes s[a]ng, without showing any dread of death, which they ... consider[ed] ... only as the passage to a life differing very little from this' (Thwaites 1959: vol. 10, 267; Axtell 1981: 202). This alternating observance of two distinct religious practices, which some sociologists of religion have termed 'alternation' (Snow & Machalek 1984: 169-74), typifies the sacred practices of many Christian Hurons and Iroquois, who were members of societies dedicated to the Virgin Mary during the seventeenth century in New France. The Virgin Mary could mean many things at the same time to converts. She could at once be a healer; a protector; an *orenda*, or guardian angel; an intercessor; Aataentsic in the Huron creation myth, the Sky Woman in the Iroquois myth; and a model of righteous living for both women and men.

The Jesuit missionaries themselves promoted the usability of Mary for all seasons and for all reasons by presenting her as a sacred spirit for veneration akin to a Huron or Algonquin *oren-*

*da.* Mothers and fathers supplicated the blessed Virgin, and asked her to restore the health of loved ones, to accept into heaven deceased members of the family, and to protect them from future calamities. Presenting Mary as a totem was particularly effective, for the Hurons and Iroquois incorporated totems and charms in their everyday sacred world. Moreover, the priests encouraged the creation of sacred societies, such as the Holy Family confraternity, which the native converts often built on the foundations of existing sacred Indian societies, such as the Brotherhood of lunatics. Although most members of these new Christian societies saw themselves as new Christians, they also viewed their new societies and their roles in them in Indian terms. For example, healer singers in the Brotherhood of lunatics changed their tunes when their society took on a Christian cast, but they continued to go about curing the sick with songs in the same manner as the 'traditional' healing society. The retention and continuity of 'traditional' sacred practices led Joseph François Lafitau, a Jesuit missionary and reliable ethnographer of early eighteenth-century Indian life in and around Kahnawake, to remark that 'traces of religion [are] still to be found well marked in their observances and by the remains which we can still find of their traditions' (Lafitau [1724] 1974: vol. 1, 95).

The most visible and perhaps most important new Christian society was the Holy Family confraternity at Kahnawake. This organization stood as a select community within a community of the elect, and reinforced the identity of the most devout converts as new Christians. It offered support to young women and men who undertook or endured 'heroic acts', which were either extreme *mea culpas* and penance inflicted upon their bodies, or tortures meted out by captors.

Some of the most devout members of the confraternity expressed their solidarity and profound love for Jesus Christ, the blessed Virgin, and God by inflicting rigorous penance on others. Take the example of Marie Oendraka, considered by many to be very devout. At one point in her life, she experienced great hardship that tested her faith in God and in the blessed Virgin: she lost her husband and, she feared, her two children in a boating accident. When she first heard the news that she had perhaps lost her entire family, Marie 'maintained her composure, and showed no agitation, seeking no consolation except at the feet of the Blessed Virgin, her sole recourse'. She asked the Virgin Mary to 'not refuse the offer ... of my boy and girl, whom I cherished above everything else in the world.' In mourning, Marie was contrite, penitent, meek, and tender, an exemplar of Catholic female behaviour (Thwaites 1959: vol. 55, 23–5).

Some time later, however, Marie's children turned up, much to her joy. Shortly after their return home, Marie's daughter found her brother 'and one of his comrades of his own age, in an act of indecency bordering on impurity'. This sent Marie into a rage. After vigorously whipping her son publicly with switches, she sought the priest's advice on further punishment. He suggested no food or water for her son for two days. Marie, who called her son 'a real *Ondechonronnon*' – meaning a 'denizen of Hell' – thought that two days was too lenient; in her opinion, her son deserved 'to burn forever in Hell ... and deserved to suffer perpetual hunger and thirst with the demons'. The priest, uncomfortable with Marie's extreme reaction, surreptitiously instructed the boy's sister to 'give the boy food in secret, as if on her own account'. Marie learned of this plot and refused to permit it. After a few days, Marie relented and agreed to end her son's punishment, but only because he began to show a 'marked weakness' from the lack of nourishment. Finally, she insisted upon a final, humiliating punishment: the boy was forced to confess his sin to the priest and to ask for God's forgiveness, which the priest said he did 'in a way that moved [him] deeply' (Thwaites 1959: vol. 55, 27–31).

Here, many of the issues surrounding the veneration of the Virgin Mary and living a pious, Christian life intersected for Marie. She prayed to the blessed Virgin, asking her either to convey her deceased children and her husband to God and heaven, or to return them safely to her. Mary responded by delivering her children unto her, and thereby offered 'proof' of her intercessionary powers. In addition, it was important to Marie that she and her family follow the edicts and taboos of the church. They were to guard against their bodies and resist 'acts of indecency'. The boy suffered multiple penalties for succumbing to this sexual temptation. His punishments – a painful whipping and the withholding of food and water – did not conform to 'traditional' Iroquois and Huron child-rearing practices, but rather mirrored punishments generally inflicted upon prisoners of war and self-imposed penance accepted by devout members of the Holy Family. Unruly children were generally chastised and embarrassed, not beaten, and close male friendships among Iroquois boys that may have carried implications of homosexuality were quite common (Axtell 1981: 34, 38–40). However, Marie found herself caught between Catholic fears of and obsession with sins of the flesh, and Iroquois practices of extreme penance inflicted upon prisoners and upon zealot converts as she faced punishing her son. Ultimately, Marie did not have to make a choice, but rather exercised both options, all the while declaring by her choices her faith in the blessed Virgin and the Roman Catholic church.

## Notes

1   Throughout this paper, I will distinguish between Huron and Iroquois peoples. Technically, Hurons were Iroquois people by virtue of their Iroquoian-based language and customs. The Hurons and the Iroquois shared similar cultural practices and beliefs, ranging from the matrilineal-matrilocal organization of their respective societies to their similar creation myths. Nevertheless, when I refer to 'Hurons', I mean those Indians who resided in western Quebec and eastern Ontario, between Montreal and Lake Ontario. When I speak of the 'Iroquois', I mean those Indians specific to Iroquoia (present-day upstate New York between Albany and Buffalo), many of whom migrated in the 1670s to the Jesuit mission of Kahnawake near Montreal.

2   Michael P. Carroll has noted that France has the largest number of shrines dedicated to the Virgin Mary of all European countries – if one discounts the shrines in Rome, which he and other historians consider 'a single object of pilgrimage'. Moreover, in France only seven shrines are dedicated to one or more saints, and only one is dedicated to Jesus Christ, which further underscores the importance and power of cults dedicated to Mary in France (Carroll 1986: 12, Table I-I).

3   According to Catholic tradition, the unforgiven descend into a real hell, with burning, torturesome fires, and experience eternal damnation.

4   Through the centuries, Mary's milk has been viewed as healthful and restorative. For a discussion of the purity of Mary's milk and how her breasts and breast milk have been represented in European paintings, see Warner (1976: 192–205).

5   The French took Saint Joseph as the 'Father, Patron, and Protector of new France'. See Thwaites (1959: vol. 11, 67; vol. 15, 223; vol. 21, 311,

87

312 n. 4).

6    For various Iroquois versions of the Iroquois creation myth reflecting various ethnic origins (e.g., Mohawk, Onondaga, Seneca), emphasizing different aspects of the myth, see Norton (1970: 88–97) for the Onondaga version; Hertzberg (1966 12–19) for the Cayuga version; and Hewitt (1903: 141–339) for the Onondaga, Seneca, and Mohawk versions. Although through the ages Mary has been referred to as the 'second Eve', the Jesuits, interestingly, did not try to link Eve, who gave birth to two boys – one good (Abel), the other evil (Cain) – with the Sky Woman's daughter, who also gave birth to two twin boys, one good, the other evil.

7    The Confraternity of the Holy Family in New France was not established until 14 March 1664, by Lavall (Thwaites 1959: vol. 57, 317 n. 5; vol. 58, 295 n. 2).

8    Le Jeune also noted that the dancers bled 'from the mouth and nostrils, or it [wa]s stimulated by a red powder they [took] by stealth' (Thwaites 1959: vol. 10, 209; Trigger 1987: 80–1).

9    Various agents caused illness, according to seventeenth-century Huron and Iroquois thought. Some illnesses were caused by unknown agents and were cured with different therapies, including the use of herbs, poultices, and sweating. Other illnesses were caused by witchcraft. Usually a shaman was called in to diagnose the illness, and remove its irritant from the body by means of incantations, rituals of purification, and legerdemain. Another form of illness was caused by one's dissatisfied soul. Once the soul's need was diagnosed, usually through a dream, and fulfilled by acting upon the dream, the patient usually recovered (Trigger 1987: 81).

10    Devout men were also known to inflict the same self-disciplinary measures upon themselves. See Thwaites (1959: vol. 53, 219).

11    For a summary of the treatment that Huron peoples accorded prisoners of war, see Trigger (1987: 70–5).

## Works cited

Axtell, J. (1981), *The Indian peoples of Eastern America: A Documentary History of the Sexes*, New York and Oxford: Oxford University Press.

   (ed.) (1985), *The Invasion Within: The Contest of Cultures in Colonial North America*, New York and Oxford: Oxford University Press.

Blanchard, D. (1982), '"...To the Other Side of the Sky": Catholicism at Kahnawake, 1667–1700', *Anthropologica* XXIV:

77-102.

Burkhart, L. M. (1989), *The Slippery Earth: Nahua-Christian Moral Dialogue in Sixteenth-Century Mexico*, Tucson: University of Arizona Press.

(1992), 'Flowery Heaven: The Aesthetic of Paradise in Nahuatl Devotional Literature', *Res: Anthropology and Aesthetics* 21: 88-109.

Bynum, C. W. (1982), *Jesus as Mother: Studies in the Spirituality of the High Middle Ages*, Berkeley, Los Angeles, London: University of California Press.

Carroll, M. P. (1986), *The Cult of the Virgin Mary: Psychological Origins*, Princeton: Princeton University Press.

Ellington, D. S. (1995), 'Impassioned Mother or Passive Icon: The Virgin's Role in Late Medieval and Early Modern Passion Sermons', *Renaissance Quarterly* XLVIII(2): 227-61.

Gehring, C. T. and W. A. Starna (1988), *A Journey into Mohawk and Oneida Country, 1634-1635: The Journal of Harmen Meyndertsz van den Bogaert*, Syracuse: Syracuse University Press.

Grant, J. W. (1984), *Moon of Wintertime*, Toronto: University of Toronto Press.

Hertzberg, Hazel W. (1966), *The Great Tree and the Longhouse: The Culture of the Iroquois*, New York: Macmillan.

Hewitt, J. N. B. (1903), 'Iroquoian Cosmology', Part I, Bureau of American Ethnology, *Annual Report, 1899-1900*, Washington, D. C.: Smithsonian: 141-339.

Lafitau, J. F. ([1724] 1974, 1977), *Customs of the American Indians Compared with the Customs of Primitive Times*, 2 vols., William N. Fenton and Elizabeth L. Moore (eds), Toronto: Champlain Society.

Norton, J. (1970), *The Journal of Major John Norton (1816)*, ed. Carl F. Klinck and James J. Talman, Toronto: Champlain Society.

Peers, L. (1996), '"The Guardian of All": Jesuit Missionary and Dalish Perceptions of the Virgin Mary'. In Jennifer S. H. Brown and Elizabeth Vibert (eds), *Reading Beyond Words: Contexts of Native History*, Peterborough, Ontario: Broadview Press.

Pelikan, J. (1996), *Mary Through the Centuries: Her Place in the History of Culture*, New Haven and London: Yale University Press.

Richter, D. K. (1991), *Ordeal of the Longhouse: The Peoples of the Iroquois League in the Era of European Colonization*, Chapel Hill: University of North Carolina Press.

Shoemaker, N. (1995), 'Kateri Tekakwitha's Tortuous Path to Sainthoood'. In Nancy Shoemaker (ed.), *Negotiators of Change: Historical Perspectives on Native American Women*, New York and London: Routledge.

Snow, D. and R. Malachek (1984), 'The Sociology of Conversion', *Annual Review of Sociology* 10: 167–90.

Spittal, W. G. (ed.) (1990), *Iroquois Women: An Anthology*, Ohsweken, Ontario: Iroqrafts.

Thwaites, R. G. (ed.) (1959), *The Jesuit Relations and Allied Documents: Travels and Explorations of the Jesuit Missionaries in New France, 1610–1791*, 73 vols., New York: Pageant.

Trigger, B. G. (1985), *Natives and Newcomers: Canada's 'Golden Age' Reconsidered*, Kingston and Montreal: McGill-Queen's University Press.

(1987), *The Children of Aataentsic: A History of the Huron People to 1660*, Kingston and Montreal: McGill-Queen's University Press.

Warner, M. (1976), *Alone of All Her Sex: The Myth and the Cult of the Virgin Mary*, New York: Knopf.

# 3

# 'Here is another marvel': Marian miracle narratives in a Nahuatl manuscript

Louise M. Burkhart

Among the many genres of religious literature translated into the Nahuatl language in sixteenth-century Mexico is the miracle narrative, the brief account of a miraculous deed executed by Christ or a saint, most typically the Virgin Mary, on behalf of a devotee. Such legends were widely used in Europe as preachers' *exempla,* as legitimating evidence for local saints and shrines, and as expressions of popular devotion not infrequently at odds with formal church doctrine. Divorced from their original context, formularized, and compiled in compendia, these narratives circulated widely across medieval Europe as editors borrowed from one another and as oral narratives passed into print and then back into oral tradition. This generalizing of the narratives applies especially to those of Mary: she was the most important and most popular saint and since according to tradition she left no bodily remains, no single shrine could dominate her cult.[1]

The Nahuas of Central Mexico had narrative traditions, including a genre of 'tale' or 'story' (*zazanilli*). But the medieval miracle narrative, introduced to Mexico by Spanish priests, was both a new narrative form and a new forum for conceptualizing and describing human encounters with the sacred, particularly Mary. This paper explores both of these aspects: the emergence of the miracle narrative as a genre in Nahuatl and the ways in which the Virgin is represented within such texts. These are not separate issues, for the Nahuas' understandings of Mary were conditioned by the texts in which information about her was conveyed to them and which they adapted to their own use.

In addition to miracle narratives, texts in Nahuatl that speak of or to the Virgin include sermons, dramas, hymns, hagiographical narratives associated with her different festivals, and prayers; the most common prayers are the Ave Maria and Salve Regina, which Christian Nahuas learned as part of the basic catechism. Miracle narratives account for only a fraction of this corpus, but are important in that they show Mary intervening directly and benevolently in the lives of (allegedly) real people. She provides an alternative to the distant and authoritative male God; the lively and relatively non-homiletic narratives provide an alternative to more formal and abstract teachings.

I will discuss Marian miracle narratives found in one sixteenth-century Nahuatl manuscript. This text, in the John Carter Brown Library at Brown University (*Doctrina* n.d.), is an anonymous and undated compilation of devotional materials: prayers, discourses and instructions regarding points of doctrine, biblical excerpts, narratives, and other genres. Many of the entries relate to the cult of Mary. The document was written by Nahua scribes who had access to a variety of religious texts but had limited facility in Latin – thus they were probably working mostly from texts already translated into Nahuatl (or possibly Spanish), including one or more compendia of miracle narratives. Some sections of the manuscript are cognate with the Franciscan Pedro de Gante's 1553 *doctrina*, a monolingual Nahuatl catechism directed at the native community (Gante 1981). It is possible that the document originally belonged to an indigenous confraternity of the Rosary, for it includes a handwritten copy of a Nahuatl account of the indulgences granted members of that sodality, apparently published in Mexico City in 1572; however, no other texts explicitly connected with the rosary are included. In any case, it appears to have been redacted with relatively little priestly input and was probably used mainly by Nahuas rather than friars. The manuscript contains ten miracle narratives, eight of which pertain to the Virgin. The eight Marian miracles fill twenty-six pages and account for slightly more than 10 per cent of the manuscript's total content. Mary also makes two appearances in a saint's legend included in the document, which I have published elsewhere (Burkhart 1995).

Accounts of miracles appear in other early Nahuatl texts (e.g., Anunciación 1577, Sahagún 1993 [1583], Bautista 1606), but usually in the context of a sermon or longer narrative rather than as individual entries. Mendicant chroniclers, in their Spanish accounts, occasionally tell of miraculous cures, visions, and rescues experienced by Christian Nahuas (Dávila Padilla 1955; Motolinía 1979; Mendieta 1980). A seventeenth-century Jesuit manuscript in the Bancroft Library contains twenty-nine narratives in Nahuatl, most of them relating to Mary and a number of these relating specifically to the rosary devotion (*Sermones y santoral en mexicano* n.d.). Fifteen narratives connected with the Mexican shrine of Our Lady of Guadalupe were appended to the Nahuatl version of the shrine's foundation legend published in 1649 (Lasso de la Vega 1649; Weckmann 1984: 343; Poole 1995; Santaballa 1995). These differ from earlier narratives in that they are set in Mexico rather than adapted directly from European sources; some involve indigenous people. I have chosen to focus here on the John Carter Brown Library manuscript because of its relatively early date and the apparently prevalent role of Nahuas in its redaction.

# The *tlamahuizolli*

English 'miracle' and Spanish *milagro* derive from the Latin *miraculum*, which in turn is based on the verb *(ad)mirari*, 'to wonder (at)'. Thomas Aquinas, based on Augustine, delineated two essential features of a miracle: the cause of the deed is hidden and the effect produced appears to go against the natural disposition of the subject (although God does not actually act against the laws of nature).[2] For Alfonso X of Castile, who included accounts of miracles in his *Cantigas de Santa Maria* (c. 1257), miracles could occur only through the power of God, acted against nature, rewarded goodness in the recipient, and had to be in conformity with the faith (Montoya Martínez 1981:24–5).

The friars and Nahuas who translated Christian concepts into Nahuatl chose the term *tlamahuizolli* to refer to miracles and the narratives that tell of them. *Tlamahuizolli* means 'something to be marvelled at' or 'something to be wondered at'; Molina's 1571 Nahuatl–Castilian dictionary defines it as *milagro o maravilla* (1971: 126r). The noun derives from the verb *mahuizoa*, 'to marvel at', and ultimately from the verb *mahui*, 'to be afraid'. It is, thus, a reasonable parallel for Latin *miraculum*, but may convey more of an attitude of awe than does the Old World concept. It does not necessarily imply any association with divinity nor any suspension, real or apparent, of natural law. I have chosen 'marvel' as a convenient English rendering.

*Tlamahuizolli* was not a colonial coinage; in indigenous discourse it could refer to anything that inspired wonder and admiration. In the *Florentine Codex*, the ethnographic encyclopedia prepared by the Franciscan Bernardino de Sahagún in collaboration with educated Nahuas (some of whom also worked on adapting Christian texts into Nahuatl), the term is applied, for example, to the ocean, the life of a newly or soon-to-be-born child, beautiful gems, a ruler's palace, a warrior's death by sacrifice, an unprecedented event, and a bean that stands on end when cast in the *patolli* game (Sahagún 1950–82: vol. 11, 247; vol. 6, 137, 138, 152, 186; vol. 11, 227, 231, 270; vol. 6, 14; vol. 1, 83; vol. 8, 30). Some other usages here reflect the Christian appropriation of the term. The appendix to Book One explains that Quetzalcoatl's deeds that were *like* marvels (*iuhqujnma tlamauiçolli*)[3] were achieved through devilish words (vol. 1, 69); that is, the native deities, unlike Christian saints, did not work authentic miracles. A dramatic representation of the Final Judgment is described as *vej tlamaujçolli vej neixcujtilli* 'a great marvel, a great example' (vol. 8, 8).[4] *Neixcuitilli* 'example' is the usual Nahuatl term for Christian dramas; it derives from Latin *exemplum* (and Spanish *ejemplo* or *exemplo*) rather than from indigenous usage (see Burkhart 1996: 46–7). As miracle narratives were also *exempla* and were the basis for some dramas, it is not surprising that a colonial chronicler would pair the two terms. The Bancroft Library manuscript refers to miracle narratives as *neixcuitillatolli*, 'example words' (*Sermones y santoral en mexicano* n.d.: 307r), as well as the more frequently used *tlamahuizolli*.

The upright *patolli* bean is also classified as a *tetzahuitl*, or omen (*cenca tetzammachoia* 'it was considered a great omen'; Sahagún 1950–82: vol. 8, 30). Although the *patolli* player would win in this instance, in most cases *tetzahuitl* portended ill fortune (Burkhart 1989: 64, 93–5). In a striking and perhaps not coincidental parallel to the miracle narrative, in Book Five of the *Florentine Codex* seventeen *tetzahuitl* are explicated in the form of a compendium of brief narratives (Sahagún 1950–82: vol. 5, 151–80). Most tell of animals or supernatural beings that bring misfortune to those who encounter them: the horned owl's cry, the weasel crossing one's path, the severed head, the human ash-bundle. They are described in separate 'chapters', except for the thirteenth and last which covers five omens. An introductory statement assigns these beliefs to the old ways of the ancestors, but the descriptions go back and forth between past and present tenses: the relegation to the past is hardly persuasive.[5] Several of the narratives associate the omens with the deity Tezcatlipoca, a trickster figure whom Catholic priests saw as particularly demonic. In Book Twelve the famous omens of the Spanish invasion, which mark the transition from the old order to the new, are also related as a compendium of brief narratives (Sahagún 1950–82: vol. 12, 1–3).

Because the term *tetzahuitl* had negative associations, it was not a suitable equivalent for the wondrous cures, rescues, and other forms of aid offered by miracle-working saints, which, though similarly anomalous and surprising, rewarded Christian devotion. The Christian use of *tlamahuizolli*, thus, designates a *type* of event – an extraordinary occurrence manifesting divine power – that Nahuas had an established tradition of naming, describing, and interpreting, but one very different in *character* from the traditional *tetzahuitl*. The Christianized concept of *tlamahuizolli*, and its associated narratives, can be seen as a colonial and Christian parallel to the *tetzahuitl*, now also gathered together in narrative collections, like *exempla*. The omens are assigned to the past and rejected as works of the demonic old deities unworthy of people's faith, and yet they continue, anomalously, to inhabit the present: the beliefs may be ongoing; the omens of the invasion are part of the established and oft-repeated lore of the conquest. The boundary between the Christian *tlamahuizolli* and other anomalous events may not have been entirely evident.[6]

## *Tlamahuizolli* narratives: stylistic formulae

The ten miracle narratives in the John Carter Brown Library manuscript (for present purposes I include the two non-Marian miracles) reveal stylistic regularities indicating that by the time the manuscript was redacted (1572 or later) the *tlamahuizolli* was a distinctive and recognized genre. Three typical features are: (1) an introductory label that includes the word *tlamahuizolli*; (2) an

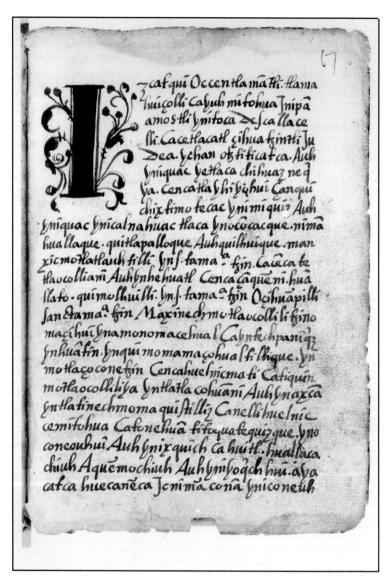

*Figure 1*    The opening page of a miracle narrative about a Jewish woman's
childbed conversion, from the John Carter Brown Library manuscript (*Codex Indianorum* 7, folio 67r). Courtesy of the John
Carter Brown Library at Brown University.

opening statement citing the source of the narrative or giving some other introductory comments; and (3) a formulaic opening to the narrative proper. Each of these features is described in more detail below.

The scribes introduce all but two of the narratives as *tlamahuizolli*. One is labelled a 'help' or 'assistance' (*ytepallehuilliztzin* 'her [Mary's] helping of people', 20v); one has no introductory statement. Some of the narratives are presented as part of numbered sequences. In a group of three, the second begins 'here is the second marvel' and the third 'here is the third marvel'. Three begin 'here is another marvel' (see Figure 1); one of these is followed by a narrative labelled 'here is a second marvel'. Others are ascribed numbers that do not make sense in the context of this manuscript, as if the scribes were selecting individual narratives from a longer compendium and simply copied the numbers along with the story. Thus there is a so-called ninth chapter (*capitollo*) which contains the ninth 'help' of Saint Mary, and other narratives labelled twelve, fourteen, and fifteen (in that order). In three cases the Spanish loanword *exemplo* appears in addition to Nahuatl *tlamahuizolli*.

Additional introductory information appears in seven of the ten narratives. Two have brief statements: 'it happened to a nun (*çihuamadre* 'woman mother')' (22v) and 'it happened long ago' (24r). Four refer to sources. Of these one states: 'Thus it appears that Saint Mary truly speaks for the sinner. It is told in a book' (64v). Another reads: 'Thus it is told in a book, the name of which is de scalla celli' (67r; see Figure 1). The third states: 'Here is told the ninth help of our precious mother Saint Mary, there it is heard, in a book called Scala celli' (70v). The book referred to is *Scala celi* by the fourteenth-century Dominican Johannes Gobius, an alphabetically arranged compilation of *exempla* that includes seventeen Marian miracle narratives, among them these two as well as another of the miracles in the manuscript (Gobius 1480). The fourth citation is as follows: 'Saint Anselm tells it in a book where the marvellous deeds of our precious mother Saint Mary lie written' (71r). The writer of the last narrative explains: 'it pertains to the festival of our mother Saint Mary which is called Purification (*porificançio*)' (75v).

The following is a list of the opening phrases of the stories themselves:

*Ce tlacatl cihuapilli* 'A person, a noblewoman' (22r)
*Ce tlacatl onnenca yntoca avatesa* 'A person there lived, who is called an "abbess"' (23r)
*Ce tlacatl pilli onnenca* 'A person, a noble, there lived' (24r)
*Ca cen*[7] *pilli hocatca tetlacuicuilliani* 'Indeed, a noble there was, a robber' (64v)
*Ca ce tlacatl çihuatzintli Judea ychan* 'Indeed, a person, a woman, resident of Judea' (67r)
*ce tlacatl sanceltode*[8] 'A person, a priest' (70v)
*ce tlacatl çivatzintli* 'A person, a woman' (71r)
*Ca cequintin Acaltica yetihuia* 'Indeed, some people were travelling by boat' (72r)
*Ca ce tlacatl Onnenca pilli* 'Indeed, a person there lived, a noble' (74r)
*Ca yn iquac monemiltiaya Ce huey teopixqui ytoca bonifancio* 'Indeed, when was living a great priest whose name was Boniface' (75r)

Clearly a formula has developed centring on the word *ce*, 'a, one' (plural *cequintin* 'some'), which is sometimes preceded by the introductory particle *ca*, 'indeed, for', and is followed by one or more words that characterize the legend's protagonist, the first of which is often *tlacatl*, 'person'. The last example departs slightly from this pattern. This is the only narrative attached to an actual historical personage, Pope (and Saint) Boniface I. But even here the protagonist is introduced with the word *ce* where one would normally expect the article *in*. *Ce (tlacatl)* was probably adopted as an analogue for Latin *quidam*, 'a certain' (person, woman, cleric, etc.).

Closing formulae are less marked, but some of the narratives end with an affirmation of the faith: the protagonist proceeds to lead a virtuous life; the audience is reminded of the importance of some aspect of Mary's worship.

In summary, the scribes who redacted these Nahuatl miracle narratives typically designated their texts as *tlamahuizolli*, placed them into a series ('a second', 'another'), legitimated them in some way by invoking a written text or the capabilities of the Virgin, and marked the beginning of the story with a formula designating a certain person as protagonist. This narrative frame informed the audience that a certain type of story was forthcoming, one in which a human being would encounter something marvellous. In contrast to the *tetzahuitl* narratives, the human actor, rather than the anomalous event, is designated the centre and subject of the story.

## Mary's marvels

The miracle narratives are distributed within the manuscript as follows. The first (number 1 below) is sandwiched between the two non-Marian miracles; all three relate to the sacrament of penance. They follow a text on Tobias and precede a discussion of the importance of confession. Numbers 2 and 3 follow Old Testament readings for the Feasts of the Visitation (of Mary to Saint Elizabeth) and Saint Mark. These are followed by additional Old Testament readings, one (apparently) for the Visitation and one for the Assumption (of Mary). Then the remaining five miracle narratives appear in unbroken sequence, followed by an excerpt from Revelation (7: 2–12) and a text on Christ's resurrection. The following are summaries of the eight Marian narratives, with quotations of some of the dialogue; the fourth is translated in full. Each is followed by a brief commentary.

1. A virtuous abbess lived with her niece, also a nun, who was deceived by the demon (*tlacatecolotl* 'human horned owl') and had sexual relations with a man. She was very ashamed and went about sad and weeping and performing penances. But she did not want to confess the misdeed, saying to herself: 'Oh how wretched I am! How will I straighten my heart?[9] Everyone speaks well of me. Let me not reveal my misdeed before the heart-straightener, so that they will not consider me to be wicked. Let me just devote myself to doing penance for it. I will pray to God. Perhaps thus he will pardon me'. She was so sad that she became ill. She confessed, omitting that one great misdeed, and took communion. Then her soul went directly to hell (*mictlan* 'among the dead'). Her aunt the abbess prayed for a year to our mother Saint Mary, asking to know where her niece's soul went. Then one time she saw Saint Mary in her sleep. Mary spoke to her and took her on a tour of hell. She saw the souls suffering in many places, smelled the awful stenches, and finally saw her niece, chained and suffering, her tongue aflame. Mary explained to the startled abbess that

the woman must suffer in this way forever because she failed to confess one mortal sin. The abbess then awakened and never again offered prayers on behalf of her niece (22v–24r).

Here Mary responds to a devotee's prayers, but the narrative is unusual in that it shows the limits of Mary's abilities. Rather than saving a sinner who might otherwise be destined for hell, as she typically does, she confirms the inevitability of infernal torment for one who failed to confess properly. Thus she upholds the formal dictates of the faith. In addition to providing a doctrinal lesson on the importance of confession, the abbess's personal vision of the underworld as a horrible place confirms the friars' depiction of it; the preconquest *mictlan* was not a place of punishment.

Nahuas were not generally allowed to become nuns, but sexual abstinence was expected of women and girls who served at the old temples and colonial Nahuas knew of the vows of chastity required of priests and nuns. Mendieta (1980: 420) tells of indigenous women who voluntarily followed their example, asserting that even in the 'Babylon' of Mexico City there were hundreds of women who had remained virgins into old age.

2. A nobleman and robber, a wicked man married to a Christian woman, was urged by his wife to fast on the sabbath in Mary's honour and to recite the Ave Maria when he passed her image. Once, en route to commit a misdeed, he entered a church and was about to say the Ave Maria before an image of Mary carrying her child in her arms, but saw blood[10] coming out and running on Mary. Mary spoke to the frightened man, explaining that he and others who are not satisfied are worse than the Jews, for the Jews only crucified her son once while they crucify him many times. Then she made the blood disappear. The man, saddened by his sins, said, 'Oh fountain of compassion, oh maiden, pray for me to your precious child'. Mary then conversed with her child, insisting repeatedly that he pardon the man's sins, because he loves her and she brought him up and he is merciful. Finally she placed him on the altar (*altal*) and knelt before him, kissing his feet. He then gave in, stating: 'As it is a commandment that people's mothers be honoured, be esteemed, and as you are my mother, it is necessary that I obey you, that I honour you.... Tru-

ly, oh my precious mother, for your sake I have compassion for this sinner. May his misdeeds be pardoned. May he live happily. And may he kiss my body where I suffered'. The man did so and the holes (wounds) closed and stopped bleeding. The man thanked Mary and Christ and went home. After giving away all his goods he became a *padre* and his wife entered a convent ('the house of the women who live in a sacred way'). They both died in goodness when their lives were over. (64r–66v)

Here Mary appears in her typical role as the 'Sinner's Friend' (Power 1928: xxvii), wheedling favours from her son and securing salvation for a person who, though flagrantly immoral, expressed devotion to her. Because it contrasts the wicked man with his Christian wife, the legend applies well to a context of recent and ongoing evangelization.

The man is designated a *pilli*, or noble in the Nahua social hierarchy, and a *tetlacuicuilliani*, 'one who customarily and repeatedly takes things from people'.[11] Molina's 1571 dictionary defines the term as 'public robber' (1971: 108r). The translator chose this term over *ichtecqui* or *ichtequini*, 'thief', perhaps to make clear that this is not an ordinary burglar but a highwayman. However, this usage also introduces an interesting ambiguity, for *tetlacuihcuiliani* (or *tetlacuihcuiliqui*) also refers to a shaman who cures by pretending to suck small objects out of his or her patient's body (López Austin 1967: 110; Siméon 1977: 522; Bautista 1979: 151). The nature of the man's sins are not identified further in the text. Thus, this wicked man could be seen as a traditional religious practitioner of a sort whom friars would identify as being in league with the devil. Yet even he, with Mary's help, makes the transition to Christianity, renouncing both his wealth and his former career to become a priest.

3. A Jewish woman of Judea was suffering greatly in childbirth and lay awaiting her death. Neighbours came and told her to pray to Saint Mary, 'for she is very compassionate'. The woman said to Mary: 'oh noblewoman, Saint Mary, have compassion for me, even though it is not my merit. For I am one of those who crucified your precious child. Very well do I know that you have compassion for sinners. And now if you will save me, truly I declare that we both will be baptized, [I and] my child'. She then gave

birth easily and fulfilled her promise. When her husband returned home he cut the child's neck with his sword (*itepuzman-
quauh*, 'his metal hand-stick').[12] The neighbours came running.
The husband fled and sought refuge in a church of Saint Mary.
Comforted at the sight of Mary's image, he threw himself on her
mercy:

> Alas! Oh how wretched I am! For I have sinned greatly, as I
> have killed my little child. Alas! Oh Mary, you are very com-
> passionate. You do not push me away. Well do I know that
> your pity is very great. And now, may it be that you have com-
> passion for me, as your precious child had compassion for
> Saint Paul when he was greatly afflicting the Christians. For
> truly I believe that Jesus became flesh inside you. And he was
> born but your maidenhood was not destroyed thereby. And I
> believe that he is the true God, whom we have been awaiting.
> He is very compassionate.

Then the authorities ('the lords, the rulers, the staff-bearers') found
him and arrested him. He asked to be baptized before his execution. The child came back to life before his[13] mother's eyes, his
neck healed, and told his mother that her husband had been
baptized. She took the child to the jail and they let the father go.
Father and child both went on to lead good lives and serve Mary.
(67r–69r)

Figure 1 is a photograph of the first page of this narrative; the
reference to the *Scala celi* is on the third to fourth lines. The
story follows its European model but is an abridged version of
it.[14] This story of a Jewish woman's conversion to Christianity
could easily serve as a model for Nahua conversions. Furthermore, the father's murder of his baptized child could call to mind
the death of Cristóbal of Tlaxcala in 1527. According to Motolinía,
the principal source, Cristóbal was the twelve- or thirteen-year-
old son and principal heir of a high-ranking nobleman named
Acxotecatl. Indoctrinated by the Franciscans, he began to harass
his unbaptized father, breaking his deity images and spilling his
vats of *pulque*, the indigenous alcoholic brew. The father finally
beat the boy severely and burned him over a fire. He looked for
his Spanish sword but could not find it; the boy expired of his

injuries the following morning. Acxotecatl also killed the boy's mother. Cristóbal's body was found to be dry and uncorrupted a year later, like that of a Christian saint. The father, unrepentant, was hanged. Two years later another noble Tlaxcalan boy and his servant were murdered while confiscating idols around the town of Tepeaca; their repentant killers begged for baptism before they were hanged. In the hands of Franciscan chroniclers, the stories of these child martyrs became homegrown *exempla* demonstrating indigenous children's innocence and aptitude for the faith.[15]

In the *Florentine Codex* orations on childbirth, the midwife tending a woman who is unable to give birth invokes the female divinities Cihuacoatl, Quilaztli, and Yohualticitl, and perhaps others: 'Who knows the ones to whom she cried out?' (Sahagún 1950–82: vol. 6, 160). Subsequently, the midwife either cuts up and removes the dead foetus from the living woman or the woman dies with the foetus inside her. In the latter case, if it is her first childbirth the woman undergoes apotheosis as one of the deities representing women who die in labour; the text continues with an account of this process (161–5). In this story, then, invocations of the old deities do not help the woman in crisis, and she may actually become one of them. In the miracle narrative, a dying woman invokes Mary and, like the saint herself, gives birth with no trouble; she then becomes a Christian. Mary replaces the old deities of female reproduction, whose sexuality contrasts strikingly with her virginity, and her own painless childbirth becomes the model for the birth experiences of her devotees. An easy delivery followed by baptism inverts the *Florentine Codex* paradigm of death followed by apotheosis as a 'pagan' deity.

The child, rescued from death in the womb, then falls victim to his father's ire but is again granted life by Mary. With Mary represented as a helper in childbirth and a restorer of dead children, the story may have had particular appeal to women as well as providing a model of a male sinner's salvation.

4. The following is a complete translation of this narrative, which is the shortest of the eight.

A person, a priest (*saceltode*, for Spanish *sacerdote*), used to pray very much to the noblewoman Saint Mary. However, he was very confused about the Holy Sacrament (*Sancto Sacramento*). Therefore he was always praying to our precious mother Saint Mary that she help him. And when it was Saturday (*Sapado*) he was saying mass (*missa*). And he was about to say the *pater noster*. Then the host (*yn ostia*), the sacrament, which he had blessed, disappeared. And when he watched this he was very frightened. He saw Saint Mary carrying her child in her arms. And she said to the priest (*teopixqui*, 'god-keeper'): 'Here is my child, the way he was born. It is he whom you have blessed. And many times you have touched him. With your hands you lift him up. Here, I am placing him in your hands. Finish the mass.' And the priest (*teopixqui*) then laid the little child on the altar. And when he would have broken the sacrament he saw that it was no longer like a child, but like a little tortilla. Thus he was very strengthened with belief, he believed very strongly in God. (70v–71r)

This narrative follows its model in the *Scala celi* very closely. Divergences from the Latin edition that I consulted include the omission from Mary's speech of a reference to the priest's eating and drinking her son, which perhaps struck the translator as too graphically cannibalistic when applied to Christ in human form, and the addition in the Nahuatl of the closing comments on the priest's faith. 'Like a little tortilla' translates *in figura panis*, 'in the form of bread' (Gobius 1480). Masses dedicated to the Virgin were customarily performed on Saturdays.

Some Nahuas, like this priest and many other European Christians, may well have been confused about the nature of the sacramental host, which they were told was the body of Christ but which certainly did look like a little tortilla. This story confirms its identification with Christ – and, thus, despite the translator's scruples, the cannibalistic nature of the rite. As in the two preceding narratives, Mary's maternal character is emphasized.

European miracle narratives feature a high proportion of Christian religious professionals as characters, a reflection of the social context in which they were developed, recorded, and used. With few exceptions, and those mostly the mestizo offspring of Spaniards and elite Nahua women, persons of native ancestry were barred from becoming priests and nuns. Thus Nahuas could not have identified very closely with such characters as abbesses and priests. The favour Mary shows to such individuals would only reinforce the religious authority of Europeans over indigenous people.

5. A woman who was very devoted to Mary prayed to her constantly that her precious child Jesus Christ might appear to her. After a long time, it happened. While the woman was standing in a church praying, Mary appeared to her and told her that her wish would be granted. Jesus Christ then appeared, looking like a little child and shimmering like an angel. The woman took him in her arms, hugging him with great delight and thanking his mother for the favour: 'Oh mother of God, Saint Mary, what will I give you, how can I return to you the way that you have so greatly favoured me? You have shown me yourself and your precious child, Jesus Christ.' The child asked her to say the Pater Noster and then the angel's (*agel*) greeting (the Ave Maria), which she did, and he prayed the Ave along with her, turning toward his mother. And when she said '*Et penedictos fructos ventris toi etc.*,'[16] very good, very fine is he who was placed inside you, Jesus Christ', the child said, 'It is I. I was inside you.' The child then disappeared, leaving the woman very content. The text concludes: 'Here it is quite evident that the angel's greeting, the Ave Maria, greatly gladdens our lord, because he wanted to say it too. Thus he taught us that we should do it willingly'. (71r–72v)

An introductory statement attributes this narrative to Saint Anselm; a version is in the fifteenth-century collection of Sánchez de Vercial (1961: 217). The Ave Maria is featured in many Marian miracle narratives; often, as in narrative 2 above, its recital by an otherwise immoral or incompetent person helps to secure Mary's favour (Power 1928: xxviii; other Nahuatl examples are Anunciación 1577: 147r–148r; *Sermones y santoral en mexicano* n.d.: 283v–284r, 287v). Here Christ participates in revering his mother, appearing, as in narratives 2 and 4 above, in the form of a child. For Christ to manifest himself as a child emphasizes his humanity and his relationship with his mother, who in turn has more authority over him as a child than as a man. The woman emulates Mary by holding the Christ child in her arms, as Mary does in so many of her images. The child himself emphasizes Mary's maternal status by speaking of how he was once inside her body.

6. Some people were travelling by boat to Jerusalem, including a bishop (*obispo*) and many nobles. When the water was about to break the boat, the bishop and some of the others got into a

lifeboat (*acaltontli*, 'little boat'), but one person fell into the water while trying to get in and sank. Those who remained in the ship were crying out to heaven; as it sank the bishop saw the souls of the drowned flying to heaven as little doves. Arriving on shore, he and his companions found their friend whom they had thought drowned alive and well. He[17] explained: 'When I fell in the water, then I called out the name of our mother, Saint Mary. When I fell I remembered her name. She does not forget her precious ones, she is very fond of them. There in the water she descended on me. She covered me with a mantle (*tilmatica*). Thereupon here to the shore she went covering me, thus she brought me here.' The survivors greatly praised Mary. The text then incorporates some additional praises of Mary and also brief references to other miracles: her having saved Rome from an epidemic following a procession with the image that Saint Luke painted of her (from Santa Maria Maggiore) and her curing a child of pestilence after he prayed the Ave Maria (72v–74r).

This shipwreck story was popular among editors of *exempla*, appearing for example in the *Scala celi* (Gobius 1480), the widely used fifteenth-century compilation by the Dominican Johannes Herolt (who borrowed it from the thirteenth-century *Speculum historiale* of Vincent of Beauvais; Herolt 1928: 64–5), and the thirteenth-century Castilian poetry of Gonzalo de Berceo (1944: 137–45). The association of souls of the dead with birds, common in the Old World (Warner 1976: 38), was also an indigenous concept: the souls of those who died in battle or sacrifice rose to the home of the sun and after four years returned as birds (Sahagún 1950–82: vol. 3, 49; Burkhart 1992). A second quasi-indigenous motif is the mantle with which Mary rescues her devotee, here labeled a *tilmahtli*, the rectangular cape worn by indigenous people and, in the colony, a marker of ethnic status.

7. A noble who had entered a convent of Cistercians (*in innecentlalliayan in padreme y motenehua cisterçiences*, 'their gathering place, the fathers who are called Cistercians') fell ill and worried about all the sins he had committed in his life outside. Mary appeared and comforted him. Later, when his abbot (*itepanicacauh*[18]) asked him why he was so happy, he explained how Mary had consoled him because he always knelt when he heard

her name, thus honouring her. He then commended his soul to Mary, praying to her. The text goes on to explain how souls in purgatory cry out to Mary, and adds another short narrative about a Franciscan who told 'me' – probably the author of the text being adapted rather than the Nahua writer himself – that, once when he was doing contemplative exercises, he looked into purgatory and saw the souls weeping and crying out to Saint Mary, intoning the Salve Regina prayer (74r–75r).

Here, again, is Mary as the 'Sinner's Friend', assuring the salvation of a sinful man who showed devotion to her. The story, without the addendum about purgatory, is in Herolt (1928: 103–4). The Cistercians, a cloistered monastic order, had no houses in New Spain, which makes this story somewhat alien to the Nahua context. However, it may be noted that this man, like the robber in narrative 2, is called a *pilli*, 'noble' (he is labelled a knight in Herolt), and he is said only to enter a convent, not actually to become a priest.

8. Pope Boniface asked the Roman emperor to allow him to assign a temple (*Diablo calli*, 'devil house') of Diana to Saint Mary. But when he was about to bless the house, Jews were arguing with the Christians, claiming that Joseph was Jesus's father and that Mary was not a virgin. A blind person was going about reprimanding the Jews. The Christians prayed that he[19] be made to see so that the Jews would believe. On the Feast of the Purification (*porificanon*) the blind person was brought out to stand before the altar. He knelt before the image of Saint Mary and sang the hymn sung on this festival. The Latin words *Gaude maria*[20] are followed by a Nahuatl translation of the song, which praises Mary for destroying heretics, believing the words of Saint Gabriel, and giving birth as a virgin. The song concludes with 'May they all be ashamed, the Jews, the wicked ones, who say that Jesus Christ is the child of Joseph'. Then the blind person was able to see. Then 6010 Jews believed (converted) (75v–77r).

Whether Mary herself had any direct role in this miracle is not specified, but the miracle was performed to uphold an aspect of her worship. A partially cognate story is told in Herolt (see notes 19 and 20). In Mexico the old temples were torn down and new churches built, but often on or near the same site and reusing the same materials. Thus, the story of the conversion of a pagan goddess's temple to Mary's worship would have had local resonance, perhaps particularly in respect to the shrine to Our Lady of Guadalupe founded in the mid-1550s: some colonial observers, most famously Sahagún, assumed (perhaps wrongly) that a temple to a preconquest goddess had previously occupied the site (Burkhart 1993: 207–9; Poole 1995: 78–81). As in narrative 3, the Jews here can symbolize any non-Christian people, including those of New Spain, especially those who have been exposed to the faith but stubbornly refuse to accept it – an attitude that many Spaniards ascribed to Nahuas, especially in more rural areas (Stafford Poole, personal communication, 1997). Weckmann describes a number of miracles attributed to friars active in the evangelization of Mexico; these include restoration of sight to the blind (1984: 281, 320–38).

The 2 February Feast of the Purification (also known as Candelaria in Spanish), which commemorated Mary's participation in the Judaic post-partum rite and the elder Simeon's recognition of Christ as the messiah (Luke 2: 22–39), was celebrated by Christian Nahuas. Texts for it are included in Sahagún's 1583 *Psalmodia christiana* (1993: 52–7) and Fray Juan de la Anunciación's 1577 *sermonario* (136v–138v); Motolinía describes Nahuas' reverence for the candles blessed at church on this festival (1979: 55).

# Concluding remarks

Exactly what Nahuas made of these stories is impossible to determine. But a certain conception of the 'marvellous', and of Mary as a sacred personage, must have been emerging. Images come to life, dead children revive, the wicked reform their ways, the drowning are rescued, the depths of the underworld are revealed. These are not chance encounters; nor are they omens of ill fortune indicating disorder in the cosmos, chaos sowed by such figures as Tezcatlipoca or the female 'filth deity' Tlahzolteotl. Rather, these encounters are fervently desired and prayed for, to a figure far less capricious and far more indulgent than preconquest deities. A representative of celestial order, Mary acts to correct crises and confusions in the earthly realm. Although she often favours Christian religious specialists, she also bestows her mercies on ordinary people, some of whom could as easily be Nahuas as anything else. Marvels occur in answer to prayers; no accompanying ritual offerings or penitential precautions, so central to preconquest encounters with the deities, appear to be necessary. One speaks directly to Mary, and she answers. Devotion is a personal, even a private, matter, and is free of danger.

These simple stories bore a message about the nature of the Christian sacred that was at once reassuring and revolutionary. Pray the Ave Maria, or perform other easy acts of devotion, and the noblewoman, our mother Saint Mary, might aid you in your time of direst need. This message was surely part of her appeal to the unschooled Europeans among whom these legends first flourished. But for Nahuas to accept this, it meant that the apparatus of communal ritual and community identity, which, as they readily accepted public and participatory modes of Christian devotion (Burkhart 1998), they had largely transferred from the old deities to the Christian saints, would become less relevant in relation to more personalized modes of devotion. And in contrast to those personal devotions that existed in preconquest religion, which typically demanded strict penitential exercises (sweeping, fasting, bloodletting, sexual abstinence), Mary responded to simple prayers and emotional appeals. Even adherence to moral dictates, whether those of traditional Nahua society or those expounded from the pulpit, was not necessarily required, provided one ultimately repented (and confessed). To the extent that any Nahuas took this message to heart, the friars' goal of undermining kinship and community bonds to promote a more individualized and personalized identity was advanced. At the same time, though, the stories undermine the friars' and the church's own authority. It was easy to forget, and miracle narratives themselves rarely point out, that Mary had no power in her own right but achieved her ends only through appeals to God. Moreover, the belief that devotion to Mary ensured one's salvation was, strictly speaking, heretical, for it overrode the more formal avenues of absolution and salvation controlled by the priesthood.

In 1572 Pedro Ocharte, a printer from Rouen, France, who published a number of Nahuatl imprints (the rosary text copied into the John Carter Brown Library manuscript is attributed to his press) was tried and tortured by the Mexican Inquisition under its zealous founder, Pedro Moya de Contreras. Ocharte was accused of reading 'Lutheran' books and questioning the intercession of the saints. Ironically, he was also interrogated for having printed, the previous year, a single-leaf woodcut of Our Lady of the Rosary that went too far in the opposite direction. At issue was the caption of the image, which read: *Estas cuentas son sin cuenta, En valor y eficacia, El pecador que os reza, Jamas le faltara gracia,* 'These beads are without limit in value and efficacy. The sinner who prays to you will never lack grace.' Ocharte insisted that he had intended no harm to the church, but his generous tribute to the Virgin helped to land him and his business in a great deal of trouble.[21]

Tensions that existed in the Old World between the popular cult of Mary and the patriarchal church hierarchy, which sought to affirm God's power by restricting her role to that of intercessor, clearly carried over into New Spain, and Nahuas were at least as likely to be confused as the unfortunate Ocharte. In this atmosphere of conflicting opinions, Christian Nahuas were left to construct, from the texts and other information made available to them, their own conceptions of the celestial noblewoman. Miracle narratives presented a Mary close to that of Ocharte's heretical woodcut, a 'Sinner's Friend' who swept into her devotees' lives to work wonders.

## Acknowledgments

Versions of this paper were presented at the University of Pennsylvania Kislak Conference and at the American Society for Ethnohistory conference, both in November 1997. I wish to thank the commentators at those events for their perceptive and helpful statements: Deborah Augsburger, Fernando Cervantes, David Ludden, and Stafford Poole. Thanks also to Samuel Y. Edgerton for his comments on an earlier draft of the paper. My initial work with the manuscript analysed here was supported by a National Endowment for the Humanities Fellowship at the John Carter Brown Library in 1988. I am grateful to Norman Fiering, Daniel Slive, and all the library staff for their help and support during my fellowship tenure and in the years since.

# Notes

1   A detailed account of the European background of Marian worship and miracle narratives is beyond the scope of this paper. My understanding of this context derives mainly from the following sources: Power (1928), Warner (1976), Christian (1981), Montoya Martínez (1981), Ward (1982), Goodich (1995), and Pelikan (1996). Original source materials I have examined include Johannes Gobius (1480), Little (1908), Bernard Pez (1925), Johannes Herolt (1928), Caesarius of Heisterbach (1929), Gonzalo de Berceo (1944), Sánchez de Vercial (1961), and Jacobus de Voragine (1993).

2   I thank Fernando Cervantes for clarifying Thomas's position.

3   In this paper when I quote a particular Nahuatl source, I reproduce the orthography of that source. I have, however, written out abbreviated words in full, inserted spaces between words, and removed spaces within words. In other contexts I employ a standardized orthography (showing glottal stops but not vowel length).

4   I am grateful to R. Joe Campbell for running a computer search of the *Florentine Codex* for me on the term *tlamahuizolli*.

5   This shifting is not evident in the Dibble and Anderson translation, which consistently uses past tense forms.

6   I thank Deborah Augsburger for pointing out that the older omens continued to coexist in the colonial present with the new miracles.

7   Variant of *ce*.

8   From Spanish *sacerdote*.

9   Nahuatl idiom for confession, used for a preconquest form as well as the Christian sacrament (see Burkhart 1989).

10  Mary's blood, but possibly the child's; the wording is ambiguous.

11  *tetlacuihcuiliani* in standard orthography.

12  In the original Latin, he first feigns joy but rises in the middle of the night to kill the child with his sword (Gobius 1480).

13  The child's gender is not specified in the Nahuatl; in Gobius the child is male.

14  The motif of a Jewish woman calling upon Mary for help in childbirth is also in Herolt (1928: 35-6), in a narrative borrowed from Vincent of Beauvais' *Speculum historiale* (Book 8, Chapter 199).

15  Motolinía (1979: 176-81) is the original and principal source; he is followed, and elaborated upon, by Mendieta (1980: 236-45), Torquemada (1975-83: V, 132-56), and others, including the Spanish judge Alonso de Zorita, a Franciscan sympathizer, who incorporated Motolinía's account into his *Relación de la Nueva España* (Baudot 1995: 390; the relationship between the two versions is documented in Motolinía 1989).

16  'Blessed is the fruit of your womb, etc.', with misspellings in the Latin.
17  The person's gender is ambiguous in the Nahuatl; in European versions it is a man.
18  The Nahuatl means 'his one who stands over people'. In Herolt's version of the story, the interlocutor is the abbot. As one of his definitions for *Abad prelado o dignidad*, 'abbot, prelate, or dignitary', Molina gives *teoyotica tepan ycac*, 'one who stands over people in a sacred way' (1971: 1r).
19  Gender is not specified in the Nahuatl but the source probably referred to a man. A cognate story in Herolt tells of a blind man named Didymus (1928: 52–3).
20  The cognate text in Herolt labels this song as the responsory *Gaude, Maria Virgo, cunctas hereses* (1928: 53). The full text is *Gaude Virgo Maria, sola interemisti cunctas haeresis in universo mundo*, 'Rejoice, O Virgin Mary, you alone have destroyed all heresies throughout the world'; this was an antiphon sung at matins in the pre-Vatican II common office of the Virgin Mary (Stafford Poole, personal communication, 1997).
21  The complete Inquisition proceedings are published in Fernández del Castillo (1982: 85–141); see also Greenleaf (1969); the woodcut is reproduced in Benítez (1984: 21); on Moya de Contreras see Poole (1987).

# Works cited

Anunciación, Juan de la (1577), *Sermonario en lengua mexicana*, Mexico City: Antonio Ricardo.

Baudot, Georges (1995), *Utopia and History in Mexico: The First Chronicles of Mexican Civilization, 1520–1569*, trans. Bernard R. Ortiz de Montellano and Thelma Ortiz de Montellano, Niwot, Colo.: University Press of Colorado.

Bautista, Juan (1606), *Sermonario en lengua mexicana*, Mexico City: Diego López Dávalos.

(1979), 'Algunas abusiones antiguas'. In Angel María Garibay K. (ed.), *Teogonía e historia de los mexicanos*, Mexico City: Editorial Porrúa.

Benítez, Fernando (1984), *Historia de la ciudad de México*, Mexico City: Salvat, vol. 2.

Berceo, Gonzalo de (1944), *Milagros de Nuestra Señora*, ed. A. G. Solalinde, Madrid: Espasa-Calpe.

Burkhart, Louise M. (1989), *The Slippery Earth: Nahua-Christian *Moral Dialogue in Sixteenth-Century Mexico*, Tucson: University of Arizona Press.

(1992), 'Flowery Heaven: The Aesthetic of Paradise in Nahuatl Devotional Literature', *Res: Anthropology and Aesthetics* 21: 88–109.

(1993), 'The Cult of the Virgin of Guadalupe in Mexico'. In Gary H. Gossen and Miguel León-Portilla (eds), *South and Meso-American Native Spirituality: From the Cult of the Feathered Serpent to the Theology of Liberation*, New York: Crossroad.

(1995), 'The Voyage of Saint Amaro: A Spanish Legend in Nahuatl Literature', *Colonial Latin American Review* 4: 29–57.

(1996), *Holy Wednesday: A Nahua Drama from Early Colonial Mexico*, Philadelphia: University of Pennsylvania Press.

(1998), 'Pious Performances: Christian Pageantry and Native Identity in Early Colonial Mexico'. In Elizabeth Hill Boone and Tom Cummins (eds), *Native Traditions in the Postconquest World*, Washington, D.C.: Dumbarton Oaks.

Caesarius of Heisterbach (1929), *The Dialogue on Miracles*, trans. H. von E. Scott and C. C. Swinton Bland, introduction by G. G. Coulton, 2 vols., London: George Routledge & Sons.

Christian, William A., Jr. (1981), *Apparitions in Late Medieval and Renaissance Spain*, Princeton, N.J.: Princeton University Press.

Dávila Padilla, Augustín (1955), *Historia de la fundación y discurso de la provincia de Santiago de México, de la orden de predicadores*, Mexico City: Editorial Academia Literaria.

*Doctrina, evangelios y epístolas en nahuátl* (n.d.), Codex Indianorum 7, The John Carter Brown Library, Brown University, Providence, R.I.

Fernández del Castillo, Francisco (ed.) (1982), *Libros y libreros en el siglo xvi*, Mexico City: Archivo General de la Nación and Fondo de Cultura Económica.

Gante, Pedro de (1981), *Doctrina cristiana en lengua mexicana (edición facsimilar de la de 1553)*, ed. Ernesto de la Torre Villar, Mexico City: Centro de Estudios Históricos Fray Bernardino de Sahagún.

Gobius, Johannes (1480), *Scala celi*, Ulm: Johann Zainer.

Goodich, Michael E. (1995), *Violence and Miracle in the Fourteenth Century: Private Grief and Public Salvation*, Chicago:

University of Chicago Press.

Greenleaf, Richard E. (1969), *The Mexican Inquisition of the Sixteenth Century*, Albuquerque: University of New Mexico Press.

Herolt, Johannes (1928), *Miracles of the Blessed Virgin Mary*, ed. and trans. C. C. Swinton Bland, introduction by Eileen Power, New York: Harcourt, Brace and Company.

Lasso de la Vega, Luis (1649), *Huei Tlamahuiçoltica omonexiti in ilhuicac tlatocacihuapilli Santa Maria*, Mexico City: Juan Ruiz.

Little, A. G. (ed.) (1908), *Liber exemplorum ad usum praedicantium*, Aberdeen: Typis Academicis.

López Austin, Alfredo (1967), 'Cuarenta clases de magos del mundo náhuatl', *Estudios de cultura náhuatl* 7: 87–117.

Mendieta, Gerónimo de (1980), *Historia eclesiástica indiana*, ed. Joaquín García Icazbalceta, Mexico City: Editorial Porrúa.

Molina, Alonso de (1971), *Vocabulario en lengua castellana y mexicana y mexicana y castellana*, ed. Miguel León-Portilla, Mexico City: Editorial Porrúa.

Montoya Martínez, Jesús (1981), *Las colecciones de milagros de la Virgen en la edad media (el milagro literario)*, Granada, Spain: Universidad de Granada.

Motolinía (Toribio de Benavente) (1979), *Historia de los indios de la Nueva España*, ed. Edmundo O'Gorman, Mexico City: Universidad Nacional Autónoma de México.

(1989), *El libro perdido: Ensayo de reconstrucción de la obra histórica extraviada de fray Toribio*, ed. Edmundo O'Gorman, Mexico City: Consejo Nacional para la Cultura y las Artes.

Pelikan, Jaroslav (1996), *Mary Through the Centuries: Her Place in the History of Culture*, New Haven: Yale University Press.

Pez, Bernard (1925), *Liber de miraculis Sanctae Dei Genitricis Mariae*, ed. Thomas Frederick Crane, Ithaca, N.Y.: Cornell University Press.

Poole, Stafford, C. M. (1987), *Pedro Moya de Conteras: Catholic Reform and Royal Power in New Spain, 1571–1591*, Berkeley: University of California Press.

(1995), *Our Lady of Guadalupe: The Origins and Sources of a Mexican National Symbol, 1531–1797*, Tucson: University of Arizona Press.

Power, Eileen (1928), 'Introduction'. In Johannes Herolt, *Mira-*

*cles of the Blessed Virgin Mary*, ed. and trans. C. C. Swinton Bland, New York: Harcourt, Brace and Company.

Sahagún, Bernardino de (1950-82), *Florentine Codex, General History of the Things of New Spain*, ed. and trans. Arthur J. O. Anderson and Charles E. Dibble, 12 vols., Santa Fe, N.M.: School of American Research and University of Utah.

——— (1993), *Psalmodia Christiana (Christian Psalmody)*, ed. and trans. Arthur J. O. Anderson, Salt Lake City: University of Utah Press.

Sánchez de Vercial, Clemente (1961), *Libro de los exenplos por A.B.C.*, ed. John Esten Keller, Madrid: Clásicos Hispánicos.

Santaballa, Sylvia (1995), '*Nican Motecpana*: Nahuatl Miracles of the Virgin of Guadalupe', *Latin American Indian Literatures Journal* 11: 34–54.

*Sermones y santoral en mexicano* (n.d.), Manuscript M-M 464, The Bancroft Library, Berkeley, California.

Siméon, Rémi (1977), *Diccionario de la lengua nahuátl o mexicana*, trans. Josefina Oliva de Coll, Mexico City: Siglo Veintiuno.

Torquemada, Juan de (1975-83), *Monarquía indiana*, Mexico City: Universidad Nacional Autónoma de México.

Voragine, Jacobus de (1993), *The Golden Legend: Readings on the Saints*, trans. William Granger Ryan, 2 vols., Princeton, N.J.: Princeton University Press.

Ward, Benedicta (1982), *Miracles and the Medieval Mind: Theory, Record and Event 1000-1215*, Philadelphia: University of Pennsylvania Press.

Warner, Marina (1976), *Alone of All Her Sex: The Myth and the Cult of the Virgin Mary*, New York: Vintage Books.

Weckmann, Luis (1984), *La herencia medieval de México*, 2 vols., Mexico City: El Colegio de Mexico.

# 4
# Cultural boundaries between adaptation and defiance: the mission communities of northwestern New Spain

Cynthia Radding

## Introduction

'Spiritual encounters' feature prominently in discussions of European and Amerindian cultural dynamics throughout the Americas. Inquisition papers and other ecclesiastical archives relinquish documentary evidence of the accusations of idolatry, witchcraft, and sorcery levelled at indigenous men and women practitioners of religious rituals that often combined Christian and native symbolic meanings. This genre of historical enquiry has yielded a substantial body of literature for the core areas of Mesoamerica and the Andes, where viceregal authorities were especially assiduous in ferreting out apostate or idolatrous behaviour, and has opened new interpretive paths for the frontier provinces where mission communities constituted the principal interface between semi-nomadic hunting, gathering, farming peoples and the Iberian authorities of church and crown (Stern 1982; Silverblatt 1987; Carmagnani 1988; MacCormack 1992; Mills 1994; Griffiths 1996; Gruzinski 1993; Deeds 1997; 1998a; 1998b). The Boltonian institutional histories of the 'civilizing' mission that characterized borderland studies of an earlier era have given way to critical ethnohistories centred on the indigenous peoples who populated the mission *reducciones*, sustained their agrarian economy, and created syncretic religious practices under colonial dominion. While it is important to note that the mission was not the only locus of cultural encounters on the borders of empire that were typified,

116

as well, by mining encampments, ranching estates, and military outposts (*presidios*), in which Indians and Iberians commingled and confronted one another under the rigours of labour recruitment and frontier defence, nevertheless it was in the missions that native peoples reconstituted enduring communities (Ortega 1985; 1993; del Río 1984; Radding 1997; 1998; Langer and Jackson 1995).

Within the broad geographic expanse and widely varied cultural traditions of Mesoamerica and the frontier provinces of northern New Spain, colonial historians have detected different symbolic spaces of political rebellion. Messianic movements whose leaders claimed extraordinary spiritual powers often envisioned a millennarian social order that would either eliminate the colonial oppressor or redress the balance of power between Indians and Spaniards. Rather than openly espouse the return of pre-Hispanic deities, rebellious leaders characteristically appropriated Christian ornaments, vestments, and eucharistic rituals in defiance of the exclusive authority claimed by the official clergy (Gruzinski 1989; Gosner 1992). Indians mounted political and religious responses to the crises occasioned by epidemics, food shortages, forced labour and tribute exactions, or the suppression of traditional leaders who performed a shamanic role of intercessor between human society and natural forces. The Pueblo revolt of New Mexico (1680) is a classic example of this kind of rebellion, rooted in religious and material grievances (Kessell 1979). Less dramatically perhaps, but nonetheless meaningfully, 'spiritual encounters' arose from the ritual practices surrounding the quotidian concerns of resource procurement, protection from disease, and maintenance of the social and cosmic order (Alonso 1994; Dehouve 1994).

This chapter engages the theme of religious interaction and confrontation in the context of the frontier society that developed in northwestern New Spain. It focuses on the dual modes of accommodation and resistance to Catholic discourse practised by the village peoples gathered in mission communities through evidence of indigenous appropriations of Christian symbols and rituals, punctuated by episodes of witchcraft and the reversal of Catholic sacrality during rebellions and uprisings. The native ethnic polities on which the discussion is centred include the Tegüima (Opata), O'odham (Pima), and some of the Cahitan peoples of the provinces of Sonora and Ostimuri, during the mid-eighteenth century when Spanish dominion was well established, but not uncontested.[1] These *serrano* peoples of the western foothills of the Sierra Madre Occidental all practised floodplain or irrigated agriculture, augmented by hunting and gathering; colonial missions and mining *reales* had altered their landscape and economy, and created zones of social and cultural *mestizaje* that led to the forging of new ethnic identities. At the same time, the nomadic frontier of Apaches, Seris, and Comanches threatened *serrano* farming villages and Spanish settlements alike, giving rise to an uneasy alliance between Indians and Spaniards through the presidial system of military rankings and auxiliary troops (Mirafuentes 1987; Radding 1997: 256–63).

Within this region of shifting borderlands across ethnic and political lines, the present discussion develops the idea of 'boundaries' to express the liminality of spiritual encounters in an ongoing counterpoint between conversion and cultural autonomy. While philosophical beliefs are difficult to define with precision from historical texts that are filtered through the transliterations of colonial authorities, the actions of indigenous peoples bespeak contrasting postures of wariness and acceptance, mimicry and contestation, partial understandings and encoded messages. Mission Indians' use of the symbols and rituals of religious practices underscores a duality of adaptation and defiance in both the material and spiritual realms of their encounters with Spanish missionaries and commanders. Above all, they were testing repeatedly the limits of the cultural boundaries within which they recreated their social and religious worlds.

## Power and the appropriation of Christian rituals

*Serrano* villagers' cautious acceptance of the material symbols of Christianity sprang, in large measure, from their search for multiple sources of spiritual power. From the earliest accounts of Jesuit endeavours to evangelize and 'reduce' the diverse Amerindian 'nations' of northwestern New Spain, beginning in 1591, to the established mission system of the eighteenth century, reports of negotiated encounters between shamans and indigenous military leaders, on the one hand, and Black Robes, on the other, suggest that the missionaries' targeted neophytes interpreted their message of exclusive conversion as an alternative resource for religious strength and insight. *Serrano* religious practitioners often derived their power from dreams; they guarded their esoteric knowledge and passed it on selectively through individual apprenticeships in the recitation of songs and chanted narratives (Underhill 1936). These intangible signs of spiritual power were closely associated with tangible relics and icons that enhanced their owners' religious efficacy. Although infrequently documented and poorly described, stone and wooden idols and shamanic paraphernalia – often hidden in caves – do appear in missionary reports from Sonora and Sinaloa in ways that suggest a duality of traditional and Christian religious structures. *Serrano* villagers embraced Catholic icons, with their visual and tactile symbolism, and imbued them with syncretic meaning. The cross, the rosary, and personalized saints introduced by Jesuit and Franciscan missionaries were appropriated as helpful talismans and intercessors in the ongoing struggle between human and cosmic forces.

The cross and crucifix, synecdoche of Christianity, figured centrally in the exchange of ritual signs that marked the earliest days of Spanish conquest in northwestern Mexico. Alvar Núñez Cabeza de Vaca, intrepid survivor of a nine-year overland trek from the Gulf of Mexico to Sonora and Sinaloa following the failed Pánfilo de Narváez expedition to Florida (1527–36), gave detailed descriptions in his *Relación* of the shamanic rituals that he and his three companions appropriated from their Amerindian captors and hosts, allowing them to travel from one tribal territory to another. The illusion of power that Cabeza de Vaca acquired came from the gift of two feathered gourds, believed to 'have healing virtues'. 'As we neared the houses [at La Junta de los Ríos] all the people came out to receive us, with much rejoicing and display, and among other things, two of their medicinemen gave us two gourds. Thence onward we carried gourds, which added to our authority, since they hold these ceremonial objects very high' (*Relación*, ch. 27, 29, cited in Ahern 1993: 221).

The gourds were exceptional items, because of their heaven-sent curing powers, within a larger cultural matrix of gift exchange. Cabeza de Vaca and his companions would have ignored that lesson at their peril, since their westward advance was accompanied by throngs of followers of distinct ethnic origins who valued these foreigners as shamans and intermediaries in a cyclical chain of looting and redistribution of goods. In one of the most famous episodes during their passage through Sonora, the Cabeza de Vaca party received 600 deer hearts, cotton blankets, and fine pieces of coral and turquoise; upon their long-awaited reunion with Spanish troops, the travellers attempted to communicate with their countrymen using the code of ritual gift giving they had learned so well. The 'Christians' received poorly Cabeza de Vaca's offering of buffalo robes, and it became evident that the Indians' network of gift exchange (although involving seizure of goods) was radically different from the Spaniards' assumed privileges of tribute, through the *encomienda*, and pillage in warfare.

The final chapters of Cabeza de Vaca's *Relación* outline the inversion of ritual signs through which the cross becomes the emblem of peaceful reception between Indians and Spaniards and, over time, the insignia of Spanish domination in this colonial frontier. During his sojourn in San Miguel de Culiacán, Cabeza de Vaca succeeded in persuading some of the Cahitan and Tahue-Totorame peoples who had fled their farming villages out of fear of the Spaniards to return, instructing them to greet their new overlords with crosses and to mark their villages with this sign (*Relación*, ch. 35, 36; Reff 1991: 27–30). The gourd, both emblem and vehicle of spiritual power, was displaced by the cross, a 'sign ... of acculturation and accommodation' and the marker of a new era (Ahern 1993: 224–5).

When juxtaposed with the gourd, the cross is an object – whether carved in wood, woven in reeds, incised in stone, or forged in metal – that carries a strong religious import. The sign of the cross is also a gesture that signifies the priestly blessing of the eucharistic sacrament or a greeting, a coded sign of recognition between priest and neophyte and among the Christian Indians who began to distinguish themselves from the *gentiles*, their unbaptized brethren (Pérez de Rivas 1985: vol. 2, 245; Merrill 1989). In both these forms, the cross continued to dominate the spiritual geography of the mission provinces of Sonora and Sinaloa. Crosses were central features of mission architecture: cruciform churches established the dimensions of sacred spaces for formal worship even as large wooden or masonry crosses placed in the central plazas of mission towns were the focal points of religious processions on Catholic feast days. The interior decoration of mission churches projected visually the lessons of Christian liturgy and belief. Although designed according to the traditions of the medieval church and the Tridentine prescriptions of the Counter-Reformation, their execution was in the hands of indigenous artisans. Typically, one of the lateral altars was devoted to themes of the Passion, dominated by the crucified Christ; the standard sacred objects inventoried for seventeenth- and eighteenth-century missions included silver-plated crosses (Nentvig 1971: 162; Pfefferkorn 1989: 240) and the bells that marked the hours of doctrinal recitation, work, and rest in the mission villages were imprinted with the cross.

As a symbol of Catholic devotion and doctrine inextricably linked to the Conquest, the cross was an emblem imposed on the *serranos'* spirituality. Nevertheless, as the proliferation of plain crosses erected in outdoor settings and individual patios suggests, indigenous peoples appropriated the symbol of a conquering god to consolidate their communities reconstituted under the shadow of the missions. Equally importantly, crosses adorned the informal spaces of worship maintained by Indians at some distance from the churches that represented the formal Catholic liturgy. Oratories and stones piled along roadways that invoked the protection of spiritual powers for travellers and pilgrims were often crowned with simple crosses; furthermore, sudden deaths at the hands of the Apaches or due to other misfortunes were marked with wooden crosses (Griffith 1992: 100–2). Finally, the cross was re-enacted in the performance of chanted processions and dances, such as the Cahitan *matachines* and Lenten *fariseos* that charged and retreated from the church in a cruciform pattern (Spicer 1980; Painter 1971).[2]

The rosary, crafted by Indian artisans, rendered the cross an amulet of personal protection and a mnemonic device for reciting the basic tenets of Christian doctrine. Andrés Pérez de Rivas, missionary and chronicler of the early Jesuit *reducciones* in Sinaloa and Sonora, gave special importance to the Christian symbols of the rosary and the cross, which he recounted in several instances of the devil's appearance to Indians who had accepted baptism. Young men who became lost while in the mountainous woodlands beyond their villages, terrified by visions of serpents and snakes, were restored to sanity by wearing a cross or rosary and confessing to the missionary. In Arivechi Padre Bartolomé Castaño brought the adults into mass by first teaching the children to recite the rosary and to sing songs of devotion to the holy sacrament in their own language. In reference to the conversion of the *nebomes* – Pimas of the uplands of central Sonora – Padre Andrés took special notice of the 'regularity and fervour' with which these neophytes recited the rosary in their homes and in the mission chapel (Pérez de Rivas 1985: vol. 2, 212, 229–31, 245, 248–9).

Over a century later Jesuits Juan Nentvig and Ignaz Pfefferkorn emphasized the devotion that *serrano* peoples evinced to the recitation of the rosary and litanies in the daily routine of mission life. These villagers, among whom Christian traditions had been established for generations, had incorporated the rosary and the symbol of the cross as a ritual of religious deference, without necessarily committing to memory the content of the words they had memorized. Nentvig observed, with a touch of irony, that 'one of the older missionaries of Sonora told me that there are no other Christians in the world who recite the doctrine so much and know it so little' (Nentvig 1971: 163–4).

The sequenced recitation of the rosary practised daily or weekly in all the missions created a time/space of sacrality that, for the missionaries, centred on the compounds of church-and-convent and seemed to mark the success of their religious endeavours. Yet, for the Indians, the rosary may have carried the power of this new Christian god to their homes and to their own bodies when they wore it as a protective talisman. Furthermore, as a symbol of divine intercession, personified in the Virgin Mary, the rosary linked its bearers to other sites of spiritual power.

Caves played a central role in Sonoran creation myths and religious practices associated with curative rites and sorcery. Among the best known stories of *serrano* hallowed cosmography, the Tohono O'odham revere the man-god of I'itoi (Elder Brother) who dwells in a cave on the west side of Baboquivari Mountain (Griffith 1992: 15–22; Nabhan 1982: 13–21). That caves were considered holy places was known to the missionaries who lived among the Sonoran highland peoples. Fray Francisco Barbastro, for example, placed the birthplace of Jesus in a cave in his Christmas sermon to the Opatas of Baviácora, elaborating on the details of the arrival of Mary and Joseph and their preparations to receive the child in this hallowed place (BL HHB M-M 483 [1792]). During the early years of Jesuit *reducciones*, their complaints of sorcery and witchcraft nearly always located these shamanic rituals in caves. Pérez de Rivas's account of Padre Francisco Oliñano's *entrada* among the *Aivinos*[3] of central Sonora in 1624 related the missionary's destruction of a cave idol commemorating the burial of a leader who had died by lightning, to whom they gave offerings to ward off a similar death (Pérez de Rivas 1985: vol. 2, 221–5). The militant language of this Jesuit chronicler reminds us that the missionaries viewed themselves in rivalry and even in battle with native religious specialists; their use of performative and artisanal symbols constituted a spiritual arsenal in their quest for the souls and the political loyalty of *serrano* neophytes.

## Power and dissent: seizing and overthrowing the symbols of Christianity

Missionaries and shamans tested their spiritual powers through witchcraft and sorcery. Repeated accusations concerning the casting of spells and the infliction of crippling and fatal diseases travelled across the Christian–pagan divide, as Jesuits imagined the work of the devil in the *hechiceros'* magic and indigenous religious leaders warned that baptism led to illness and death. The enduring belief in *hechicería* arose from fear, fear of supernatural powers to injure individuals, create storms, or bring on drought that could endanger the livelihood of an entire community. Andrés Pérez de Rivas referred to this power in his account of the early years of missionization in Sinaloa: 'They only obey certain Indians like themselves, either because of their [military] valor or because they have been *hechiceros* or physicians, insofar as they have cured them in their illness or refrained from casting spells and bringing them harm.' (González Rodríguez 1987: 74; 1977: 60)

Padre Joseph Neumann, who witnessed the uprisings of the 1690s in the Tarahumara Alta, condemned particularly the following that sorcerers gained among their people. He wrote that during these years of epidemics and widespread rebellion, 'there were detected several magicians who had evil spirits as their familiars, and who were tormenting many persons by their witchcraft. By their magic arts they obtained influence among the people and struck terror into everyone who refused to obey their commands.' It was sorcerers, Padre Neumann contended, who had persuaded Tarahumara villagers to flee the missions for the hills and canyons of the Sierra Madre, away from the 'church bells which, they said, attracted diseases', and from the prying visits of missionaries and military captains (Sheridan & Naylor 1979: 45–50).

Even as these *hechiceros* and oracles maintained ascendancy over their brethren, like one old man who brought on thunderstorms and danced in the air, they could train their powers on the missionaries themselves. Padre Carlos de Rojas, Jesuit Rector stationed in central Sonora during the mid-eighteenth century, described vividly the suffering of two missionaries in his district, Padre Marcos de Loyola of Teuricachi and Padre Cristóbal de Cañas of Arizpe, both of them victims of a sorcerer's spell. The last two years of Cañas's life were wracked by psychological anguish and physical maladies of 'unnatural' causes. The shaman who had tormented him was settling accounts over an earlier dispute concerning the native governorship of the pueblo. Against the missionary's will, the shaman had been elected governor of Arizpe, a large and important Opata village. When the priest interfered with the shaman's corporal punishment of another Indian, he vowed revenge against the Black Robe. Some years later, when the shaman himself faced death, but refused to confess his sins to the priest, Padre Rojas denied him a Christian burial in the church cemetery. The old sorcerer's family took his remains to the fields beyond the village, but even the earth rejected his bones, a sign that Rojas imbued with religious significance (Carlos de Rojas, Arizpe, 1744, BL M-M 1716, v. 1–77).

That this episode was chronicled in fairly lengthy detail in a report that responded to a province-wide survey covering general mission affairs in Sonora and Sinaloa in 1744, suggests that witchcraft weighed heavily on the minds of these Sons of Loyola. It further shows that the power to command and punish exercised by priests and by Indian governors created fissures of political and religious authority in the mission villages (Padre Juan Nentvig to Padre Visitador General, José de Utrera, 1754 [BNAF 33/692] in Nentvig 1971: 201–2). If, indeed, witchcraft was a 'weapon of the weak' – especially when practised by women (Behar 1989: 178–208; Scott 1985) – it also represented a complex mixture of ritual practices and beliefs that blurred the boundaries between Christian and pagan, Spaniard and Indian, priest and neophyte.

Spanish missionaries and military commanders alike feared that covert resistance personified in the bewitching powers of *hechiceros* could easily flare into open rebellion. In the provinces of Nueva Vizcaya and Sonora-Sinaloa, where missions, mining camps, and *presidios* were established precariously among village agriculturalists and surrounded by different bands of nomadic hunters and raiders, colonial power was contested on both religious and political grounds, creating an enduring frontier that was never completely subdued. The underlying motives for rebellion readily come to light in multiple historical accounts from the seventeenth and eighteenth centuries: forced labour, whether under the guise of *encomienda* or regulated by the *repartimiento* that drafted workers from the missions and sent them to the *reales de minas*; epidemics and the spectre of death in the mission towns, worsened by resentment over the Jesuits' meddling in conjugal relations that weakened kinship networks; and the cruelty of pre-emptive strikes and exemplary punishments meted out by Spanish commanders against suspected rebels.

Often these uprisings were inflammatory spiritual encounters as much as they were planned rebellions with a defined set of grievances. Shamans urged their followers to flee into the woods and caves, not only to escape dreaded pestilence, but also to feed and venerate stone idols and other sacred objects. The Acaxée revolt of 1601 illustrates well this kind of explosion, in which shamans took a leading role. Jesuits and lay Spaniards were targeted for death, churches were burned, and Acaxée rebels seized Catholic vestments, chalices, bells, and crosses (Deeds, 1998a: 37–40). In the Tarahumara rebellions of the end of the century, mentioned above, angry insurgents broke into the church of Echoguita, burned a large cemetery cross, smashed religious statuary, shredded vestments, broke the carved wooded altars and even destroyed the stone baptismal font. Rebels who invaded the village of Cocomórachic, in turn, were accused of stealing the priest's vestments and chalice (Sheridan & Naylor 1979: 53–5, 67).

Religious icons themselves became focal points of rebellion, both to defy the Spaniards' claim to imperial dominion and to acquire the spiritual power that flowed through these sacred objects. Three rebellions that shook Spanish control in mid eighteenth-century Sonora, involving Hokan (Seris), Cahitan (Yaquis) and Piman peoples, used Christian emblems as the ostentatious signs of a world turned upside down, of the reversal of the colonial realm. Each of these movements was sparked by secular grievances involving access to land and water, freedom of movement, and the betrayal of negotiated compromises; nevertheless insurgents turned their wrath against the symbols of the Catholic order during each of these episodes.

An incipient rebellion of lower Pimas with strongly messianic overtones was discovered and suppressed by Spanish presidial forces during the spring of 1737. Jesuit Felipe Segesser learned during his preparations for *Semana Santa* that a considerable number of his neophytes from the mission of Tecoripa had abandoned their villages and joined a pilgrimage to a shrine newly created in the Cerro Prieto, a cluster of hilly outcroppings in the desert frequented by both Seris and Pimas. They were following a prophet named Ariscibi from the Guaymas band of Seris, who led a cult to the god Moctezuma and predicted a new millennarian order in which Indians would rule over Spaniards, the infirm should be healed, and the land would render food and water in abundance. Ariscibi had built a modest oratory that housed the wooden figure of Moctezuma, dressed notably in the garb of Christian saints, and decorated with ornaments taken from the Guaymas mission of Belén. The prophet received his followers with the sign of the cross and performed an elaborate ritual based on the Catholic mass, embellished with the ceremonial smoking of cigarettes. During its brief existence, it was estimated that the cult attracted several thousand Indians from northern and western Sonora. These pilgrims of mixed ethnic origins journeyed to the desert shrine bringing with them livestock to slaughter and share among the gathered worshippers. The movement dissolved when Spanish troops, under the command of Juan Bautista de Anza, assaulted the Cerro Prieto, scattered the Indians gathered there, and captured Ariscibi. Interrogated and beaten, the prophet attributed his religious inspiration to demonic deception and revealed the location of his shrine. He was subjected to a public execution by hanging, in what was meant to be an exemplary punishment (Mirafuentes 1992: 123–41). Notwithstanding the Spaniards' severity, unrest continued to seeth in the province, in movements that combined religious and political motives.

The Cahitan revolt of 1739–41 represented the first major uprising of Yaquis since the establishment of the Jesuit mission regime in their territory in the early seventeenth century. Yaqui insurgents, joined by Mayos and Pimas, inflamed the provinces of Ostimuri and Sonora, forcing the temporary abandonment of mines and estates and the mobilization of presidial troops from Sinaloa. Their grievances were clearly spelled out in formal petitions presented to the newly appointed Governor of Sonora and Sinaloa and carried all the way to the viceregal court in Mexico. Yaquis demanded the removal of specific missionaries against whom they harboured resentments; the right to bear arms; the expulsion of non-Indians from their villages; the termination of compulsory labour in the missions without pay and, conversely, the freedom to sell their own produce and to work outside the missions. In short, they upheld the political autonomy of their pueblos even as they sought greater access to colonial markets (Spicer 1980: 41–2).

The first signs of what would become a widespread rebellion occurred in the theft and appropriation of religious icons from the mission churches of the Yaqui Valley. During the late spring of 1739, armed warriors from the pueblo of Guirivis broke into the missionary's house in Belén and stole the priestly vestments and sacred ornaments. They tore the cloths used to dress the saints and cover the altar, and refashioned them into shirts and pants ('camisa [y] calzones de género') that were donned by *matachines*, who danced with them on the eve of Corpus Christi in the pueblo of Ráhum (AGN *Californias*, 64, 8, f. 136–56). The ensuing investigation of this ostentatious reversal of sacrality revealed several layers of meaning. *Matachines*, in the Cahitan tradition, create sacred spaces through their dancing; in contemporary practice, their choreographed movements sanctify the atria and patios where religious ceremonies take place (Spicer 1980: 59–113). On this occasion, however, the *matachines* paraded their stolen garments openly before assembled Indians and Spaniards on the eve of Corpus Christi. Jesuit Ignacio María Nápoli elaborated on the gravity of the Indians' defiance, linking this act of symbolic vandalism with their increasingly militant rejection of the missionaries' temporal authority invested in the loyal governors who held the canes of office for each village (AGN *Californias*, 64, 8, f. 148–9, testimony of Juan Matheo Pinto, *maestro y governador que ha sido deste pueblo* [Ráhum] 1 July 1739).

The uprising swelled during the following year; total insurgent forces may have numbered as many as 14,000, and the territory they covered extended from the middle Yaqui river to the lower Fuerte valley (Spicer 1980: 32–58; Hu-Dehart 1981: 68–70). Yaquis and Spaniards reached a negotiated peace late in 1740, only after the defeat of rebel forces in Tecoripa and the return of two Yaqui emissaries who had been granted a hearing by the Viceroy and claimed to bring with them written approval for some of their petitions. In 1741, however, the new governor of Sonora raised charges of sedition against these Yaqui leaders, Juan Ignacio Usacamea (Muni) and Basoritemea (Bernabé) and summarily had them executed. Similarly arbitrary policies focused on the lower San Miguel valley of Sonora, where Seris and Pimas had gradually adapted to mission life, provoked the Seri revolt of 1748 that led to intermittent unrest lasting well over a century.

Seris (whose indigenous name is *cunca'ac*), coastal nomads who lived by fishing, hunting, gathering and trading with the inland farming peoples of Sonora, resisted the constraints of mission *reducciones* to return to their *rancherías* and seek their livelihood from nature's bounty. Nonetheless, several hundred Seri families had settled in the Pima villages of Nacameri, Pópulo, and Los Angeles, missions that shared the floodplain with Spanish ranches and haciendas. At mid-century, royal visitor José Rafael Rodríguez Gallardo ordered the military garrison at Pitic moved to San Miguel, a site wedged in between Pópulo and Los Angeles, for which he arranged for the relocation of Seris from Los Angeles to Nacameri and the transferal of their land to the presidial soldiers who would man the garrison. This betrayal of the terms under which the Seris had entered the missions was aggravated by their forced recruitment – under pain of lash – to build the *presidio*. During the following year increasing numbers of Seris fled the mission pueblos and joined the uprising, which had spread to the lower Sonora valley. The rebels trained their attacks on Spanish mines and estates, reserving their most destructive assaults on the properties of Spanish militiamen who led punitive expeditions against Seri forces. During the attack against the Real del Aguaje, southwest of the Presidio of Pitic and north of the Seris' desert fortress in the Cerro Prieto, insurgents turned their fury against the church. Having burned and pillaged the town, they 'spattered holy oil and, with an infernal rage, thrust spears nine times into a painting of Our Lady of Guadalupe'. After desecrating the communion chalice by eating on it, they flung it into the fire (AGN *Jesuitas* 1-12, exp. 2; Mirafuentes 1994: 119; Mirafuentes 1987: 18-29).

Spanish forces failed to subdue the Seris, merely pushing them into low-intensity guerrilla warfare and, in 1751, they faced open rebellion in the Pimería Alta, Sonora's northern frontier. Numerous bands of Pima warriors, totalling over 1000, burned mission churches and attacked scattered mining and ranching settlements. Two Jesuit missionaries lost their lives in this uprising: Tomás Tello of Caborca and Enrique Rúhen of Sonoitac were deliberately murdered, victims of the Indians' wrath and of their villages' isolation from the rest of the province. Hostilities lasted several months during the winter of 1751-52, leaving several hundred Pima warriors and Spanish settlers dead, and Spanish properties pillaged and torched (Mirafuentes 1989, 106-15; Spicer 1962: 129-30).

Contemporary accounts of the rebellion focused on the charismatic figure of its principal leader, Luis Oacpicagigua, governor of Sáric. Luis had built a following among the Pimas by hosting lavish feasts and giving generously from his harvests and livestock herds. He gained the confidence of Spanish military commanders during the 1750 campaign against the Seris, and was rewarded with the title of captain-general, which gave him considerable sway over the village governors. Luis vaunted the insignia of prestige that befitted his office, including the privilege of riding a horse, dressing in the Castilian manner, and even carrying a sword and musket. He rebuffed the moral authority of the Jesuits, refused to confess, and disdained any gesture of reverence during mass. His defiance of the customary deference that missionaries expected from their neophytes reached the audacity of desacralizing the sacramental ornaments of the church at Sáric, by putting them to vulgar uses. Padre Juan Nentvig recounted, 'with tears in his eyes', that Luis had put cigarettes in the silver cup reserved for the baptismal oil (*crismera*), allowed his followers to tie their hair with the cords that bound the priests' vestments, and taken the cloth painting of Santiago to place under his saddle as a sweat blanket (BNAF 33/692 in Nentvig 1971: 202-4; Mirafuentes 1989: 107-24).

# Conclusions: boundaries and spiritual encounters

The brief narratives of encounters between Spaniards and Indians summarized here, exhibiting different degrees of accommodation and resistance, suggest that the cultural boundaries between colonizers and colonized were porous and fluid. The divergent forms of religious expression that emerged in the frontier province of Sonora composed over time a palimpsest of symbolic meanings that were complex and even contradictory in their implications. Missionaries found it necessary to place biblical stories in natural settings, such as caves, that corresponded to native cosmologies; conversely, Yaqui, Pima and Seri rebellious leaders embedded Christian symbols in their rituals of defiance. Thus, Ariscibi, the self-proclaimed prophet of Moctezuma, created a syncretic cult with ornaments and vestments 'borrowed' from the church of Belén and may have transposed the figure of Moctezuma through Spanish accounts of the Mexica lore of their origins and odyssey to the valley of Mexico. His followers offered to this god the rosaries they wore as talismans against illness and injury. The fury of Spanish reprisals against this rather ingenious messianic movement probably stemmed from their anger at such a mixture of Christian and pagan icons (Mirafuentes 1992: 129–34; see also Gosner 1992: 122–59 on the brutal repression of the Tzeltal rebellion of Chiapas, 1712). Again, the powerful image of the cross served both to bind Sonoran peoples to Catholicism and to signal their resistance to Spanish rule. Seris who had defied Spanish troops on Tiburón Island in the summer of 1750, repudiated Governor Ortiz Parrilla's offer of peace by returning one of the messengers he had sent to them with a cross and the message that they would never surrender (Mirafuentes 1994: 121; AGN *Provincias Internas* 176, 4).

The symbolic interpretation of ritual acts cannot be divorced from the direct confrontations of historical actors, nor from the geographic and temporal contexts in which they took place. From the preceding discussion we can highlight Cerro Prieto and the Yaqui Valley as sites of important military confrontations and of cultural encounters. The harsh contours of rocky canyons and slopes in the Cerro Prieto, like the relative distance of Tiburón Island, provided a refuge for Seris and Pimas who had grown weary of the rigours of mission life and were fleeing Spanish punitive campaigns. By way of contrast, the Cahitan peoples of southern Sonora, Ostimuri, and Sinaloa tried to turn the Jesuit *reducciones* into a protective shield around the fertile deltas of the lower Yaqui, Mayo, and Fuerte rivers. The Yaquis, in particular, developed elaborate rituals based on the Catholic ceremonies they had learned, and made the mission towns focal points of the ethnic territory they so staunchly defended (Spicer 1980: 164–76). Among all *serrano* peoples of Sonora and Sinaloa, the histories they lived and narrated drew and effaced different cultural boundaries in a colonial frontier that was itself permeable and changing.

## Notes

1   The *serrano* peoples, known variously as Tegüima (Opata), O'odham (Pima), and the Cahitan peoples (Yaqui and Mayo) spoke languages that were part of the Uto-Aztecan family of languages and were village-dwelling agriculturalists. Prior to Spanish conquest they had warred among each other over territory, but they were similar in material culture and social structure. They distinguished themselves from the nomadic peoples like the Seris of the Gulf coast and the mountainous Apaches.

2   *Matachines* are ritual dancers who sanctify religious spaces, including church atria used in the performance of ceremonies outside the formal Christian liturgy. *Fariseos* (pharisees) play a prominent role in Cahitan observances of Lent and Holy Week. See Spicer (1980: 59–113) and Lolaz (1997: 59–77).

3   A local designation for Eudeves, an ethnic group who were linguistically distinct from but culturally related to the Opatas.

## Works cited

AGN     Archivo General de la Nación (Mexico City)
BNAF    Biblioteca Nacional Archivo Franciscano (Mexico City)
BL      Bancroft Library, University of California, Berkeley

Ahern, Maureen (1993), 'The Cross and the Gourd. The Appropriation of Ritual Signs in the *Relaciones* of Alvar Núñez Cabeza de Vaca and Fray Marcos de Niza'. In J. M. Williams and R. E. Lewis (eds), *Early Images of the Americas. Transfer and Invention*, Tucson & London: University of Arizona

Press.

Alonso, Marcos Matías (ed.) (1994), *Rituales agrícolas y otras costumbres guerrerenses*, Mexico: CIESAS.

Behar, Ruth (1989), 'Sexual Witchcraft, Colonialism, and Women's Powers: Views from the Mexican Inquisition'. In A. Lavrín (ed.), *Sexuality and Marriage in Colonial Latin America*, Lincoln: University of Arizona Press.

Carmagnani, Marcello (1988), *El regreso de los dioses. El proceso de reconstitución de la identidad étnica en Oaxaca. Siglos XVII y XVIII*, Mexico City: Fondo de Cultura Económica.

Deeds, Susan M. (1997), 'Double Jeopardy: Indian Women in Jesuit Missions of Nueva Vizcaya'. In S. Schroeder, S. Wood and R. Haskett (eds), *Indian Women of Early Mexico*, Norman and London: University of Oklahoma Press.

(1998a), 'Indigenous Rebellions on the Northern Mexican Mission Frontier: From First-Generation to Later Colonial Responses'. In D. J. Guy and T. E. Sheridan (eds), *Contested Ground. Comparative Frontiers on the Northern and Southern Edges of the Spanish Empire*, Tucson: University of Arizona Press.

(1998b), 'First-Generation Rebellions in Colonial Nueva Vizcaya'. In S. Schroeder (ed.), *Native Resistance and the Pax Colonial in New Spain*, Lincoln: University of Nebraska Press.

Dehouve, Danièle (1994), *Entre el caimán y el jaguar. Los pueblos indios de Guerrero*, Historia de los pueblos indígenas de México, Mexico: CIESAS.

González Rodríguez, Luis (1977), *Etnología y misión en la Pimería Alta, 1715–1740*, Mexico: UNAM.

(1987), *Crónicas de la Sierra Tarahumara*, Mexico: SEP.

Gosner, Kevin (1992), *Soldiers of the Virgen. The Moral Economy of a Peasant Rebellion*, Tucson: University of Arizona Press.

Griffith, James S. (1992), *Beliefs and Holy Places. A Spiritual Geography of the Pimería Alta*, Tucson: University of Arizona Press.

Griffiths, Nicholas (1996), *The Cross and the Serpent. Religious Repression and Resurgence in Colonial Peru*, Norman and London: University of Oklahoma Press.

Gruzinski, Serge (1989), *Man-Gods in the Mexican Highlands*, Stanford: Stanford University Press.

(1993), *The Conquest of Mexico. The Incorporation of Indian Societies into the Western World, 16^{th}-18^{th} Centuries*, Cambridge: Polity Press.

Hu-Dehart, Evelyn (1981), *Missionaries, Miners, & Indians. Spanish Contact with the Yaqui Nation of Northwestern New Spain*, Tucson: University of Arizona Press.

Kessell, John L. (1979), *Kiva, Cross, and Crown. The Pecos Indians and New Mexico, 1540-1840*, Washington, D.C.: US Department of the Interior.

Langer, Erick and Robert Jackson (eds) (1995), *The New Latin American Mission History*, Lincoln: University of Nebraska Press.

Lolaz, Thomas M. (1997), 'Tohono O'odham Fariseos at the Village of Kawori'k', *Journal of the Southwest* 39(1): 59-77.

MacCormack, Sabine (1992), *Religion in the Andes. Vision and Imagination in Early Colonial Peru*, Princeton: Princeton University Press.

Merrill, William (1989), 'Conversion and Colonialism in Northern Mexico. The Tarahumara Response to the Jesuit Mission Program, 1601-1767'. In R. W. Hefner (ed.), *Conversion to Christianity. Historical and Anthropological Perspectives on a Great Transformation*, Berkeley: University of California Press.

Mills, Kenneth (1994) 'The Limits of Religious Coercion in Mid-Colonial Peru', *Past & Present* 145: 85-121.

Mirafuentes Galván, José Luis (1987), 'Elite y defensa en la Provincia de Sonora, siglo XVIII'. In *Memoria del XI Simposio de Historia y Antropología de Sonora*, Hermosillo: Universidad de Sonora.

(1989), 'El "enemigo de las casas de adobe", Luis de Sáric y la Rebelión de los Pimas Altos en 1751'. In *XIII Simposio de Historia y Antropología de Sonora*, Hermosillo, Universidad de Sonora, vol. 1.

(1992), 'Ägustin Ascuhul, el profeta de Moctezuma. Milenarismo y aculturación en Sonora (Guaymas, 1737)'. In *Estudios de Historia Novohispana*, Mexico: UNAM, vol. 12.

(1994), 'Colonial Expansion and Indian Resistance in Sonora: The Seri Uprisings in 1748 and 1750'. In W. B. Taylor and F. Pease G. Y. (eds), *Violence, Resistance, and Survival in the Americas. Native Americans and the Legacy of Conquest*,

Washington and London: Smithsonian Institution.

Nabhan, Gary Paul (1982), *The Desert Smells like Rain. A Naturalist in Papago Indian Country*, San Francisco: North Point Press.

Nentvig, Juan ([1764] 1971), *Descripción geográfica, natural y curiosa de la provincia de Sonora*, ed. G. Viveros, Mexico: Archivo General de la Nación.

Ortega Noriega, Sergio (1985), 'El sistema de misiones jesuíticas: 1591–1699'. In *Historia General de Sonora. II.*, Mexico: Gobierno del Estado de Sonora.

(1993), *Un ensayo de historia regional: El Noroeste de México, 1530–1880*, Mexico: UNAM.

Painter, Muriel Thayer (1971), *A Yaqui Easter*, Tucson: University of Arizona Press.

Pérez de Rivas, Andrés ([1645] 1985), *Historia de los triunfos de nuestra santa fé entre gentes las más bárbaras y fieras del nuevo orbe*, Hermosillo: Gobierno del Estado de Sonora, vols. 1 and 2.

Pfefferkorn, Ignaz ([1795] 1989), *Sonora. A Description of the Province*, Tucson: University of Arizona Press.

Radding, Cynthia (1997), *Wandering Peoples. Colonialism, Ethnic Spaces, and Ecological Frontiers in Northwestern Mexico, 1700–1850*, Durham and London: Duke University Press.

(1998), 'The Colonial Pact and Changing Ethnic Frontiers in Highland Sonora, 1740–1840'. In D. J. Guy and T. E. Sheridan (eds), *Contested Ground. Comparative Frontiers on the Northern and Southern Edges of the Spanish Empire*, Tucson: University of Arizona Press.

Reff, Daniel T. (1991), *Disease, Depopulation, and Culture Change in Northwestern New Spain, 1518–1764*, Salt Lake City: University of Utah Press.

Río, Ignacio del (1984), *Conquista y aculturación en la California jesuítica*, Mexico: UNAM.

Scott, James, C. (1985), *Weapons of the Weak. Everyday Forms of Peasant Resistance*, New Haven: Yale University Press.

Sheridan, Thomas E. and Thomas H. Naylor (eds) (1979), *Rarámuri. A Tarahumara Colonial Chronicle, 1607–1791*, Flagstaff: Northland Press.

Silverblatt, Irene (1987), *Moon, Sun, and Witches. Gender Ideologies and Class in Inca and Colonial Peru*, Princeton: Princeton University Press.

Spicer, Edward H. (1962), *Cycles of Conquest*, Tucson: University of Arizona Press.

(1980), *The Yaquis. A Cultural History*, Tucson: University of Arizona Press.

Stern, Steve J. (1982), *Peru's Indian Peoples and the Challenge of Spanish Conquest*, Madison: University of Wisconsin Press.

Underhill, Ruth ([1936] 1985), *The Autobiography of a Papago Woman* (Memoir 46 of the American Anthropological Association, reprinted as *Papago Woman*), Prospect Height, IL: Waveland Press.

# 5
# 'Telling lives': confessional autobiography and the reconstruction of the Nahua self[1]

J. JORGE KLOR DE ALVA

## Introduction

Sometime around 1570 a Franciscan friar claimed that the natives of New Spain had uncluttered, parallel lives. He argued that 'they had none of the deals, contracts, and tangles the Spaniards have' and that a hundred or more of their confessions could be heard in a day because they committed 'such few types of sins ... [which were] so well known by the confessors ... [that they] would rather confess twenty of them than one Spaniard' (*Códice franciscano* 1941: 86, 89). About six years later another Franciscan, Bernardino de Sahagún, sadly admitted that – the faith having made little progress among them – many if not most of the natives continued their ancient practices and beliefs behind a thin veil of Christianity (Sahagún 1975: 578–85). These positions are not necessarily contradictory; instead, I will attempt to show that together they affirm that, to Europeans, Indians were no good at telling lives.

Sahagún, the missionary most familiar with native ethnography, came to believe the patterned, terse stories Indians confessed to priests were not true. I believe the question is not so much about truth as it is about error. Since 1526, when the sacrament of penance was formally introduced in Mexico (Motolinía 1971: 128), baptized natives were required to recount the story of a moral self that was not theirs. The narrative of the self expected during a confession was modelled after an ideal image of the Christian life, where every word, deed, and thought had a sinful side, where sin threatened eternal damnation, and where only tearful remorse followed by a vocal recitation of one's darkest secrets held the promise of reconciliation. No native, who had constituted himself out of very different self-forming practices than those used in the West, could see himself reflected in this image. In effect, to the extent that acculturation – that is, the acceptance of the new regime of self-formation – did not follow baptism, the Indian self was not reconstructed enough to recite a Christian autobiography. Therefore, natives who in Sahagún's eyes confessed to lives they did not live may not have been telling lies. Instead, those who were attempting to tell the truth may have been telling the life of a self they hardly knew and who was certainly not kneeling before the priest.

## Fragmenting selves

With the introduction of Christianity, two contrasting ways of making up and representing the self were pitted against each other. The differences were obvious to the confessors who routinely heard natives and Europeans emplot their biographies in fundamentally distinct forms, and who could not avoid inciting conflict between the two as they sought to impose one by delegitimizing the other in the course of establishing a penitential system of discipline. Furthermore, the narratives the natives told could themselves be understood in opposite ways by those who engaged in eliciting them. On the one hand, they suggested a failure in the conversion process (Sahagún's complaint), because the story told did not fit the behaviour observed. On the other, they led to a naïve belief in the success of the Christianization process, as the natives repeated by rote idealized episodes from an imaginary life that was so poorly understood it could only be mechanically outlined, making it appear as though they lived a dull, monotonous existence.

To move beyond the telling but limited observations of the missionaries, in order to explain the relation between native confessional autobiography and the priests' attempts to reconstruct the self of the Nahuas (the so-called 'Aztecs' and their linguistic and cultural neighbours), I will begin by comparing the manner in which the members of each cultural group were expected to form themselves into ethical subjects and conduct themselves as moral agents. The contrast between the ways in which each group experiences itself can be outlined by drawing on a useful methodological approach employed by Michel Foucault (1985: 25–32) to clarify the distinction between classical Greek and early Christian modes of self-formation.

## Ethical substance

Because Roman Catholicism rests on the premise of a free will, the moral agent is the individual. Therefore, freedom of choice means that the subject, plagued by illicit inclinations but intent on being moral, must concern himself with his desires – of concupiscence, greed, gluttony, and so on. The aspect of the self one must work on in order to act in an ethical manner is what Foucault calls the 'ethical substance'. By giving primacy to the will, Christianity made *desire* a more critical focus of moral attention than feelings (of pleasure, self-fulfilment, or well-being) or the performance of moral acts.

As the Christian faith distanced itself from its Jewish roots, *behaviour* came increasingly to be seen primarily as a sign of the internal state of the self, becoming less the centre of the moral terrain and more the marker pointing to the stirrings of the soul. By the thirteenth century, when heresies flourished that flirted with predestination and the belief that matter was intrinsically evil, the church re-emphasized its commitment to the belief in personal responsibility and the importance of internal states by making contrition, that is, personal sorrow, rather than the performance of penitential acts, the most important part of the Sacrament of Penance (Tentler 1977: 16–21). In 1215 the Fourth Lateran Council, called to respond to the popular heresies, made annual private confession obligatory, thereby declaring that more than ever the church would focus its attention on the individual's desires as the substance that needed to be relentlessly disciplined to create the moral self. Though some desires were understood to have an external object, their origin was made traceable solely to the subject. God's grace or Satan's evil could not move one to act morally without an independent exercise of the will; therefore, desire as cause and effect of the will's movements had to be brought in line if one was to make oneself a moral agent.

Despite the fact that much of the early missionization in New Spain took place with little attention paid to native volition (Gómez

Canedo 1977: 177–80), individual responsibility, the core of Christian moral philosophy, was preached to the neophytes from the start. The early doctrinal works and practical manuals used for this purpose explained that the human will, suspended between the opposing temptations of devils and angels, and forced to be the site of the struggles between body and soul, was alone held responsible for moulding desire. Pedro de Córdoba's *Doctrina christiana*, written in the second decade of the sixteenth century, summarizes the issues when, in the course of describing the fifth Article of Faith, God is quoted admonishing Adam and Eve as follows: 'The inclinations of the body and the desires of the soul are contrary to one another. So that from without and from within, you are subject to much great wretchedness, anguish and tribulation. But ... contrary to the quality of your nature [nothing] can come against your will ... as long as you remain firm and persevering in keeping the law that I shall give you' (Córdoba 1970: 70). In effect, the Nahuas were being taught that the essence of the Christian self was its segmentation into warring parts. Consequently, their conversion implied taking sides against a part of their self by arming their will ('the desires of the soul') to do battle with their natural desires ('the inclinations of the body'). Nothing could have been further from pre-contact Nahua belief.

Though an understanding of the Nahua self was critical if one wished to make sense of their self-presentation, whether in a casual encounter or during sacramental confession, it was poorly apprehended by the missionaries, who unavoidably interpreted it through the Christian categories of the person that were assumed to be universal. However, the problem was not solely ideological. A reading of the extant Nahua documentation makes clear that the evidence needed to analyse the Nahua self was usually indirect, implied rather than asserted, and always in need of interpretation. This observation should make superfluous the proviso that the interpretations and conclusions that follow are and will remain necessarily tentative.

The Nahua self, like that of the Christians, was also partitioned, but the nature and geography of the parts and the relations among them had little resemblance to the essence, map, or politics of the Christian self. It follows that the ethical substance the Nahuas worked on to become moral agents had to be different. As was the case for the Christians, desires were problematic, but what the Nahuas worried about when they strove to make themselves ethical subjects was desire itself, which they believed could originate from forces beyond their control. Therefore, they were preoccupied with the need to balance the desires; that is, the moral subject was one who attended to the personal and ritual *acts* that balanced the forces acting within him or her in order to restrain any one desire from overcoming the others. Unlike the mendicant priests, whose Christian ideal was the obliteration of all earthly desires, the Nahuas sought to survive in this life by prolonging them through careful management. For the natives there was no autonomous will at the core of the self since every human being was a microcosm reflecting the forces that made up the cosmos at large. Indeed, there was no boundary, no clear distinctions between personal will and the supernatural and natural forces that governed the universe. For this kind of self, one crisscrossed by forces, many of which emanated from (or constituted) the gods, *acts* that were believed truly to harmonize the contrary influences of external and internal forces, rather than right *intentions*, mapped out the terrain of the ethical subject. Therefore, behaviour, performance, and punctiliousness, rather than will, responsibility, or motivation, were the key concerns of the Nahua moral self.

This self was believed to be·composed of many physical and supernatural elements. However, three major animistic entities, the *tonalli*, the *teyolia*, and the *ihiyotl*, all shared with animals, plants, and certain objects, constituted its core (see López Austin 1980: 221–62). The *tonalli*, whose animistic centre appears to have been located in the head, originated as a light-heat force in the heavens and remained the key link between the individual and the gods. The nature of this link, always defined by the will of the deity or, more precisely, the time when it was ritually infused in the child, was the major determinant of an individual's destiny. Among other things, the *tonalli* was responsible for each person's vital power, physical growth, temperament, and cognition or rationality. As is well known, each of the 260 days of the religious calendric cycle called the *tonalpohualli* ('the count of the *tonalli*') was a different *tonalli* that radiated throughout the surface of the earth. The specific *tonalli*, fixed for any individual in the course of a ceremony, formed a part of the same animistic force that seems to have affected everything in the world when the same *tonalli* once more radiated throughout the earth. Consequently, the boundary between the singular self, other selves, and what Westerners would consider non-animate objects was extremely permeable. Human beings physically and supernaturally formed part of a universal continuum linking their fortunes directly to the cosmic whole. Free will made little sense in this cosmology, and individual acts, moral or immoral, always had a social, if not cosmic, significance.

In contrast, in the sixteenth century the *teyolia* was defined with good reason as 'el alma, o ánima' by Fray Alonso de Molina (1970: 95). After all, it was considered by the Nahuas to be the part of the self that survived mortal life and, unlike the flighty *tonalli* – always subject to being scared off and sporting an independent volition – it was the vivifying force *par excellence*, the one that could never abandon the living being. Centred in the heart, it shared with it its qualities of cognition, sentimentality, and desire. But as with the heart, the *teyolia* was susceptible to those diseases – originating with illicit sexual acts or excesses – said to compress or darken the heart, or that were caused by sorcerers who magically devoured or 'twisted' hearts. It was to cure these afflictions or imbalances that the Nahuas confessed and did penance in a ritual aptly named *neyolmelahualiztli*, 'the act of straightening out the heart'.

The *ihiyotl*, a luminous gas that emanated from living or dead bodies, is the least understood of the animistic forces we assume made up the Nahua self. It was considered dangerous because it had the power to over-stimulate, causing the self to be destabilized. After all, since its centre was the liver, where passion, sentiment, and vigour resided, the *ihiyotl* was closely associated with anger, hatred, desire, and, in particular, envy. To keep the *ihiyotl* under control and thereby to become a healthy, fortunate, and moral human being, an individual had to keep all three forces functioning harmoniously. This was a difficult task, calling on one to fix his or her gaze on the many moral obligations equilibrium required. However, unlike the classical Greeks who pursued the ideal of the golden mean, the Nahuas sought to balance extremes in order to take advantage of their virtues while escaping the effects of their excesses. In the Nahuas' context the act linking desire to survival was the ethical substance they focused on in order to make moral agents of themselves; that is, in order to become members of the society who could maintain themselves healthy, respected, and well off, and could assist the community to do likewise.

## Mode of subjection

How one makes the truth of the ethical substance one's own and thereby becomes concerned with it is what is meant by mode of subjection. Sixteenth-century Christians were moved to recognize their moral obligations by learning the rudiments of what the church preached as divine and natural law. The former was based on the precepts found in the Bible, the doctrinal sins and virtues contained in the catechism and other devotional literature, and the codified rules of the church heard in sermons and declaimed by the local priests. The commands of natural law were drawn primarily from the accumulated tradition of Western rationalizations about what is and is not natural and, therefore, what is and is not acceptable for decent humans to do. Because of the warring nature of the Christian self, with the natural desires of the body struggling against the other-worldly desires of the soul, the saintly teachers of the church had made renunciation of the self, particularly the flesh, the ideal mode of subjection. It was this lofty goal that the austere mendicants sought to inculcate in the minds of the natives. Short of that ascetic ideal, an acceptance of and compliance with the church's basic precepts was the mode by which the Christian was expected to work on his desires in order to make himself a moral actor.

Because the Nahua self was believed to be fundamentally unstable, the native modes of subjection, that is, the way they recognized their obligation to put equilibrium or harmony into practice, appears to have rested on their belief in the principles of a cosmic order. Rather than a world divided between the forces of good and evil, the Nahua cosmos was formed of opposing forces, all of which were necessary and each of which was capable of harm. Consequently, each force had to be constantly balanced by the others if stability were to be preserved.

As the Nahuas made clear in the myths handed down to us, the macro-order of the present age, the epoch of the Fifth Sun, was considered possible only because the divine forces of each cardinal direction and the centre were taking turns radiating their influences across the universe. The Nahuas promoted this mac-

ro-order at the local or micro-level by performing public ceremonies, beyond the watchful eyes of the friars, that fortified each
of the forces according to the ritual or, more precisely, balancing
cycle. In turn, at the level of the individual body, harmony or
well being was maintained through a complex calculus of equili-
brations, primarily of a divinatory sort, that took into consideration gender, age, *tonalli*, physical states (like pregnancy, exhaus-
tion, sexual excitation, or extreme desire), and moral, condition.

The threat to equilibrium posed by the moral condition of
the self did not come from a belief that immoral acts or thoughts
were intrinsically evil – an idea more closely in tune with the
assumptions about natural and divine law made by faithful Christians – but from the likelihood that an excess of the forces that
made up either sexuality or personal exuberance would destabi-
lize the harmony required by the self. In effect, the danger of a
sexual transgression did not result from sex itself; instead, it resided in a form of contamination called *tlazolmiquiztli*, 'death or
disease from refuse/what is worn out'. The post-contact *Códice
carolino* glosses the term as follows: 'a false general omen applied to anything that is damaged or any effort that is not successful ... was *tlazolmiqui*, because it took place before a sinner, especially a fornicator, or also before someone considered to have
an excess of nature, like twins or their parents ... or if some man,
especially a young one, gave himself too much to his wife' (*Códice
carolino* 1967: 46). This suggests that the disease or death produced by a breach of sexual conduct is, like garbage, the product
of a physical wearing down or something superfluous, an excess
that can pollute the guilty as easily as the innocent.

It is here that we see the Nahua concept of transgression in
sharpest contrast with the Christian idea of sin. What is problematic for the Nahua who fails to live up to the principles that order
the cosmos is not that he or she offends the gods, who themselves are hardly paragons of morality, but that by doing so one
puts oneself, others, and the things and events around one in
danger. From a wider perspective, a transgression – whether the
result of human, natural, or supernatural causes – precipitated a
*tetzahuitl*, defined by Molina as a 'cosa escandalosa, o espantosa,
o cosa de agüero' and by Frances Karttunen as 'something extraordinary, frightening, supernatural; an augury, a bad omen'
(Karttunen 1983: 237). I believe a *tetzahuitl* was a rupture in the

cosmic whole, a form of destabilization that could result from an immoral act, affecting the perpetrator, those around him or her, and, as the *Códice carolino* notes, those contaminated by the *tlazolmiquiztli* that was sure to follow. To reduce the frequency and effects of these unavoidable personal and cosmic disturbances, Nahua society had techniques by which the self could be transformed into an ethical subject rather than remain a mere object of the amoral forces of the universe.

## Asceticism

To be moral the individual must engage in exercises that permit him or her to work on the ethical substance. These ascetic practices include not only what a person does to him or herself in order to follow the moral code, but also what any person must work on within themselves in order to become the author of their respective actions. From the beginning, Christian asceticism was closely tied to the techniques of the self that permitted baptized sinners to be forgiven and thereby saved. These mental exercises and their ritual manifestations were always associated with the moral ideal upon which the church was founded: the renunciation of the self through the eradication of desire. Though the personal and ritual mechanisms employed in the process of forgiveness underwent many changes over the centuries, they maintained throughout a fourfold structure of self-examination (contrition), oral narration of the sinful self (confession), successful performance of disciplinary acts (satisfaction), and priestly absolution (reconciliation).

Contrition was the core of the late medieval confession brought to New Spain. It required penitents to undergo a systematic, thorough, and detailed self-decipherment that would uncover all illicit desires, their circumstances, and the nature of the acts that accompanied them. This hermeneutic of the self was meant to be complete, based on techniques of self-examination that were carefully outlined in a variety of summas and manuals for confessors that circulated widely in the Old and New Worlds. The ultimate goal of this introspection was to bring one to a tearful acknowledgement of all one's sins as sorrowful experiences offensive to God and therefore disgusting to the individual. In contrast to the goal of personal growth implied by the Greek command 'know thyself', the end of this investigation into the self was to repudiate it. This probing of the self in order to eradicate it, founded on the need to identify one's illicit desires so as to be distressed at their appearance, was the ideal upon which sacramental confession rested and, therefore, constituted the main self-forming activity required by Christian asceticism. In effect, a Christian could make him or herself into a moral subject only through the development of techniques of self-discovery and self-mastery.

Nahua asceticism was logically founded on native beliefs concerning the nature of the self. A self composed primarily of elements shared with entities external to it was necessarily susceptible to influences and effects over which it had little control. Consequently, any practices that aimed at (1) bringing conduct in line with the rules and (2) transforming one into the subject rather than the object of one's behaviour required both hermeneutic and disciplinary exercises. But contrary to Christian asceticism, in this case hermeneutics was necessary to make sense of the internal *and* external forces. And discipline was required to manipulate their influences in order to empower the self, not negate it.

Thus, instead of self-examination in order to discover one's faults, Nahua practices called for the mastering of complex sets of moral rules, an understanding of the ordering of the calendric and natural cycles, and a working knowledge of the characteristics of supernatural and natural entities. This hermeneutic of the cosmic order, as reflected in the individual and the world, was undertaken by learning, memorizing, and assimilating a vast body of cultural information. This information, going far beyond the realm of moral codes to address the very practical needs of everyday life, had to be understood if one were to be considered moral. After all, the only proof of the ethical subject's truth was its being well off, and one was well off by knowing how to balance forces, symbolically and practically, that resided beyond the range of one's immediate control. The ability to interpret at least the rudiments of the *tonalamatl* complex was only one part of what a person needed to master. The interpretation of local topography, animal habits, divine inclinations, and human acts formed other critical fields for exegetical self-formative efforts. Without going into details, I believe that this reading of the moral significance of the Nahua understanding of their temporal and supernatural worlds may help to explain the religious and ethical roles played by both the *huehuehtlahtolli* ('speech of the elders') narratives and the ethnographic data which the native informants provided Sahagún for his *Historia general* (see Klor de Alva et al. 1988).

Nahua asceticism is the subject of an insightful study by Miguel León-Portilla (1993) on the concept of *tlamacehua*, 'to do penance, to deserve something'. He explains the ideology behind the native disciplinary practices by studying the use of *macehua* derivatives in the pre-contact Nahua creation myth, a story of reciprocity fundamentally at odds with its Christian counterpart:

> The key concept of *tlamacehua* denotes the primary and essential relation human beings have with their gods. These, with their own penance and sacrifice, deserved – brought into existence – the human beings. The gods did it because they were in need of some beings who would be their worshipers, the providers of sustenance to foster life on earth. Man also had to perform *tlamacehualiztli*, 'penance, the act of deserving through sacrifice,' including the bloody one of human beings. If the gods ... 'did penance for us,' we ought to follow their example, deserve our own being on the earth with our blood and life.
>
> [Thus,] ... everything in life ... has to be deserved through penance and sacrifice. (León-Portilla 1993: 75)

This analysis is given additional support by Molina's sixteenth-century definition of *macehua* as 'to obtain or to deserve what is desired' or 'to do penance' (1970: 50; cf. Karttunen and Lockhart 1987: 31).

Without doubt, the key self-forming activity of the Nahuas was the performance of public and private disciplinary acts (bloodletting, sleep deprivation, etc.) through which they sought to 'make themselves worthy'; that is, by which, through 'penitential' exercises, they trained the various parts of the self to function harmoniously in order to balance the self's desires with those of the gods. The extreme forms of Nahua asceticism required a compelling politico-religious ideology capable of eliciting from each member truly severe sacrifices. Not surprisingly, with the waning of the influence of the native religious leaders that followed the introduction of Christianity, the rigorous techniques for self-mastery suffered a precipitous decline in popularity. This decline, which the imposition of Christian penitential rites could not arrest, was deeply lamented by Sahagún and others who saw the Nahuas reject the mendicant friars' austere regime in favour of 'bodily desires and natural inclinations' (Sahagún 1975: 580). By the second half of the sixteenth century even the Archbishop of Mexico began to despair of saving from the torments of hell any native who was not a recently baptized child (García Pimentel 1897: 425).

## Telos

The ethical subject worries about the ethical substance and subjects itself to ascetic practices for some purpose. This end, or *telos*, is the type of self one seeks to form when one engages in ethical behaviour. The Christian *telos* is to be immortal with a pure self, a self free of the taint of mortal sin. In this state the individual can fulfil the transcendent aim of gaining eternal salvation for his or her soul. However, the Nahua *telos* was to be well off in this life – as healthy, wealthy, and wise as the gods permitted. Eternal salvation required that the fragmented Christian self split forever apart, allowing the soul, the ultimate metaphor of the ethical subject, to be free at last of the body and the desires that were the obstacles to a glorious end. On the other hand, temporal survival required that the Nahuas struggle constantly against the fragmenting tendencies of their precarious selves. Only the aggregated self, in concert with other united selves, could struggle against the obstacles to personal, social, and cosmic order posed by destiny. These opposing *telos* implied dissimilar moral concerns and contrasting relations to the self; in turn, they resulted in distinctive autobiographies. It is to the nature and meaning of these different narratives of the self that I now turn my attention.

# The reconstruction of the Nahua self

### Straightening hearts

Christian morality and the attainment of eternal salvation rested on the individual's willingness to undergo periodic self-examinations. These introspections and subsequent confessions served important social and religious ends that justified the church as the most pervasive institution in the late medieval world. Individually, the painstaking reconstruction of one's life and its narration were meant to console the faithful in this life as they made salvation in the next possible. Socially, the penitential system contributed so extensively to the transformation of Christians into peaceful, loyal, and moral members of the society that neither church nor state could have done without it, as was proven during the Reformation when the system was put in question. Consolation and discipline, the two key tasks of sacramental confession, were frequently opposed to one another and so fraught with practical and spiritual dangers that the history of the Sacrament of Penance is one of disagreement concerning the significance – and at times the nature – of every theological and ritual aspect of the Sacrament except its fourfold structure: contrition, confession, satisfaction, and reconciliation (Tentler 1977).

No matter how much disagreement existed between the authors of summas or confessional guides, and no matter how poorly the process was understood or how well the basics of the confessional ritual were memorized, late medieval Europeans were taught to examine their desires in detail, to chart their behaviour, to dissect their motives, and to tell priests all about it. These exercises were so ubiquitous and conditioned the meaning of Christian life so fundamentally that Foucault's claim (1980) that they are the roots of modern psychology and of other nineteenth-century sciences of the self has the appearance of a truism. These were powerful cultural practices deeply affecting the self's relation to itself and others, even if one confessed rarely or not at all. Indeed, without them one could hardly be called a Christian.

Although the ascetic self of some priests was not identical to that of most European peasants, nobles, or crown officials, it was cut of the same Christian cloth. But since the regime of self-decipherment and autobiographical discourse was first deployed in Mexico, two dramatically different selves, generally with opposed social or political agendas, began to face each other. Spanish priests worked diligently to impose not only a new way to live, but also a new way to represent one's life in discourse; while bewildered or resistant natives, attempting to live a life familiar to them, were bent on telling it their way. While this struggle over the proper fabrication and subsequent rendition of an autobiography was being waged, the Christianization of indigenous Mexico hung in the balance, and with it the moral and civic foundation of the new society.

Sacramental confession implied that would-be native penitents had to be convinced to tell Europeans about themselves and others, but equally important for the individual, they had to be taught the European techniques of self-examination and autobiographical representation which, when successfully accomplished, transformed them into Christian actors on the social stage. Psychologically speaking, a good confession required the mastery of a number of difficult self-forming and, figuratively, self-destructive practices.

First, the unstable Nahua self, composed of a collection of forces that constituted the cosmic *and cyclical* continuum of which it was a part, needed to be destroyed and replaced by an autonomous bipolar self, whose two aspects were antagonistic. One of the new poles required that the physical body, as polysemantic microcosm of the universe, be replaced by the semantically restricted desiring body as centre of libidinal and deviant inclinations. Thus the transformation of the Nahua body into a morally and physically corruptible entity called for the transfer of many of its former qualities to its new antithesis: the Christian soul. With this modal self, that Nahua narrative of self-representation familiar to ethnohistorians and ethnographers – with all its digressions, its symbolic chronology, its tropological exuberance, and its focus on the seemingly insignificant details of everyday life – was traded in for a two-part discourse on the self: the story of the desiring body, what Christianity characterized as the life of sin, and the story of the soul, the tale of salvation.

Second, in order to shorten the narrative on the body, the reconstruction of the Nahua self into a Christian one required the cultivation of a preoccupation with the surveillance of its desires. To be a Christian, inspection of the self had to go on continuously; no word was too innocent, no deed too ephemeral, and no thought too transitory that it should be permitted to escape the gaze of the probing self. Although the lion's share of the study of Nahua self-consciousness still lies ahead, already we know much about the mechanisms used to develop it into a tool of self-discipline. From the earliest and most popular *Doctrinas*, like Córdoba's of 1544 and Molina's of 1546 (*Códice franciscano* 1941: 29–54), and the most widely used manuals for the confessors of Indians, like those of Molina (1565; 1984 [1569]) or Juan Bautista (1599: 1600), we learn the steps that were taught to all baptized natives old enough to sin, however badly they were followed and however infrequently Nahuas formally sought penitence.

Molina begins his *Confessionario mayor* with a prologue that captures the meaning of the practice of self-examination: the priest is to admonish all penitents to remember that, 'whoever you are ... in order for you to gain eternal life, it is necessary that you know and remember that you are a sinner in the eyes of our Lord' (1984: 3). What Molina was asking for is not an exercise of mere memory, but of conscience: 'whoever justifies himself by not holding himself as a sinner, and states that his conscience accuses him of nothing ... engages in a great falsehood and is beside himself' (1984: 4). It is the development of a (painfully) probing conscience, *neyoliximachiliztli* or 'the act of knowing one's heart', not a long memory, *tlalnamiquiliztli*, 'the act of recollecting something', that Christian discourse on the self required. Therefore, the confession of the reconstructed Nahua self was supposed to be a *neyolmelahualiztli*, 'a straightening of one's heart', rather than a *tlapohuiliztli*, 'a recounting [or] reciting of something'. The part of the unreconstructed Nahua self that was centred on the heart was responsible for reason, but, even more so, for emotional sensitivity and the passions. Christian autobiography was to be, first and foremost, the story of the heart, of feelings, and all other details were relevant only to the extent that they elucidated, contextualized, and helped explain the emotive life.

## Telling sins

So far I have avoided the consequences of distinguishing between the categories used to characterize persons, selves, and individuals; or those that make it possible to contrast public and private selves or social roles and personae (see Carrithers et al. 1985; Heller et al. 1986). Instead, I have stated on the basis of substantial evidence (see, for instance, the discussion concerning the *tonalli* and *nagualismo* in López Austin 1980: 223–51, 416–32) that the Nahuas imagined their multidimensional self to be an integral part of their body and of the spiritual and physical world around them. This belief necessarily negates the idea that an autonomous individual can exist who charts the course of his life at will. However, I have assumed without hesitation that sixteenth-cen-

tury Europeans had a more developed sense of individual autonomy than most scholars ordinarily grant them.

In *The Civilization of the Renaissance in Italy*, the *locus clas-
sicus* on the subject, Jacob Burckhardt argues that 'In the Middle
Ages ... Man was conscious of himself only as a member of a race,
people, party, family or corporation – only through some general
category', but in the Renaissance 'man became a spiritual individual, and recognized himself as such' (1945: 81-3). This position has been assailed for being too quick to recognize mature
individualism during the early Renaissance (Greenblatt 1986: 35)
and for disregarding the role that social context, power, and wealth
(or their absence) played in the formation of the self (Davis 1986:
53). Though in this essay I cannot go into the details necessary to
support my position, I believe sufficient data exist to suggest that
Natalie Zemon Davis' observation concerning sixteenth-century
France is applicable to the Europeans in Mexico: '[I]n a century
in which the boundary around the conceptual self and the bodily
self was not always firm and closed, men and women nonetheless
could work out strategies for self-expression and autonomy; and
... the greatest obstacle to self-definition was not embeddedness
but powerlessness and poverty' (Davis 1986: 53).

Indeed, while the unacculturated conceptual self of the Nahuas was even more weakly bounded than that of Burckhardt's
medieval man, forming what was believed to be a physical and
conceptual continuum with others, the body, and the world beyond it, Christians, to the extent that their local situation permitted, seem to have been quite capable of being conscious of themselves as ethical subjects and social actors. As is evident from even
a superficial survey of the literature, Christianization and this more
autonomous self went hand in hand. In this conceptual scheme
there was little room for the unreconstructed Nahua self. Consequently, its elimination was a fundamental part of the struggle to
determine truth and deploy power that made up the colonial
situation.

Contact with Europeans, if not always harrowing, was never
neutral. The good intentions of the missionaries are well known:
many sought to save the natives from both the pains of hell and
the abuses of crown officials or Spanish settlers. However, with
the exception of the forms of social, economic, and political organization that could be adapted to colonial ends, most aspects

of native culture that articulated the meaning, the symbolic structure, and the hopes and fears of the spiritual *and* everyday lives of
the Nahuas were considered sins. This position led to some un-
derstandable paradoxes, such as the case of Fray Bernardino de
Sahagún, who tirelessly undertook the detailed compilation of
every aspect of Nahua culture (overtly) in order to eradicate it. As
he specifically noted, he wrote about the Nahuas and their world
so as to teach the confessors what and how to ask the natives
about their public and private lives (Anderson and Dibble 1982:
45-6). This identification of native imagination and practice with
sin, common among those who saw the hand of Satan wherever
indigenous culture flourished, implied that sacramental confession among the Nahuas functioned not only to console and discipline, but also to destroy the Nahua self and the cultural context
of which it was a part. Thus, in more ways than the obvious (i.e.,
as a Christianizing process), confession among the Indians was
meant to be a process of conversion in the Pauline sense of death
and resurrection.

The telling of one's sins, or confessional autobiography, has
dominated Western discourse on the self since Augustine's *Confessions*. But long before the *Confessions* was written, St Paul
had made conversion the subject matter of the Christian narrative
of the self. Keeping both of these points in mind, John Freccero
has argued that 'conversion ... was theologically defined as the
destruction of a former self ... [and] this theme is inherent in the
autobiographical genre, which ... implies the death of the self as
character and the resurrection of the self as author (1986: 16–17).

It follows from this that in sixteenth-century New Spain, where
the conversion of the natives was ostensibly the *raison d'être* of
colonization and where the success of the colonial regime depended on some semblance of it, the power of the links that
joined autobiography, confession, and conversion into a single
narrative are not only apparent – in the very rare literary representations of the self that exist (see, for instance, Bautista n.d.;
Chimalpahin Cuauhtlehuanitzin 1965, 1983; Alvarado Tezozomoc 1975a, 1975b; Muñoz Camargo 1972; Alva Ixtlilxóchitl 1975)
– but are also particularly salient as expressions of hegemony especially as the penitential system assumed the role of a central
socio-political locus of power. Even more than in Europe, autobiographies in New Spain were about the death of a former self.

As noted above, conversion required the rejection of much of the native culture that responded to the Nahua 'heart': for instance, ways of reasoning logically (with regards to categories of reality, types of acceptable evidence for truth claims, assertions of reality concerning the empirical world, etc.), spiritually, axiologically, and aesthetically; modes of expressing, experiencing, and evaluating emotions; ways of organizing the sexual, domestic, social, and public life; rituals associated with technology (including medicine) and occupations; and cognitive frameworks and semiotic fields relevant to time, space, colour, direction, and temperature. The Nahua subject could not survive a successful challenge to these elements that constituted its object and field of action. Consequently, since conversion was the central topic of the narrative expected by sacramental confession, every Nahua who participated in the Sacrament of Penance necessarily engaged in an ethnocidal and, figuratively speaking, a suicidal act.

Since the conversion narrative, as the Augustinian prototype makes clear, was structured in two parts, the story of sin and death, and the tale of resurrection and salvation, students of literature have pointed out that it requires an 'absurd pretense: the story of one's life is definitively concluded, yet one survives to tell the tale' (Freccero 1986: 20). But in colonial Mexico more than a literary fiction was involved. The telling of sins not only exposed native lives to the judgement of priests, but also, as Sahagún noted, it made possible the friars' attempts to root out the culture that sustained them. However, the two-part representation of the self had other negative implications even for those who gladly embraced the Christian message.

A close examination of the canons of confessional narrative, found in the many manuals for confessors of Indians, doctrinal works, and devotional texts that circulated widely in New Spain, reveals that the discourse that was expected was supposed to be linear, chronologically ordered, punctuated by conflict between the desires and the moral will, and final, that is, concluding with a firm commitment to sin no more (see Molina 1565: 19). Yet, as the ethnohistorical (e.g., Durán 1967; Ruiz de Alarcón 1982) and ethnographic (e.g., Madsen 1960; Montoya Briones 1964; James Taggart 1983) record discloses, the Nahua self we described above, even after extensive exposure to Christianity, could adapt its particular mode of subjection and asceticism to the Christian *telos* of salvation without rejecting its ethical substance: the part of itself at the centre of the heart-*teyolia*/head-*tonalli* complex. Consequently, for this Nahua ethical subject, whose key preoccupation was to balance the desires and thereby to promote harmony between the opposing influences of external and internal forces, the bifurcated Christian autobiography, focused on the scrutiny of intentions and the elimination of desires, was no way to tell the story of the true self.

Nahua self-portraiture was of necessity chronologically discontinuous, non-linear in structure or content (since the logic of conversion/separation was not always there to sustain the sequentialized narrative), more concerned with harmony than conflict (given that the conceptual self lacked an autonomous moral will), and more semantically charged with tropes and symbols than was expected to result from self-examination exercises modelled on sacramental confession. In effect, the data we have suggest that the sharp break that the logic of conversion required between the past life of the sinner and the new life of the saint – the clear separation in the narrative between the object who is the protagonist of the story of sin, and the subject who narrates the tale – was missing or only haltingly present until acculturation took place. No wonder the Franciscans preferred to baptize twenty Indians rather than one Spaniard; after all, as Sahagún sadly noted, they were faster at telling sins because they were not confessing (Christian) truths. Their inability or unwillingness to follow the linear outline or narrative structure of the well-told life meant the friars had to consider them either saintly or sinful for their too-brief stories of sin.

## Subjecting lives

Human beings are made to conform by many means. In a highly influential work Foucault persuasively traces the history of the subjection of the body by analysing three sequential moments: torture, punishment, and discipline (Foucault 1979). Although inquisitorial confessions could make use of torture, and criminal confessions employed punishment, sacramental confessions had access to what Foucault has shown to be a far more powerful mechanism of subjection. While in the early colonial period torture and punishment were used to impose a semblance of Christianity on recalcitrant natives, these approaches were quickly condemned as both wrong and ineffectual (Gómez Canedo 1977: 178). However, because so many missionaries supported some form of coercion, during the first fifty years of the colonial regime physical force and light to brutal punishments were sometimes used to make the natives hear mass, attend catechism classes, and confess. After the 1560s, however, its almost complete disappearance was deeply lamented by many friars who genuinely believed in the utility of Christ's command: *compelle eos intrare*, 'compel them to come in' (Luke 14: 23). There are many reasons why physical punishments and brute force became rare, but perhaps the most important is connected to the disciplinary capacity of the penitential system and to the particular nature of its object: the soul (or, in today's language, the self), rather than the body.

This disciplinary system rested on the *idea* of conversion, not conversion itself (about which, as St Thomas was quick to point out, one can make no judgments since only God can see into a man's heart). I have been arguing that the idea of conversion as a narrative process of separation, death, and resurrection had to be the subject matter of a successful confession, that is, one that a priest could accept as sincere, complete, and worthy of forgiveness. At the base of the penitential system of subjection were the self-forming practices I have described. Consequently, the discipline of the confessional depended on teaching natives how to subject their desires to the relentless surveillance and the inescapable pain of the conscience. By promising forgiveness, the priests could relieve the penitents of the very suffering they had taught them to impose on themselves. This was a mechanism of control far more pervasive, efficient, economical, and subtle than torture or punishment.

But teaching natives to impose the pangs of conscience on themselves was no easy matter, as the proliferation of manuals and *advertencias* for confessors, the constant complaints of the priests, and the historical record suggest. First, natives had to see themselves as sinners, a pedagogical task undertaken by those who sought to convince the Nahuas to equate many, if not most, of their cultural practices with sin. Second, they had to be taught to fragment their selves so that one part could keep a constant vigil over the other, deciphering its every move. When these panoptical and hermeneutic exercises were mastered, the confessant had to learn how to narrate the story of the sinful self. No matter how much or how little they accepted the basic tenets of Christianity, they could not present themselves as Christians if they could not tell the two-part tale a conversion narrative required. The incomplete, backsliding, alternating, atemporally confused confession enshrined in Durán's anecdote concerning the state of *nepantla* would never do. Because it serves as an excellent example of a genuine, but unacceptable confessional conflict, Durán's frequently quoted text bears repeating in full:

> Once when I was questioning an Indian (with good reason) about certain things, particularly about his dragging himself about begging for money, passing bad nights and worse days and, after having collected so much money with so much effort, why he had put on a wedding and had invited the whole town and spent everything and, thus, reprehending him for the evil he had done, he responded: 'Father, do not be astonished since we are still *nepantla*.' And although I understood what he meant by that term and metaphor, which means 'to be in the middle,' I insisted he tell me what 'middle' it was they were in. He answered that since they were not yet rooted in the faith, I should not be astonished that they were still neutral; that they neither responded to one law nor the other or, better yet, that they believed in God and at the same time kept their ancient customs and the rites of the devil. And this is what he meant by his abominable excuse that they were still 'in the middle and were neutral'. (1967: 237)

Confessional autobiography implied a variety of forms of subjection. However, a particularly potent type resulted from the imposition on all penitents of a common set of categories of sin by which they were to narrate their different lives. As the guides for confessors (e.g., Molina 1565; 1984) make clear, all confessants were to portray the singular and discontinuous content of their real lives as a coherent and unified (ideal) story ordered by the Ten Commandments, the Seven Deadly Sins, and, time permitting, the Commandments of the Church, the Corporal and Spiritual Works of Mercy, the Five Senses, the Three Powers, and the Theological and Cardinal Virtues. Following Hayden White (1987), I suggest that the restricted form of this confessional discourse helped to shape the content and narrative of the lives represented through it, moulding the representation of heterogeneous experiences into the pattern of 'uncluttered, parallel lives' some Franciscan friars praised so highly around 1570 (*Códice franciscano* 1941: 86, 89). Implicit in this description, of course, is the progressive destruction of the expression and perhaps experience of much of the individuality that Nahua penitents could have possessed during the sixteenth century.

The perception of native faults through the prism of standardized Christian sins reduced Indian subjects, in the eyes of Europeans, to undifferentiated objects, free to be exploited, trained, disciplined, normalized, or, at best, ignored. Excluding the biographical information we have in wills (Cline and León-Portilla 1984; Cline 1986) and in official records (e.g., Lockhart et al. 1986), the post-contact native biographies or mere names known to us today refer almost exclusively to the very few who managed to exalt themselves by noteworthy service to the Europeans or by signatory, virtuoso performances of sinfulness. To the former category belong the names of literate Indians like Chimalpahin Cuauhtlehuanitzin (1983) and Alvarado Tezozomoc (1975a), or the trilingual assistants of Sahagún, Martín Jacobita, Antonio Valeriano, Alonso Vegerano, and Pedro de San Buenaventura (Anderson and Dibble 1982: 55). Among others, the latter category includes the victims of the Inquisition, including Don Carlos Ometochtzin, the *cacique* (native ruler) of Texcoco, who was burned at the stake in 1539 (Greenleaf 1961: 68-74), or Martín Ocelotl, the clandestine cult leader who died on the way to his exile in Spain (Klor de Alva 1981: 128-41).

The deployment of the penitential system, with its sacramental confession, its diffusion of a consciousness of new modes of deviant behaviour, its insistence on autobiographical discourse aimed at divulging the most private thoughts and acts of the individual, and, most importantly, its imposition of self-forming practices of introspection, contributed to the transformation of the Nahuas into the Other not only of the Europeans, but of themselves. The new techniques of self-constitution introduced by the confessional practices created new subjects who recognized a now alienated part of themselves (their body, their desires) as the object of their will. This new truth about the native self, made up of novel self-conceptualizations drawn in the image of the Christian sinner, reformulated native self-identities and generated a new knowledge of themselves as actors in a significantly restricted cosmos. Christianized Nahuas could no longer be sure of the importance of their role as an essential force of balance in a precarious universe when sacramental confession shrank their world to tragicomic clashes between good and evil played out on the tiny stages of their desiring bodies and their repentant souls. Bodies, which were once the microcosm of the cosmic dramas that made and destroyed universes (León-Portilla 1966; López Austin 1980: 58–98), became the 'Other' of those Christian natives pursuing personal purity and individual salvation.

However, in the diminutive theatre of the Christian ethical subject, a universal drama was indeed re-enacted, as Nahuas who were taught to sin in the same process that required them to be sorrowful, repentant, and loquacious about their trespasses, were made to understand their phenomenological lives as reflections of a coherent story of Sin, Redemption, and Salvation. From this it followed that insistence on conversion as the theme of confessional autobiography gave rise to a humbling new truth about the self and its representation. New Nahua identities as sinners in search of forgiveness tended conceptually to delimit the possible actions open to them to resist, accommodate, or redefine the truth of the Europeans.

The ideology of the confessional thus promoted the subjection of the *self* through self-discipline and the subjugation of the *body* through the assent to the claims of those who asserted an expertise in the ways of bodies and souls. To tell one's life to another is always a dangerous thing, and in sixteenth-century Mexico the risk was particularly high, even if not always apparent. Confessional autobiography, when successfully implanted, led to the reconstruction of the Nahua self, and this transformation contributed in subtle and not so subtle ways to the solidification of the European world's hold on native bodies, selves, and fortunes. The ultimate result of this confessional regime was to make Nahua selves disappear from public life and individual consciousness in order to reappear as indistinguishable poor peasants – labourers whose voice rarely claimed the attention of those in power except when heard in the confessional.

## Notes

1    This essay, which appears here in English for the first time, is a revised version of 'Contar vidas: La autobiografía confesional y la reconstrucción del ser nahua', *Arbor* 515-16 (1988): 49-78 (Consejo Superior de Investigaciones Científicas, Madrid) and 'Raconter des Vies: L'autobiographie confessionnelle et la reconstruction de l'être nahua', *Archives des Sciences Sociales des Religions* 77 (janvier-mars, 1992): 111-24 (CNRS, Paris).

## Works cited

Alva Ixtlilxóchitl, Fernando de (1975), *Obras históricas*, ed. Edmundo O'Gorman, Mexico: Instituto de Investigaciones Históricas, UNAM.

Alvarado Tezozomoc, Fernando (1975a), *Crónica mexicana*, ed. Manuel Orozco Y Berra, Mexico: Editorial Porrúa.

(1975b) *Crónica mexicayotl*, trans. Adrián León Mexico: Instituto de Investigaciones Históricas, UNAM.

Anderson, Arthur J. O. and Charles E. Dibble (eds) (1982), *Florentine Codex: General History of the Things of New Spain by Fray Bernardino de Sahagún, Introduction and Indices*, Salt Lake City: The School of American Research and the University of Utah, Santa Fe and Salt Lake City.

Bautista, Fray Juan (1599), *Confessionario en lengua mexicana y castellana*, Mexico: Melchior Ocharte.

(1600), *Advertencias para los confessores de los naturales*, Mexico: Melchior Ocharte.

Bautista, Juan (n.d.) Diario. Ms. in the Archivo Capitular of the Basílica de Guadalupe, Mexico: Colección Boturini.

Burkhardt, Jacob (1945), *The Civilization of the Renaissance in Italy*, trans. S. G. C. Middlemore, London and Oxford: Phaidon Press/Oxford University.

Carrithers, Michael, Steven Collins, and Steven Lukes (eds) (1985) *The Category of the Person: Anthropology, Philosophy, History*, Cambridge: Cambridge University Press.

Chimalpahin Cuauhtlehuanitzin, Domingo Francisco de San Antón Muñon (1965), *Die Relationen Chimalpahin's zur Geschichte México's*, transcription by Günter Zimmerman, Abhandlungen aus dem Gebiet der Auslandskunde, Hamburg:

Cram, De Gruyter & Co.

(1983), *Octava relación*, ed. and trans. José Rubén Romero Galván, Mexico: Instituto de Investigaciones Históricas, UNAM

Cline, S. L. (1986), *Colonial Culhuacan, 1580-1600: A Social History of an Aztec Town*, Albuquerque: University of New Mexico.

Cline, S. L. and Miguel León-Portilla (eds and trans.) (1984), *The Testaments of Culhuacán*, UCLA Latin American Center Publications, Nahuatl Series no. 1, Los Angeles: University of California.

*Códice carolino* (1967), 'Códice carolino', *Estudios de Cultura Náhuatl* 7: 11-58.

*Códice franciscano* (1941). In *Nueva colección de documentos para la historia de México*, Mexico: Salavador Chavez Hayhoe.

Córdoba, Fray Pedro de (1970), *Christian Doctrine for the Instruction and Information of the Indians*, trans. Sterling A. Stoudemire from 1544 original, Coral Gables: University of Miami.

Davis, Natalie Zemon (1986), 'Boundaries and the Sense of Self in Sixteenth-Century France'. In Thomas C. Heller et al. (eds), *Reconstructing Individualism*, Stanford: Stanford University Press.

Durán, Fray Diego (1967), *Historia de las Indias de Nueva España e islas de la tierra firme*, 2 vols., ed. Angel María Garibay K., Mexico: Editorial Porrúa.

Foucault, Michel (1979), *Discipline and Punish: The Birth of the Prison*, trans. Alan Sheridan, New York: Vintage Books.

(1980), *The History of Sexuality, Volume I: An Introduction*, trans. Robert Hurley, New York: Vintage Books.

(1985), *The History of Sexuality, Volume 2: The Use of Pleasure*, trans. Robert Hurley, New York: Pantheon Books.

Freccero, John (1986), 'Autobiography and Narrative'. In Thomas C. Heller, et al. (eds), *Reconstructing Individualism*, Stanford: Stanford University Press.

García Pimentel, Luis (ed.) (1897), *Descripción del arzobispado de México*, Mexico: José Joaquín Terrazas e Hijas.

Gómez Canedo, Lino (1977), *Evangelización y conquista: Experiencia franciscana en Hispanoamérica*, Mexico: Editorial

Porrúa.

Greenblatt, Stephen, (1986), 'Fiction and Friction'. In Thomas C. Heller et al. (eds), *Reconstructing Individualism*, Stanford: Stanford University Press.

Greenleaf, Richard E. (1961), *Zumárraga and the Mexican Inquisition, 1536–43*, Washington, D.C.: Academy of American Franciscan History.

Heller, Thomas C. Morton Sosna, and D. E. Wellbery (eds) (1986), *Reconstructing Individualism: Autonomy, Individuality, and the Self in Western Thought*, Stanford: Stanford University Press.

Karttunen, Frances (1983), *An Analytical Dictionary of Nahuatl*, Austin: University of Texas.

Karttunen, Frances and James Lockhart (eds) (1987), *The Art of Nahuatl Speech: The Bancroft Dialogues*, Los Angeles: Latin American Center, University of California.

Klor de Alva, J. Jorge (1981), 'Martín Ocelotl: Clandestine Cult Leader'. In David G. Sweet and Gary B. Nash (eds), *Struggle and Survival in Colonial America*, Berkeley: University of California Press.

Klor de Alva, J. Jorge, H. B. Nicholson, and E. Quiñones Keber (eds) (1988), *The Work of Bernardino de Sahagún: Pioneer Ethnographer of Sixteenth-Century Aztec Mexico*, Albany and Austin: Institute for Mesoamerican Studies, State University of New York /University of Texas.

León-Portilla, Miguel (1966), *La filosofía náhuatl estudiada en sus fuentes*. 3rd edn, intro. by Angel María Garibay K., Mexico: Instituto de Investigaciones Históricas, UNAM.

——— (1993), 'The Great Tradition at the Time of the Conquest: The Mexican Central Plateau.' In Gary H. Gossen and Miguel León-Portilla (eds), *South and Meso-American Native Spirituality*, vol. 4 of *World Spirituality: An Encyclopedic History of the Religious Quest*, gen. ed. E. Cousins, New York: The Crossroad Publishing Co.

Lockhart, James, F. Berdan, and Arthur J. O. Anderson (eds. and trans.) (1986), *The Tlaxcalan Actas: A Compendium of the Records of the Cabildo of Tlaxcala (1545–1627)*, Salt Lake City: University of Utah.

López Austin, Alfredo (1980), *Cuerpo humano e ideología: las concepciones de los antiguos nahuas*, 2 vols., México: UNAM.

Madsen, William (1960), *The Virgin's Children: Life in an Aztec Village Today*, Austin: University of Texas.

Molina, Fray Alonso de (1565), *Confessionario breue, en lengua mexicana y castellana*, Mexico: Antonio de Espinosa.

(1941), *Doctrina christiana*. in *Códice franciscano*, Mexico: Salvador Chavez Hayhoe.

([1571] 1970), *Vocabulario en lengua castellana y mexicana y mexicana y castellana*, Preliminary study by Miguel León-Portilla, Mexico: Editorial Porrúa.

([1569] 1984), *Confesionario mayor en la lengua mexicana y castellana*, intro. by Roberto Moreno, 2nd edn, Mexico: Institutos de Investigaciones Filológicas e Históricas, UNAM.

Montoya Briones, José de Jesús (1964), *Atla: Etnographía de un pueblo náhuatl*, Mexico: Instituto nacional Antropología e Historia.

Motolinía, Toribio de Benavente or (1971), *Memoriales o libro de cosas de la Nueva España y de los naturales de ella*, Mexico: UNAM.

Muñoz Camargo, Diego ([1892] 1972), *Historia de Tlaxcala*, ed. Alfredo Chavero, Guadalajara: Edmundo Aviña Levy.

Ruiz de Alarcón, Hernando (1982), *Aztec Sorcerers in Seventeenth-Century Mexico: The Treatise on Superstitions*, ed. Michael D. Coe and Gordon Whittaker (trans.) Albany: Institute for Mesoamerican Studies, State University of New York at Albany.

Sahagún, Fray Bernardino de (1975), *Historia general de las cosas de Nueva España*, ed. Angel María Garibay K., 3rd edn, Mexico: Editorial Porrúa.

Taggart, James M. (1983), *Nahuat Myth and Social Structure*, Austin: University of Texas Press.

Tentler, Thomas N. (1977), *Sin and Confession on the Eve of the Reformation*, Princeton: Princeton University Press.

White, Hayden (1987), *The Content of the Form: Narrative Discourse and Historical Representation*, Baltimore: The Johns Hopkins University Press.

# 6
# Contesting the power to heal: angels, demons and plants in colonial Mexico

Osvaldo F. Pardo

## I

In 1562 an enigmatic Spaniard, Gregorio López, arrived in New Spain with the purpose of leading a solitary life in the wilderness of the newly discovered territories. In 1580, this same Gregorio López fell ill and was admitted to the Hospital de Santa Cruz of Huaxtepec, an institution run by the Hermanos de la Caridad that cared for the physical and spiritual well-being of both Spaniards and Indians (Muriel [1956] 1990: vol. 1, 211–13). At this hospital, according to his biographer and friend Francisco de Losa, López penned 'a book of Medicine, containing numerous remedies for different diseases, drawn from his varied experiments and vast knowledge of the properties and natural virtues of the herbs' (Losa 1642: 23v).

López's purpose in this book was to help make up for the shortage of surgeons and accredited physicians in the area.[1] Further, according to Francisco de Losa, the book put at the reader's disposal knowledge derived both from experiments and from López's familiarity with plants. As to the ultimate source of López's medical wisdom Losa offered a telling anecdote: when asked to name the book from which he had acquired his knowledge of natural remedies, the hermit's answer pointed to God, rather than to any written source (Losa 1642: 24). Nonetheless books played a crucial part in López's life. For the hermit was in the habit of borrowing books from his acquaintances and commiting them to memory in a remarkably short period of time. This unusual talent of Gregorio López elicited Losa's remark that 'the way he

163

read was peculiar, somehow supernatural and closer to a kind of angelic comprehension' (Losa 1642: 15). That Losa should compare Gregorio López's understanding to that of the angels is surprising, and I will return to the issue later. Here I am interested in pointing out the peculiar status assigned to the book as a source of knowledge. Both López and his biographer obviously esteemed its authority, but in López's case the book, more than simply a primary source of knowledge, was also something of a complement to his unique way of comprehending.

Losa shaped Gregorio López's biography by following closely the lives of the Desert Fathers that López himself had set out to imitate. Like the wisdom of the Desert Fathers, Losa asserted, so too the knowledge of Gregorio López, which embraced medicine, history and the scriptures, derived entirely from his conversations with God, and corresponded to the higher state of existence he had been able to achieve.[2] His understanding of nature had been acquired in the course of an unusual life. In the wilderness he had learned to survive by feeding upon fruits, herbs, and roots, as his spiritual forebears had done (Losa 1642: 14). On one occasion a visitor had the chance to observe López at work in his garden surrounded by angels (Losa 1642: 7v). To the holy man in the desert, God had revealed the inner workings of nature so as to bring about not only his servant's survival, but also the perfect harmony that existed between him and his surroundings.

It is clear that Gregorio López intended his book to help the friars at the hospital in the treatment of their patients, but his own personal influence also manifested itself in more direct and dramatic ways. A sick man, for example, had his health restored after following López's advice that the Gospel of St. John be recited to him (Losa 1642: 24). Losa also reported that several miraculous cures effected by López's relics took place shortly after his death.

López's treatise on medicinal herbs was meant to circulate for others to use. The cures he himself accomplished, on the other hand, were exclusively his own, for they did not involve medicines of any kind but derived entirely from his individual sacred power. This placed him on a quite different plane from the brothers at the hospital, for whereas López, alive or dead, worked his cures by sacred power, the brothers could do no more than follow the instructions of others in the matter of curing.

Familiar as the typology of Losa's biography of López is to any student of Christian hagiographical tradition, the work makes strange reading in the context of New Spain. The region of Huaxtepec where the Hospital de Santa Cruz was located was famous from pre-conquest times for its indigenous physicians and herbalists, who passed on their experience to early colonial successors. Indeed, Huaxtepec was said to have enjoyed the best herbalists of the region, and it was here that Moctezuma's botanical garden was located. Although López's *Tesoro de medicinas* consists for the most part of remedies taken from European sources, a manuscript from the Vatican Library revealed a section wholly dedicated to the *materia medica* of New Spain (Guerra 1982: 27).

Early in 1571, only a few years before López's arrival, the *protomédico*[3] Francisco Hernández came to gather from Nahua herbalists in Huaxtepec an impressive amount of information regarding the uses of medicinal herbs (Somolinos D'Ardois 1960: 159). Like many Europeans, Francisco Hernández thought that indigenous knowledge was practical rather than theoretical, which is why he was critical of Nahua expertise regarding plants and their applications. In his translation of Pliny's *Natural History* he commented on the striking contrast between what he saw as the rude intellect of the Indians and the puzzling fact that they were able to name almost any plant (Hernández 1976: vol. 2, 425); the latter being an observation that is nowadays commonplace in ethnobotanical literature (Berlin 1992: 5-8).

Hernández's reservations towards Nahua botanical knowledge sprang in part from his adherence to Galenic medicine and classifications that, more often than not, were at odds with the uses he found so widespread among the Indian herbalists. Hernández did not hide his contempt for the practices of the *ticitl*, a type of Nahua physician, who, according to him, tended to ignore the cause of illnesses, and whose prescriptions for cures were wanting in method (Hernández 1926: 53).[4] For the *protomédico* the failure of native medicine resided in the ways by which the *ticitl* attained and used his knowledge: 'They are just empiricists, and for any disease they use only those herbs, minerals or parts of animals, which they have received from their elders, as some inheritance which has passed from hand to hand.'(Hernández 1926: 53) The lack of method and what Hernández considered a disregard for the causes of diseases are part of the contemporary definition of the 'empiricist'. These two features had come to differentiate the medical practitioners known as empiricists from professional doctors trained in universities.[5] This characterization originated in the dispute of the empiricists with the medical school of the dogmatists or rationalists in the Hellenistic period, a dispute on which Galen reported at length (Frede 1985: 8–10; Mudry 1982: 22–4).[6]

Hernández's comment echoes the standard objections raised by those professional physicians who, following Galen, saw research into the causes of disease and an overall theory of the nature of the body as a necessary part of the art of medicine – features that native medicine seemed to lack. The investigation of causes was at the centre of what in Hernández's times continued to be defined as the main activity of those engaged in *scientia*, an intellectual realm which Aristotle had conceived as separate from that of the *artes*, and further removed from experience. Both science and art involved rational activity rather than experience. Art differed from science in that it involved production, technical skills, and also had a practical end (Aristotle NE: VI, iv, 2–6). Science, on the other hand, sought to unravel universal causes based on first principles (Aristotle: NE: VI, iii, 4). Medicine had both a practical and a theoretical side (Huarte de San Juan [1575] 1989: 493–523). With the consolidation of natural philosophy in academic circles, it was the theoretical component – chiefly represented by Galen's writings on method, which were the core of university courses – that granted medicine its status as a science, and its practitioners professional prestige (García Ballester 1995: 127–9).[7] The importance of this aspect of medicine is clear in the view of the layman Vargas Machuca, who recommended 'buena Filosofía' to accompany the empirical search for medical remedies (Vargas Machuca 1599: 43v).

Moreover, if the *ticitl* was deprived of theoretical knowledge, his relationship with practical knowledge also seemed problematic. Hernández here also points out another flaw in the intellectual make-up of the *ticitl*: the depreciation on his part of the value of direct observation, which was an essential thread of what the ancient empiricists referred to as *experience*. Not direct observation (*autopsia*) but exclusive reliance on received reports (*historia*) and notions, to borrow the language of the empiricists, was for Hernández the way the *ticitl* had arrived at his particular

brand of knowledge (Frede 1985: ch. 2).[8] Hernández's letters to
Philip II bear witness to the important place that experiments
and direct observation had in his evaluation of newly found medicinal plants (Hernández 1937: 14, 18). For the king's physician,
both experience and rational method seemed absent from native
medicine. By highlighting the *ticitl*'s dependence on tradition –
a charge often levelled at other areas of Nahua behaviour – instead of experimentation, Hernández was attacking an essential
part of the process involved in the recruitment of healers in their
communities.

Hernández went to New Spain at the request of Philip II who,
in 1570, instructed the then *médico de cámara* to identify local
surgeons, herbalists, and physicians in order to elicit from them
information regarding local herbs and medicinal plants (Somolinos D'Ardois 1960: 146).[9] Hernández's mission should be understood in the framework of the wider entreprise that under
royal sponsorship would produce the vast compilation of scientific and historical information on the Americas known as the
*Relaciones geográficas*. An instruction similar to that given to
Hernández by the king is found in the questionnaire attached to
these *Relaciones*, which extended the enquiry to include a study
of the most common diseases in the land, and their causes (Acuña
1985: vol. 1, 20). Thus, local healers and herbalists were recognized as legitimate sources of knowledge about their natural environment and the medicinal herbs to be found in it. This was true
even in religious quarters, as is illustrated by the *Codex Badianus*, a herbal manual produced by the Mexican physician Martín de la Cruz under the auspices of the Franciscan friars in 1552.
Significantly, in the opening of his work Martín de la Cruz distanced himself from university-trained physicians by declaring that
he was 'nullis rationibus doctus, sed solis experimentis edoctus'
(Cruz [1552] 1940: 205). The crown's interest – scientific as well
as economic – in the gathering of information on local diseases
and medicines had been preceded by a not-uncommon practice
among Spanish settlers who, given the absence of Spanish physicians, had much earlier begun to make use of the native *materia
medica* in their frequent consultations with Indian physicians
(Motolinía 1985: 179).

Such recognition of Nahua medical and botanical knowledge
was not widely accepted. Native practices concerning the identifi-

cation, understanding and treatment of disease posed a direct challenge to the authority of priests and missionaries. Healing in mendicant hospitals such as the Hospital de Santa Cruz was thought of as a continuum which extended from the body to the soul. Treatment of illness was part of an overall programme of pastoral care that carried with it the introduction, among the native population, of a new conception of the relationship between the body and the natural and supernatural powers. In 1585 the Third Council of the Mexican Church recommended that 'sacramenta quoque pauperibus suorum Hospitalium Rectores administrent' (Lorenzana 1770: 228). The care of the body was to be secondary to the care of the soul upon which salvation in the afterlife depended, especially in those cases where the chances of recovery were deemed low. This long-lasting tension between bodily and spiritual health in Christian thought, which was eloquently expressed by Archbishop Juan de Zumárraga in his comment on the divergence between the precepts of Avicenna and those of Christ,[10] was brought home to the friars in the hospitals of New Spain. A series of epidemics which decimated the local population throughout the sixteenth century reduced the friars' activities to providing care for the dying and their souls. It is not surprising therefore to find the physician López de Hinojoso, including in his treatise on surgery advice on the administration of the sacraments to those victims of the deadly pestilence referred to by the sources as *cocoliztli* (López de Hinojoso 1595: 152r; Gibson 1964: 448-9). Doctors were to encourage ailing patients to confess to a priest (Farfán 1579: 10v). Secular medical practice did not rule out resorting to religion in the treatment of patients, as is apparent from Vargas Machuca who expressed his fondness for the use of prayer ('santo ensalmo') to achieve miraculous cures (Vargas Machuca 1599: 43v).

The wide variety of native physicians came under the scrutiny of friars and priests who saw them as agents of the old religious beliefs that they were trying so hard to uproot. Time and again the ministers pointed out in their manuals and accounts the threat posed by these healers, reporting in detail on their practices so as to help their peers in eradicating them. Given the religious dimension which lent coherence to the beliefs and treatments that characterized the different aspects of the healing process in Nahua society, the ministers' suspicion about Indian physicians also fell upon the efficacy of the herbs and plants which they employed, for the most part unknown to Europeans. In some cases this same suspicion found its counterpart in the Mexican Indians' distrust of Spanish medicines. Martín Ocelotl, who in 1536 was tried on charges of idolatry and *hechicería*, openly expressed his belief that medicines from Castile were lethal (*Procesos*: 26).

Ministers and other observers puzzled by the practices of local healers devoted special attention to the question of the origin of the practitioner's knowledge, and to whether any actual knowledge worth the name was involved in their trade. For some friars and parish priests, the lack of familiarity with indigenous plants, together with the religious features apparent in the practices of Nahua healers, such as their use of spells and states of hallucination, forced upon them an interpretation of the healing process in which the natural order, as they understood it, was being challenged.

## II

When speculating about the origin of Nahua botanical knowledge, Spaniards often invoked possible sources other than observation and experimentation. The physician Juan de Cárdenas, praising the medicinal properties of *picietl* or tobacco, could not help but imagine who might have been the first person to inhale the smoke from this plant. In a somehow awkward way, he ventured 'that some angel advised its use to the Indians, or some demon who was also an angel was involved; since it liberates us from diseases, it truly seems to be like an angelic medicine, or a remedy created by demons'(Cárdenas [1591] 1965: 172). For Cárdenas it was not a human being, but rather a superior agent who had handed this medicine to the Indians. His hesitancy in identifying this agent definitively as an angel or as a demon reveals the cautious attitude of a secular physician vis-à-vis matters religious. Where was the line to be drawn? Cárdenas, for example, brought upon himself an attack from the Dominican Dávila Padilla for having advanced the opinion that the drinking of chocolate – also a new plant – was incompatible with the observance of fasting (Dávila Padilla [1596] 1955: 626).

The association of angels with healing had a long history in Christian tradition.[11] Angels were known for having effected cures

either by means of their supernatural power or simply by following the strict procedures that any other medical practitioner would
apply (Flint 1991: 163). Sometimes they just limited themselves
to imparting to someone the knowledge necessary to cure the
sick. Whatever the circumstance, there was always a lesson to be
learnt: miraculous cures reminded human beings of the incom-
mensurable power of God; an angel acting as a physician made
clear the resources available in God's creation.

Nicolás Monardes had earlier commented upon the power of
*picietl*, warning also against the possibility of intoxication, a state
not unknown to Nahua priests when advising their lords and no-
blemen on serious matters. Monardes writes: 'Since the devil is a
deceiver and knows the virtues of herbs, he taught the Indians
about the virtue of this particular plant so that by using it they
might experience those visions and images which lead them to
error' (Monardes 1574: 47v). López de Hinojoso concurred with
Monardes' judgment (1595: 151r). Monardes compared *picietl* to
other plants with similar hallucinogenic effects found in Dioscorides' *Materia medica*. Among them he listed the *solano furioso*
[*solanum manicum*], the same plant that Andrés Laguna had referred to in his commentary on Dioscorides as the one used by
witches to induce visions that they claimed were actual happen-
ings (Dubler 1955: III, 421).

In describing the appearance and therapeutic properties
of another Mexican plant, *ololiuhqui* [*rivea corimbosa*],
Hernández did not fail to make reference to its narcotic uses
among the Nahuas.[12] *Ololiuhqui*, Hernández added, was also
known among the Nahuas as *coaxihuitl* or 'snake herb' [*herbam
serpentis*] because of its resemblance to this reptile (Hernández 1790: III, 32). In the *Prolegomena* to Recchi's revised
compendium of Hernández's work we find a similar reference to *ololiuhqui*. Dealing with nomenclature here the author showed the connection between the name *coaxihuitl* and
the plant's hallucinogenic properties based on the association
of the serpent with prudence and wisdom [*prudentiam et sa-
pientiam*], which in turn illuminated another name in use:
'plant of the wise' (Hernández 1651: 8). This wisdom was not
however from this world, since the plant was used when the
Indians wanted to contact superior beings [*volebant versari
cum superis*]. The content of this communication consisted

of apparitions [*phantasmata*] and the faces of demons [*demonum obversantium effigies*].

*Ololiuhqui*, although recognized as a different plant, did not fail to evoke in Hernández a comparison with the well-known effects of the *solanum manicum*. He found *ololiuhqui* to be hot in the fourth degree, which set it apart from the plants with a high degree of coldness that were associated – as in Laguna's comment on the *solanum manicum* – with drugs that deprived the body of sensation, inducing states of stupor and hallucination (Dubler 1955: III, 8).[13]

The Dominican friar Diego Durán reached a similar conclusion when reporting on the administration of a concoction to cure illnesses made with *picietl* and *ololiuhqui*. Together with their hallucinogenic properties, Durán reported also on their anesthetic qualities (Durán [1570] 1967: I, cap. 5, 52). It should be noted that in spite of these warnings concerning *ololiuhqui*, its name is not absent from home-remedies prescribed in works such as those of Gregorio López (Guerra 1982: 377), Farfán (1579: 105) and Juan de Barrios (1607: trat 4, 60v).[14] Morover, in some sources references to the hallucinogenic properties are altogether absent (Acuña 1985: vol. 1, 180, 303).

Angels and demons, superior agents that shared a common origin, played an essential role in the consideration of the nature of divine and human knowledge as formulated by Aquinas. According to him, angels do not possess discursive knowledge as men do; that is, angels do not acquire knowledge by investigating a series of causes and effects, since all these things are for them present at once (Aquinas 1948: 1a., Q. 58, art. 3, res). Their incorporeal nature allows them to dispense with acquiring knowledge through sense-experience – the primary source of human knowledge about the world – instead, they possess intellectual cognition [*intellectiva cognitio*] (Aquinas 1948: 1a. Q. 54, art. 5, res.) through which they are able to apprehend purely incorporeal 'species' that are 'connatural' to them (Aquinas 1948: 1a. Q. 55, art. 2, res.).[15] For Aquinas angels, properly speaking, cannot be thought to have 'experience', which itself requires sense-perception, except in a figurative manner [*per similitudinem cognitorum, etsi non per similitudinem virtutis cognoscitivae*] (Aquinas 1948: 1a., Q. 54, art. 5, ad.). In angelic knowledge there is no room for falsehood; in the case of demons, however, although they know everything about natural matters, they are not able to grasp all that is in the supernatural realm (Aquinas 1948: 1a. Q. 58., art. 5, res.).[16]

It is within this intellectual tradition that Kramer and Sprenger at the end of the fifteenth century set themselves the task of explaining the workings of demons in their widely read treatise on witchcraft, which shaped European notions about witches during the sixteenth and seventeenth centuries. In trying to delimit the scope of what demons could accomplish with their powers and knowledge, the *Malleus maleficarum* provided a conceptual scheme that sought to map, within the narrow limits of human understanding, the domain to which natural phenomena belonged.

Kramer and Sprenger asserted that angels, as purely intellectual entities, gravitate around human understanding, and through them men can acquire truths that would otherwise remain out of their reach, as is the case of the interpretation of obscure passages in the scriptures that are revealed in sleep (Kramer and Sprenger 1971: part 1, Q. 16, 81; part 2, Q. 1, 92). Such possible cases of supernatural assistance helped Francisco de Losa to account for the insights that Gregorio López demonstrated in his commentary on the Apocalypse.[17]

Although the content of their revelations might vary, with regard to the workings of nature both angels and demons possess an understanding that surpasses that of man. This is an important issue because it acknowledges, following the scholastic tradition, the possibility of a variety of phenomena within the natural realm, the exact explanation of which, however, is uncertain (Clark 1984). A classic example of this kind was the attraction of iron to the loadstone, which was explained by the action of some occult or unknown quality (Kramer and Sprenger: part 1, Q. 2, 13). By the term 'occult', scholastic philosophy understood what was either unintelligible or unobservable (Millen 1985: 186–9). Occult qualities were often invoked in the case of herbs and medicines whose efficacy could not be explained according to the basic properties laid out by Galen.[18] Angels and demons, both of whom were deemed to possess a thorough understanding of nature, may in some instances transmit this knowledge to men, be it by dreams, sudden revelations or visions (Horozco y Covarrubias 1588: 142v). Dreams of non-supernatural provenance, it should be noted, were also thought to furnish information about certain bodily conditions, such as illnesses and their remedies, thus showing nature's inclination towards the preservation of the body (Kramer and Sprenger: part 1, Q. 16, 81).[19]

Along these lines Francisco de Vitoria indicated that the discovery of the successful application of some medicinal herbs unknown to the majority could be traced either to medical tradition or to the revelation of a demon (Vitoria 1960: 1256). Dreams and apparitions of demonic origin were, more often than not, sources of deception and confusion, and, unequivocally, damnation. This precise set of ideas is behind what Monardes and Cárdenas expressed when trying to account for the way in which the knowledge of some plants reached the Mexican Indians. Deriving their explanation from the observed effects of certain hallucinogenic plants, these two writers doubted the native practitioner's ability to acquire practical knowledge through experimentation.

This particular perception of the nature of native botanical lore as a domain outside the realm of experience carried with it the identification of Nahua healers with a cast of characters familiar to Spaniards in the Peninsula. These embraced a colourful variety, from potion peddlers to those individuals specializing in curing by the particular means after which they were named, such as the *saludadores* (Durán [1570] 1967: I, 52). Theologians on both sides of the Atlantic, although suspicious of the efficacy of these practitioners, were not ready to condemn them outright because of the difficulty they encountered in deciding whether the cures were produced by natural virtue or by demonic intervention (Vitoria 1960: 1259–60; Veracruz 1557: 300). More frequently in the ministers' minds, Nahua medical practitioners became associated with those popular figures which the treatises of demonology suspected of dealing with demons.

Theologians preoccupied with demarcating legitimate areas of human enquiry from those that could attract suspicion on religious grounds, could rely on the method of achieving and transmitting knowledge, for such a method provided an indication of the nature and value of what was being transmitted. Warning those who might expect to learn something about the actual practice of witchcraft by reading their tract, Kramer and Sprenger pointed out that witchcraft could not be learned from books, being a tradition that belonged entirely to the unlearned (Kramer and Sprenger: part 2, Q. 1, 95). In this respect literate culture appears as a legitimate domain of knowledge differentiated from the unruly practices, opinions, and curiosity of those deprived of proper instruction. In strict terms, to teach, to transmit knowledge that belonged to *scientia*, was to teach about causes.[20] Transmission based on experience could not aspire to produce scientific knowledge in another person, it could only produce opinion (Aquinas 1961: I, L.1: C30, 15). According to this definition, whatever the operations wrought by witches or magicians, they did not have true knowledge of the phenomena before them. The script for their actions had been passed down to them; in some instances demons did the work (Vitoria 1960: 1258).[21] Similarly, the *ticitl* portrayed by Hernández owed his skills and relationship to natural remedies to a blind adherence to what had been handed on to him. In this sense he was removed both from theoretical and practical knowledge.

Although Gregorio López's book on home remedies was intended for circulation, a portion of his knowledge remained with him. Not only was he familiar with the properties of herbs, but he was also able to change and improve their qualities by adding homemade liquors, a skill that he kept to himself. As noted by his biographer, the reason for this secrecy was based on prudence, since only a curious and good Christian with a fear of God would not yield to the temptation of turning the herbs into poisonous substances (Losa 1642: 34).

## III

That demons might instruct Nahua healers and herbalists on natural matters was a possibility that Spanish observers could not overlook, since demons, after all, were in no short supply in America. Thus, Francisco de Vitoria relied upon the widely reported Amerindian belief in demons as evidence to refute Aristotle's opinion against their existence (Vitoria 1960: 1250). This opinion was later taken up by the part-time demonologist Jean Bodin (Bodin 1581: lib. 1, cap. iii, 28).

Ministers and religious authorities in their fight against Nahua healers were trying to overturn a fundamental set of beliefs and practices, the special resilience of which was linked to the core of questions that disease as an individual and social experience brings to the fore. Hernando Ruiz de Alarcón, a parish priest working in Mexico during the first half of the seventeenth century, left a detailed account of his personal crusade to challenge the authority and social space of the local healers.

The *ololiuhqui* seed occupies an important place in his report, since it was employed not only in the treatment of diseases, but also as a means to determine the nature of them by divination. Among the Nahuas a disease could have its origin in a spell, a conception also familiar to Europeans acquainted with the works of witches. The state induced by the ingestion of the seed, either by the *ticitl* or the patient, yielded the identification of the person who had cast the spell. This divinatory aspect was especially troublesome since it paved the way for demonic intervention, but also, and more importantly, because it could lead to what Ruiz de Alarcón took as the disruption of social ties through accusations (Ruiz de Alarcón [1629] 1953: trat. I, cap. vii, 49).[22]

For the conversion of the general population Ruiz de Alarcón relied on the teaching of the *doctrineros* ([1629] 1953: trat. I, cap.ix, 55). Healers and diviners, however, had to be dealt with by means of coercion because of their stubborn resistance to revealing the nature of their trade to the Spanish priests and authorities (trat. I, cap. ii, 33). Upon pressing Mariana, a woman known as a *ticitl*, to confess to having used *ololiuhqui*, she declared to Ruiz de Alarcón that she had learned her art from her sister, who in turn had received it from an angel when sick and after having used the seed (Ruiz de Alarcón [1629] 1953: trat. I, cap. vii, 52). This gift was bestowed upon the woman so that she may not lack for 'chili and salt'. This was the call which gave her the means to earn her living as a healer.

A similar case involved a blind man who, on his deathbed, confessed to having been taken to hell where he received the herbs that cured him and that he continued to use to help other people (Ruiz de Alarcón [1629] 1953: trat. VI, cap. xx, 160). Jacinto de la Serna, a priest whose zeal equalled Ruiz de Alarcón's, reported stories similar to these (Serna 1953: 99). There is a common pattern in these as well as other stories: the healer had experienced a disease that triggered a contact with superior beings and resulted in a cure, the acquisition of medicinal herbs, and the assumption of a new social role in the community. Ruiz de Alarcón attributed these tales, uncannily familiar to a priest, to the works of demons always ready to confuse the Indian's understanding of reality, making it difficult for them to embrace Catholicism. These tales nonetheless encompass a basic narrative which contains important features of the recruitment process undergone by native healers and diviners which can still be observed today in Mesoamerica. Such features may include the experiencing of a series of dreams as well as the suffering and recovery from specific diseases (Tedlock 1982; Fabrega and Silver 1973).[23]

Ruiz de Alarcón informed his readers that the natives still continued to believe that clouds, winds, and geographical features were in fact angels and deities with control over natural phenomena and therefore objects of individual worship (Ruiz de Alarcón [1629] 1953: trat. I, cap. i, 23–4; and also Acuña 1984: vol. 1, 189). The concept of 'angel' in Ruiz de Alarcón's assessment of Nahua beliefs derived from his observations of contemporary practices that had been touched by Christian teaching. The occurrence of the word 'angel' incorporated in a Nahua charm together with the names of saints certainly did not escape his attention (Ruiz de Alarcón [1629] 1953: trat 5, cap.1, 125).

On one occasion, after having confiscated some seeds of *ololiuhqui* from an Indian woman, Ruiz de Alarcón fell ill. According to his account, the people of the town thought of his disease as a punishment inflicted by the god *ololiuhqui* for the priest's actions against the plant. After recovering from his ailment, he waited for an important holiday to burn a huge amount of the plant before the Indian crowd (Ruiz de Alarcón [1629] 1953: trat. I, cap.vi, 43).

As with the miraculous cures and the destruction of pagan temples carried out by Martin of Tours in sixth-century Gaul, Ruiz de Alarcón delivered a clear message with his public display: that Christianity was a stronger religion than that of the Nahuas, and that he, as a Christian priest, could outshine the Nahua physicians's deeds. In order for this form of persuasion that sought to make visible the superior power of Christianity to be effective, it had first to be intelligible to the audience. Ruiz de Alarcón might not have proved the invincible power of Christianity, but rather a more personal feature, that of his own spiritual force. From his own observations of the readiness with which patients would submit to the healers's demands, Ruiz de Alarcón was well aware of the ascendancy that local doctors had over the community (Ruiz de Alarcón [1629] 1953: trat. I, cap. i, 24). The authority of Nahua healers sprang from a knowledge and spiritual – as well as physical – strength that allowed them to communicate and interact with superior beings and forces.

Ruiz de Alarcón's stories registered the confrontation of two systems of legitimation, a confrontation that in the particular case involving those whom the community trusted to handle disease or crisis, did not take place in the realm of religious ideation, but in that of everyday life, where religious beliefs take root (Berger 1969: 41). They also describe a negotiation between asymmetrical forces, in which Nahua healers had to translate a social experience into a narrative – rendered within the framework of Christianity and decoded as a judicial confession – that explained the nature of their legitimate role in the community and eroded it at the same time.

Ruiz de Alarcón and Jacinto de la Serna pressed their charges to denounce healers, and, in confronting them, enquired about the origins of their knowledge. These priests did not concern themselves with the assessment of any particular plant's powers, but rather with the actors and participants who contributed to shaping and maintaining a particular symbolic universe rooted in a social order that had undergone deep transformations. Far removed from Francisco Hernández's scientific interest, these recorded episodes of 'discovery', modelled on inquisitorial procedures, betray a more urgent preoccupation with the need to build authority and legitimacy in a context in which both Nahua and Christian beliefs and practices were still redefining their boundaries.

In 1626 in Tenantzingo, an Indian maid in the service of Jacinto de la Serna started to experience an intense bleeding from her mouth. Seeing her servant close to death the priest handed her water with a small piece of bone to drink. As a result of this action the Indian woman vomited an object composed of wool, coal and hair, after which she recovered (Serna 1953: 97). It was later that Jacinto de la Serna found out that his maid's sickness had been the result of a spell cast by another woman known as a physician after both had been involved in an argument (Serna 1953: 98). The portion of bone that helped cure the maid happened to be taken from a bigger piece that Serna treasured: in life it had belonged to Gregorio López. In this way López's relics found a new context to display their power.

177

# Notes

1　For an overview of the practice of medicine in sixteenth-century New Spain see Risse (1987). Lanning (1985) contains a series of essays on the legal aspects of medical practice in the Spanish colonies.

2　'He had committed to memory all the Historical Books of the Scriptures, and word by word all the Gospels – St. Matthew's and St. John's, as well as the other two – plus those things not reported in them; and St. Paul's Epistles, and the Apocalypse' (Losa 1642: 29).

3　The *protomédico* was a royal official in charge of the regulation and supervision of all aspects of medical practice in towns or provinces. In Castile the *protomédicos* were also *médicos de cámara* – physicians who attended the royal family. F. Hernández was a *médico de cámara* before becoming a *protomédico*.

4　For Galen's discussion of method, see Gilbert (1960: 13–24). For humanist interpretations of Galen on this issue, see Gilbert (1960: 98–107).

5　'The person who heals based only on experience, without having studied or practised medicine or surgery' (Covarrubias [1611] 1943). John Cotta characterized the empiricists as follows: 'The Empiricke is he who reiecteth the disquisition of disease and remedies, their cause, natures and qualities according to iudgement and understanding '(Cotta 1612: 10).

6　For a succinct account of the debate between the different medical schools as reported by Galen, and his own position about them, see Temkin (1973: 15–23). Frede (1985) offers a fine analysis of the philosophical underpinnings of the dispute.

7　Addressing the issue of the state of the sciences in his time, Simón Abril believed that medicine was the one discipline not in need of a substantial reform since the teachings of Hippocrates and Galen had always been followed (Simón Abril 1905: 296).

8　Underlying these two sources – *historia* and *autopsia* – is the key role of memory, which was the basis of what the empiricists understood as experience, upon which the art of medicine should rest.

9　On the king's interest in medicinal plants, see Goodman (1988: 233–8).

10　'Very different indeed are Avicenna's precepts, and sometimes quite contrary to those of Jesus Christ our redeemer. The reason is very simple: Avicenna and those who share his profession work to restore health to the body, by being kind to it; the Evangelic Law, however, seeks to heal the soul by suppressing the forces and passions of that beast which inhabits our body' (Zumárraga [1547] 1951: 173–4). On the reception of Hippocratic medicine in Christianity and the manifold set of responses that it elicited, see Temkin (1991: chs 10–12).

11 'Angels and Archangels have also occupied themselves with the exercise of Medicine: St. Michael with Aquilinus, St. Raphael with Tobit, and more, and those Angels mentioned by Jeremiah in connection with Babylon, and some others who, according to St. John Chrysostom, are referred to in the Canonical texts' (Muñoz 1751: 21). Angelic help did sometimes get physicians into trouble. Such was the famous case of the Doctor Torralba to whom the angel Zaqiel had provided medical secrets about the uses of herbs. He faced charges by the Spanish Inquisition in 1528 (Caro Baroja 1992: I, 243–61).

12 Francisco Ximénez, Hernández's translator, omitted information about where *ololiuhqui* grows (Hernández 1615: 78r).

13 Hernández made a similar observation when referring to *picietl*, which he describes as being hot in the fourth degree, and its power to induce sleep a consequence of this quality (Hernández 1790: lib. III, cap. cix, 160). *Tlapatl*, on the other hand, induces sleep, and could lead to madness because of its coldness (Hernández 1790: III, 19). The assigning of the four basic properties – cold, hot, moist and dry – to plants was alien to Dioscorides. It was Galen who introduced this type of classification (Riddle 1985: 171).

14 The last *tratado* in Barrios's work is an abridged and reworked version of Hernández, taken from Ximénez's translation. Descriptions have been omitted, and the therapeutic uses of particular plants recast in a list of remedies for specific illnesses and ailments.

15 While for Aquinas angels are incorporeal, lacking bodies and matter, Bonaventure attributed to them form and matter, since all things created had to have a composite nature (Gilson 1965: 222–3). However, for Bonaventure, this distinction of form and matter does not imply that angels possess bodies. Matter, in this case, should be taken as an indication of 'an absolutely indeterminate potentiality' (Gilson 1965: 225).

16 A suggestive passage in Martín del Río's treatise on magic depicts demons as having superior knowledge, not entirely based on direct apprehension, but rather on extended experience and observation, in addition to their knowledge derived from both angels and men (Río 1991: 223–4).

17 About the circumstances surrounding Lopez's composition of his commentary, Losa writes: 'It is even worthier of praise that a man without formal studies should have written such a great work. It is indeed current opinion among the learned and pious that such an explanation of the Apocalypse had come to light by revealed science and a state of supernatural illumination (Losa 1642: 31v).

18   Aquinas postulated the influence of superior substances on inferior bodies to explain those cases in which certain effects could not be ascribed to the properties of a thing. Angels and demons would be examples of such superior and separate substances (McAllister 1939: 191). In the case of some medicinal plants, occult qualities were thought to be at work, rather than a superior influence (McAllister 1939: 193).

19   The empiricists acknowledged the possibility of discovering cures through the help of dreams (Frede 1985: 4). Pliny tells the story of a mother who dreamed of a root that would cure her son from rabies (Hernández 1966: lib. XXV, cap. ii, 502).

20   For a contemporary critique of this notion of scientific knowledge, see Sánchez ([1581] 1988: 195-8).

21   According to Vitoria, in the case of demons revealing some natural secret, once the secret is passed down to the next generation, the original demonic intervention becomes irrelevant.

22   As anthropologists have observed, the set of beliefs behind notions of witchcraft in certain societies seem to work in exactly the opposite direction (Evans Pritchard 1976).

23   It is worth mentioning that in Zinacantan the medical practitioner's incorporation into the community involves interrogation by the authorities of the presumptive *h'lol* or physician. This interrogation is accompanied by the testimony of witnesses regarding the *h'lol*'s ability to effect cures (Fabrega & Silver 1973: 33-5).

# Works cited

Aristotle (1982), *Nichomachean Ethics,* trans. H. Rackham, Cambridge: Harvard University Press.

Acuña, René (1984-85), *Relaciones geográficas del siglo XVI: Tlaxcala,* 2 vols., Mexico: UNAM.

Aquinas, Thomas (1948), *Summa Theologiae,* ed. Sac. Petri Caramello, 3 vols., Rome: Marietti.

   (1961), *Commentary on the Metaphysics of Aristotle,* trans. John Rowan, 2 vols., Chicago: Henry Regnery.

Barrios, Juan de (1607), *De la verdadera cirugia,* Mexico: Medicina y Astrologia.

Berger, Peter (1969), *The Sacred Canopy,* New York: Anchor Press.

Berlin, Brent (1992), *Ethnobiological Classification. Principles of Categorization of Plants and Animals in Traditional Societies,* Princeton: Princeton University Press.

Bodin, Jean (1581), *De Magorum Daemomani*, Basileae.

Cárdenas, Peter ([1591] 1965), *Problemas y secretos maravillosos de las Indias*, Mexico: Bibliófilos mexicanos.

Caro Baroja, Julio (1992), *Vidas mágicas e Inquisición*, 2 vols., Madrid: Istmo.

Cervantes, Fernando (1994), *The Devil in the New World*, New Haven: Yale University Press.

Clark, S. (1984) 'The Scientific Status of Demonology'. In Brian Vicker (ed.), *Occult and Scientific Mentalities in the Renaissance*, Cambridge: Cambridge University Press.

Cotta, John ([1612] 1972), *A Short Discoverie of the Unobserved dangers of severall sorts of ignorant and unconsiderate practicers of Physicke in England*, Amsterdam:Theatrum Orbis Terrarum.

Covarrubias, Sebastián de ([1611] 1943), *Tesoro de la lengua castellana o española*, Barcelona: S. A. Horta.

Cruz, Martín de la ([1552] 1940), *The Badianus Manuscript*, ed. Emily Walcott Emmart, Baltimore: The Johns Hopkins Press.

Dávila Padilla, Agustín ([1596] 1955), *Historia de la fundación y discurso de la Provincia de Santiago de México*, Mexico: Academia Literaria.

Dubler, César E. (1955), *La 'Materia Médica' de Dioscórides traducida y comentada por D. Andrés Laguna*, 3 vols., Barcelona.

Durán, Diego (1967), *Historia de las Indias de la Nueva España*, 2 vols., Mexico: Porrúa.

Evans-Pritchard, Edward (1976), *Witchcraft, Oracles, and Magic Among the Azande*, Oxford: Oxford University Press.

Fabrega, Horacio and Daniel B. Silver (1973), *Illness and Shamanistic Curing in Zinacantan*, Stanford: Stanford University Press.

Farfán, Augustín (1579), *Tractado breve de anathomia y chirugia, y de algunas enfermedades, que mas communmente suelen haver en esta Nueva España*, Mexico: Antonio Ricardo.

Flint, Valerie I. J. (1991), *The Rise of Magic in Early Medieval Europe*, Princeton: Princeton University Press.

Frede, Michael (1985), *Three Treatises on the Nature of Science*, Indianapolis: Hackett Publishing Company.

García-Ballester, Luis (1995), '*Artifex factivus sanitatis*: health and medical care in medieval Latin Galenism'. In Don Bates (ed.), *Knowledge and the scholarly medical traditions*, Cambridge: Cambridge University Press.

Gibson, Charles (1964), *The Aztecs Under Spanish Rule*, Stanford: Stanford University Press.

Gilbert, Neal W. (1960), *Renaissance Concepts of Method*, New York: Columbia University Press.

Gilson, Etienne (1965), *The Philosophy of St. Bonaventure*, Paterson, NJ: St. Anthony Guild Press.

Goodman, David C. (1988), *Power and Penury*, Cambridge: Cambridge University Press.

Guerra, Francisco (ed.) (1982), *El tesoro de medicina de Gregorio López 1542-1596*, Madrid: Ediciones Cultura Hispánica del Instituto de Cooperación Iberoamericana.

Hernández, Francisco (1615), *Quatro libros de la naturaleza, y virtudes de las plantas, y animales que estan recevidos en el uso de Medicina en la Nueva España, y la Methodo, y correccion, y preparacion, que para administrallas se requiere con lo que el Doctor Francisco Hernández escrivio en lengua latina*, Mexico: Diego Lopez Davalos.

(1651), *Nova plantarum, animalium et mineralium Mexicanorum*, Rome.

(1790), *Opera*, 3 vols., Madrid.

(1926), *De Antiquitatibus Novae Hispaniae*, Mexico: Talleres gráficos del Museo Nacional de Arqueología, Historia y Etnografía.

(1937), *Correspondencia del Doctor Francisco Hernández dirigida desde México al Rey Don Felipe II*, Chapultepec: Universidad Nacional de México, Instituto de Biología.

(1966-76), *Historia Natural de Cayo Plinio Segundo trasladada y anotada por el Doctor Francisco Hernández*, 2 vols., Mexico: UNAM.

Horozco y Covarrubias, Juan de (1588), *Tratado de la verdadera y falsa prophecia*, Segovia.

Juan Huarte de San Juan ([1575] 1989), *Examen de ingenios*, Madrid: Cátedra.

Kramer, Heinrich and James Sprenger (1971), *The Malleus Maleficarum*, translated and with an introduction by Montague Summers, New York: Dover.

Lanning, John Tate (1985), *The Royal Protomedicato. The Reg-*

ulation of the Medical Profession in the Spanish Empire,
ed. John Jay TePaske, Durham: Duke University Press.

López Austin, Alfredo (1980), *Cuerpo humano e ideología: las
concepciones de los antiguos nahuas*, 2 vols., Mexico: UNAM.

López de Hinojoso, Alonso (1595), *Summa y recopilacion de
cirugia, con un arte para sangrar, y examen de barbero*, Mexico: Pedro Balli.

Lorenzana, Francisco A. (1770), *Concilium Mexicanum Provin-
ciale III*, Mexico: José Antonio de Hogal.

Losa, Francisco de (1642), *Vida que el siervo de Dios Gregorio
Lopez hizo en algunos lugares de la Nueva España*, Madrid:
Imprenta Real.

McAllister, J. B. (1939), *The Letter of Saint Thomas Aquinas
'De Occultis Operibus Naturae'*, Washington: The Catholic
University of America Press.

Millen, Ron (1985), 'The manifestation of occult qualities in the
scientific revolution'. In Margaret J Osler and Paul Lawrence
Farber (eds), *Religion, science, and worldview. Essays in honor
of Richard S. Westfall*, Cambridge: Cambridge University
Press.

Monardes, Nicolás (1574), *Primera y segunda y tercera parte de la
historia de las cosas que se traen de nuestras Indias Occiden-
tales que sirven en Medicina*, Sevilla: Alonso Escrivano.

Motolinía [Toribio de Benavente] (1985), *Historia de los indios
de la Nueva España*, Madrid: Historia 16.

Mudry, Philippe (1982), *La Préface du 'De Medicina' de Celse*,
Lausanne: Institut Suissse de Rome.

Muñoz, Miguel Eugenio (1751), *Recopilación de las leyes, prag-
máticas reales, decretos, y acuerdos del Real Proto-Medica-
to*, Valencia: Viuda de Antonio Bordazar.

Muriel, Josefina ([1956] 1990), *Hospitales de la Nueva España*, 2
vols., Mexico: UNAM/Cruz Roja Mexicana.

*Procesos de indios idólatras y hechiceros* (1912): Mexico: Publi-
caciones del Archivo General de la Nación, vol. 3.

Riddle, John M. (1985), *Dioscorides on Pharmacy and Medicine*, Austin: University of Texas Press.

Río, Martín del (1991), *La magia demoníaca (libro II de las Dis-
quisiciones mágicas)*, Madrid: Hiperión.

Risse, Guenter B. (1987), 'Medicine in New Spain'. In Ronald L.
Numbers (ed.), *Medicine in the New World*, Knoxville: The

*Osvaldo F. Pardo*

University of Tennessee Press.

Ruiz de Alarcón, Hernando ([1629] 1953), 'Tratado de las supersticiones y costumbres gentílicas que oy viven entre los indios naturales deste Nueva España'. In Francisco del Paso y Troncoso, *Tratado de las idolatrías, supersticiones, dioses, ritos, hechicerías y otras costumbres gentílicas de las razas aborígenes de México*, Mexico: Fuente Cultural.

Sánchez, Francisco ([1581] 1988), *That Nothing is Known*, Cambridge: Cambridge University Press.

Serna, Jacinto de la (1953), 'Manual de ministros de indios para el conocimiento de sus idolatrías y extirpación de ellas', in Francisco del Paso y Troncoso, *Tratado de las idolatrías, supersticiones, dioses, ritos, hechicerías y otras costumbres gentílicas de las razas aborígenes de México*, Mexico: Fuente Cultural.

Simón Abril, Pedro (1905), 'Apuntamientos de cómo se deben reformar las doctrinas'. In *Obras escogidas de filósofos*, Madrid: Biblioteca de autores españoles, vol. 65.

Somolinos D'Ardois, Germán (1960), 'Vida y obra de Francisco Hernández'. In Francisco Hernández, *Obras completas*, Mexico: UNAM, vol. 1.

Tedlock, Barbara (1982), *Time and the Highland Maya*, Albuquerque: University of New Mexico Press.

Temkin, Osei (1973), *Galenism. Rise and Decline of a Medical Philosophy*, Ithaca: Cornell University Press.

(1991), *Hippocrates in a World of Pagans and Christians*, Baltimore: The Johns Hopkins University Press.

Vargas Machuca, Bernardo de (1599), *Milicia y descripción de las Indias*, Madrid: Pedro Madrigal.

Veracruz, Alonso de la (1557), *Phisica speculatio*, Mexico.

Vitoria, Francisco de (1960), 'De la magia'. In *Obras. Relecciones teológicas*, ed. Teófilo Urdanoz, Madrid: Biblioteca de autores cristianos.

Zumárraga: Juan de ([1547] 1951), *Regla christiana breve*, Mexico: Editorial Jus.

# 7
# Andean *curanderos* and their repressors: the persecution of native healing in late seventeenth- and early eighteenth-century Peru

NICHOLAS GRIFFITHS

Once, as a child, sleeping in a field, Juan Vásques was visited in his dreams by an old white man with a cross in his hand. This man, whom he believed to be St. John, instructed him to look carefully at his own arm, where he too would find a cross. Astonished, Vásques discovered four black marks like moles on his right arm, apparently in the shape of a cross. In this same dream, the old man taught him to recognize certain herbs and the illnesses for which they should be administered. Some time later, seeing a young Indian in great pain and remembering the dream, he went to look for one of these herbs, the *yerba de San Juan*, and prepared an infusion for the boy to drink, by which means alone he recovered. For some years after this Vásques performed no more cures but came to Lima to earn his living.[1]

This account of his own initiation as a *curandero* (native healer) was given by the Indian Juan Vásques, native of Cajamarca, when he was brought before the court of the *provisor* (vicar-general) of the archbishopric of Lima in 1710, accused of the superstitious use of herbal remedies.[2] An examination of this trial yields significant insights; first, into the intellectual framework which Spanish clerics sought to impose on the activities of native *curanderos*, second into the extent to which defendants adapted to the terminology and world view of their accusers during the course of their trials, and finally into the manner in which Andean healers understood the relationship between indigenous and Christian supernatural power. What follows will examine, then, both the conceptual apparatus Spaniards used to interpret native healing and how *curanderos* reaffirmed their own native principles in the face of repression.

One of the most interesting aspects of Vásques's trial is his contention that his cures were performed with the sanction of Christian authority. He explained that one day when he told his confessor that he was apprehensive about using his knowledge of healing techniques, the cleric reprimanded him and refused to absolve him until he used his talent as a gift of charity for others. In spite of this, he ignored the advice until he himself fell ill. Then, in a dream, a 'little angel' (*angelito*) appeared to him, telling him to look for a medicinal plant, the *yerba de San Juan,* at the mountain of San Gerónimo, and there indeed he found it with a cross emblazoned on it. Imbibing a drink he prepared from it, he recovered, for which, he said, 'he gave thanks to God'.

It was not unusual for *curanderos* who were tried by the *provisor* to attribute the success of their healing powers to God. What is more original about Vásques's experience is the role of figures of Christian authority as the apparent guarantors of the orthodoxy of his activities. For, if he was still reluctant to make use of his powers, the insistence of a second cleric convinced him. One day in Lima, seized by a conviction that he should cure the sick with herbs, he went to confess in order to settle his conscience. The cleric refused him absolution until he had provided the sick with the benefits of his abilities. Administering to a crippled Indian a drink prepared from the *yerba de San Francisco*, he enabled the man to walk again. He took no payment from the man since his confessor had insisted that his cures should not be performed for personal gain. That Vásques's doubts were apparently assuaged by the reassurances he received from Catholic clerics might at first sight be interpreted as a justification for his cures, an attempt to curry favour with his accusers by invoking the sanction of Christian power and demonstrating his respect for Catholic authority. However this would not be a sufficient explanation. Rather, Vásques's experience, as we shall see later, was an original and genuine attempt to legitimize his healing skills within the context of the only source of supernatural power that he knew.

In fact, Vásques's interrogators were unimpressed by his deference to clerics, since his healing involved superstitious observances. By his own admission, his cures were always preceded by praying the creed. He also stated that he was able to discern 'as clearly as if it had been reflected in a mirror' the origin of an ailment by examining a client's spittle and taking his pulse.[3] In this way, he perceived not only the nature of the affliction but also which herb would be most appropriate for the cure. This testimony suggested that Vásques did not employ purely natural means in his cures and led his interrogators to question him closely on the origin of his knowledge. Vásques affirmed that he had possessed his knowledge since he had experienced the vision in his dreams; he had had no master nor had he communicated with or invoked the devil, and had only used the method of the saliva and the creed.[4] Still not satisfied, the prosecution threatened him with torture unless he confessed the truth, which was that he had made a pact with the devil who had taught him his tricks through illicit means. Vásques repeated that he had had no master other than the insight which had been communicated to him in his vision, that he had only used the herbs already declared and that he could not be forced to say anything else.

Alarmed by the accusations of diabolism which his communications with his spiritual guardian had provoked, Vásques attempted in a subsequent statement to disavow his earlier confession. Instead of attributing his extraordinary abilities to the old man of his dreams, he now credited his grandfather with imparting to him the knowledge of which herbs to apply to which illnesses. He retracted his earlier account of the vision he had experienced, claiming that he had only invented this story in the belief that it would help him escape punishment. He had had the moles on his arm since he was a child; they were natural and were not formed in a vision as he had previously said. His ability to see the nature of afflictions as clearly as if human bodies were open to the eye was innate and could only be the will of God. He denied that, in performing one of his cures, he had summoned the old man of his dreams, extinguishing the candle since his guardian would refuse to enter while there was light. Confronted with the testimony of witnesses, he admitted that, in the darkness, he had changed the pitch of his voice and pretended to be the old man, but he insisted that it was only a trick that he had been taught to earn money. He also denied having said he had eighteen devils, who appeared at graves and at *huacas* (native shrines), to help him with his cures; nor was it true that he had performed cures by offering blood to the sun or to the devil. He emphatically denied any type of diabolical pact.[5]

The accusation of the diabolical pact forced Vásques to adapt his account so that he could plausibly attribute the origin of his knowledge to natural, not supernatural, causes. It is interesting that the discourse of diabolism introduced by the prosecution did not encourage Vásques to confess to the pact; on the contrary, he was allowed to disavow his spirit and deny the significance of his old man figure. His accusers were not looking for a genuine demonic presence. The accusation of diabolism was the logical consequence of the accused's insistence on the role of supernatural forces in his initiation; if, on the other hand, natural causes were the origins of his powers, then there was no need to resort to the discourse of demonology.

This dichotomy between the natural or supernatural origins of healing powers was the principal issue for the repressors of native *curanderos*. It is important to note that it was not the act of healing in itself that was condemned by church authorities; indeed numerous authors had written on the subject of the lore of plants and concluded that its use *per se* did not necessarily involve superstition. The great Dominican theologian Francisco de Vitoria considered many cures made with special herbs to be efficacious on the basis of their natural virtues. Although such knowledge could be imparted by the devil, it could also be acquired through the tradition of learned authorities. Furthermore, once acquired, this knowledge could also be used in a natural way without aid from either good or bad spirits. These conclusions thus allowed the use of herbs in certain circumstances. Even so, such a position was ambivalent since it left open to debate how in any particular instance the source of knowledge could be determined. (Vitoria 1960: 1256–7).

Vitoria's tolerance was reflected in the resolutions of the Council of Lima of 1567, where it was stipulated that those *curanderos* whose healing derived from 'empirical' experience were to be provided with written permission to practise. The only condition was that it should be verified that they did not employ 'superstitious' words or ceremonies (Vargas Ugarte1951–54: vol. 1, 255).

It is difficult to determine whether such licences to practise were in fact granted, but many other commentators were similarly indulgent of non-superstitious healing. The native Andean chronicler Felipe Guaman Poma de Ayala distinguished between common *hechiceros* (sorcerers) and *curanderos*. Because of their skill with plants, the latter were able to practise as effectively as doctors of medicine. Although it was common for the priest or *corregidor* (judicial and administrative official) to bring proceedings against them, calling them *hechiceros*, in fact they were only Christians, and it would be far better if they were given a licence to practise. (Guaman Poma de Ayala 1980: vol. 2, 769). According to the Jesuit provincial and extirpator of native Andean religions, Pablo José de Arriaga, the sin of the native *curanderos* lay not in the cures they aimed to effect but in the superstitious or idolatrous methods they employed. Indeed such was his respect for their knowledge of native herbs that he proposed that priests should provide practitioners with instruction and thus remove any suspicion of superstition. In this way full advantage could be taken of their abilities without the danger of sin (Arriaga 1968: 238). This view was reflected in the instruction issued by the archbishop of Lima, Pedro de Villagómez, to his Visitors-General of Idolatry that, whereas the Indian *hechiceros* and ministers of idolatry should by no means be allowed to cure the sick, the healing activities of other Indians, whose practice rested on expert knowledge of the virtues of plants, should be approved. Such approval would always be conditional on an investigation by the village priest of the methods of curing so as to ensure the absence of all superstition (Villagómez 1919: 268).

It is within the context of this relatively tolerant attitude towards the practice of healing with herbs that we should situate the attempts made by the *procuradores de los naturales* (attorneys who acted on behalf of the native population) to construct rigorous justifications for the use of herbal remedies by reference to natural origins. For example, the accusation of murderous *maleficio* brought against two Indian women, Francisca de Ribera and María de la Cruz, in 1691 was dismissed as false by the defence since they had been engaged in nothing more sinful than an attempt to cure afflictions which had been ailing them. The coca found in their possession had not been directed to superstitious ends, but had been used as a remedy for de Ribera's toothache, for which it was commonly held to be effective.[6] Similarly, in defence of María de la Cruz and Augustina Barbola, the *procurador* argued that neither healing with herbs nor the chewing of coca was an offence of superstition. The former was a common custom among Indians on account of the impossibility of obtaining better medicine, and the latter was an everyday practice among Indians at work. The issue was not the use of herbs in themselves but rather the properties of these herbs (whether they could produce the claimed effects) and the words of invocation used. Since the accused had employed no diabolical spells, they had practised not magic or superstition, but natural philosophy.[7]

This defence was harder to maintain when, as in the case of Vásques, defendants attributed their powers to the communications of a guardian angel or spirit. Juana Agustina, tried in 1697, provoked the censure of the authorities for the superstitious observances which she employed in her cures and divination. Invoking the apostles Saint Peter and Saint Paul, she would spit chewed tobacco into her hand and, merely by moving the saliva with her fingers, she was able to deduce from the course it took across her hand whether a client's lost item would reappear or not. But her greatest sin had been her communication with a guardian angel who appeared to her whenever she prayed the *Paternoster*, the *Ave Maria* and the *Salve Regina* (three of the basic Catholic prayers) She had been taught how to summon this spiritual guardian by her stepfather and it had appeared to her several times after his death, usually whenever she was at a certain stream. It was from the angel that she had learned how to attract good fortune and the love of men, both for herself and her clients, by taking baths in herbs. Communication with this spiritual guardian provoked an accusation of demonic pact. In order to escape this charge, the initial strategy of her defence was to deny the reality of the angel. She had learned the use of herbs, not from any angel, which was a story she had invented, but from her stepfather, and, although she had divined with tobacco and saliva, it had been mere trickery in order to earn a living. When it became clear that her accusers were not convinced, she returned to her original story. The angel with whom she communicated had been bequeathed to her by her stepfather, who had been a doctor and not a sorcerer, in order that she might earn her livelihood. She begged forgiveness for her deeds, abominating her pact with the angel and promising not to repeat her superstitions with herbs since they were 'the work of the devil'. Her submission to the discourse of diabolism of her accusers was the sign of her true contrition. In this case, the role of the 'angel' led to the conclusion that the origin of her powers was supernatural rather than natural.[8]

The trial of Juan Vásques was also dominated by the dichotomy of the natural or supernatural origin of healing powers, but, as we have seen, this defendant was permitted to retreat from his initial confession of the central role of his old man figure.[9] The accusation of superstition did not infer any genuine contact with spirits or demons but only foolish convictions contrary to the faith. The issue was not the existence of the spiritual guardian but rather Vásques's sincere belief in the efficacy of his cures. On one level, the accused was clearly guilty of superstitious acts, for example his insistence on performing cures only on certain days, believing them to be propitious, or his examination of the spittle of the sick in order to learn of future events or to reveal hidden things. The prosecutor argued that, on account of the methods by which Vásques had learnt of the nature of the illnesses of his clients, he could be held to be a heretic. On the other hand, in repeated examinations he had been found to be firm in the faith, and one who remained true to the faith *in his mind*, could not be called a heretic since heresy implied *interior consent*. Furthermore, the prosecutor conceded that the accusation of divination which he himself had brought against Vásques had not been sufficiently proved, and that therefore the resolution of this question should be left until such time as there might be more evidence.

In order to demonstrate the absence of superstition from his client's practices, the *procurador de los naturales* sought to provide an explanation in purely natural terms. Vásques did not know the origin of his knowledge which he had possessed since he was a child and which he had attributed to the will of God. His moles had not been formed in a vision but had been with him since the day of his birth. If he had reserved certain days for his cures, it was not for any superstitious reason, but because the occupations of his patients only permitted them to attend on those days. He knew well that all days were equal for the purposes of his cures. As for recognizing the illnesses of patients from their saliva, it was well known that doctors could do the same. Vásques's ability with herbs was not to be taken as evidence of superstition or of dealings with the devil, since knowledge of the properties of herbs had been given by the Lord to some individuals in his divine providence. In their pagan state, without doctors, the Indians had possessed this knowledge and used it to cure illnesses. Other heathen peoples, such as the Ethiopians, had known of the properties of plants and had used them for medicinal purposes. Since the medicinal virtues lay in the herbs themselves, and the accused had learned of them from his grandfather through the grace of God, it could not be demonstrated that he had committed any offence against the faith.

The prosecution proposed to resolve the issue of the natural virtues of the herbs Vásques had used by summoning a *protomédico* (officer appointed to supervise the practice of medicine) and a professor of medicine to offer their professional opinions. They were asked to consider if the herbs mentioned in the confessions could have the medicinal effects claimed by the accused, and if he could reasonably have acquired knowledge of these effects. They concluded that the herbs did indeed possess natural virtues for curing serious ailments, that doctors had successfully used them, and that knowledge of their virtues could be obtained by natural means through continual observance of their effects. Although current medical knowledge of some of the herbs was incomplete, it was quite possible that, through the tradition of his ancestors, an individual might have acquired a detailed understanding of their virtues. However, the experts felt unable to give any opinion as to how Vásques himself had made use of the herbs, since it was a matter of religion, and therefore under the jurisdiction of the *provisor*. Their evidence was deliberately non-committal and ambiguous, since they wisely did not wish to appear to usurp the authority of the church. Although their testimony appeared to vindicate the defendant, the prosecutor was not deterred. He insisted that, even if it was true that the effects of herbs could be known by natural causes, there was no proof that this particular defendant had acquired his knowledge in this manner. The expert testimony was incapable of resolving the question. Indeed, it is clear that the question was fundamentally irresolvable, since Spaniards were aware that they were ignorant of many of the properties of herbs. This detailed examination of the question of the natural virtues of herbs, the most complete of its kind existing in the documentation on colonial idolatry trials, had brought the dispute to no effective conclusion.

The final sentence passed against Vásques failed to resolve the question of the origin of his powers. Although it found him guilty of using 'illicit and superstitious means' in his cures, it neglected to reach a verdict either about the diabolical pact or the significance of the vision of the old man. The failure to resolve the central theoretical questions of the case is an indication that the priority was not to engage in theological disputes about the nature of diabolical intervention, but to prevent individual subjects from engaging in deviant behaviour. If the question of the natural or supernatural origin of herbal knowledge was not explicitly addressed, it may have been because of the latent contradictions it evoked, evident in the sentence and punishment imposed. On the one hand, the fact that Vásques was ordered never to perform such cures again, or to pass on his knowledge of herbs to any other person, suggests a conviction that this knowledge was reprehensible *in itself* and not simply by association with superstitious practices. On the other hand, the leniency of the penalty in relation to the apparent seriousness of the accusation implicitly recognized the plausibility of natural causes as the explanation of Vásques's cures. His punishment was restricted to two years service in the convent of the Bethlehemites, where he would be instructed in Christian doctrine (curiously, the Bethlehemites were a hospital order, suggesting a continuing ambivalence on the part of the authorities with regard to Vásques's medical knowledge). The full weight of the law would only be brought against him if he relapsed into superstitions in the future. Such forbearance was not wholly consistent with a sentence that had spoken of 'illicit and superstitious acts'. By the logic of the prosecution's own argument, if demonic intervention was excluded as the real source of Vásques's acts, and the superstition lay only in the frame of mind in which he had performed them, what other explanation remained but that of natural causes? In effect, the outcome of Vásques's case was a tacit recognition of the role of natural causes in the use of herbal remedies.

At the outset of his analysis, the prosecutor had posited two possible explanations, excluding mental illness, for the apparent successful outcome of Vásques's cures: natural causes or the illusion of demons. Yet his own account concentrated on an argument, that of reprehensible superstitious beliefs, which, while providing a plausible pretext for punishment, could not account for the outcome of exterior acts. The prosecutor was ensnared in the contradictions of his own philosophy. The rejection of the intervention of demons by minds that were, in any event, highly sceptical of the powers that *curanderos* attributed to themselves, strengthened the case for natural causes. Yet, at the same time, acceptance of natural causes attributed a dangerous efficacy to the actions of *curanderos*. Their expertise in medical matters was a major source of prestige in native communities. If the Christian faith of the bulk of the Indians was not to be undermined, the alternative supernatural power offered by native *curanderos* had to be delegitimized. The most effective means of disempowerment was to denounce them as frauds and tricksters. Conceding success to *curanderos* in the sphere of healing was to recognize their access to genuine supernatural power. Thus, the natural origin of healing powers proved as unsatisfactory as the supernatural origin, since both conferred too much power on native religious specialists. It seems that having posited two alternative theories to explain native healing, the authorities were not happy with either, unconsciously acknowledging, through their unease, that the terrain of the empirical evidence did not quite fit the map of their intellectual constructs.

Vásques's relationship with the old man of his dreams testifies to the resilience of the bond between *curandero* and tutelary deity, a bond that survived the increasing atomization of the native world. Vásques differed from many of his fellow healers in his isolation from any traditional intellectual framework or collective indigenous context for his abilities. Whereas many *curanderos* performed their roles within the context of their traditional communities, from which they drew their inspiration, Vásques worked alone in the alien environment of the capital, cut off from the network of references which gave meaning to his office. It was true that he had been awakened to the possibilities of his calling by the example of his grandfather, but he had not begun to practise until he was alone in Lima. Once he began to receive intimations of his vocation, he was plunged into a crisis of doubts and uncertainties and a sense of existential unease which only the validation of an authoritative voice could assuage. In the normal course of events, the budding healer would receive his spiritual initiation only in the context of the intellectual and physical preparation provided by the sustaining beliefs of his community. Vásques stood outside such a secure environment. He enjoyed the support of no master in his adult life to communicate to him, and sustain in him, a conceptual understanding of his powers. Therefore, it seems he was ineluctably drawn to an alternative source of numinous authority. In order to validate his unnerving experiences, he sought legitimacy from representatives of the strongest supernatural force he knew: Catholic clerics. In the climate of tolerance demonstrated by the church toward the practice of healing without superstition, it is not implausible that a cleric might have given his approval to Vásques's cures. Other defendants in these trials also claimed that their healing rites had received the sanction of the Christian church. In 1660 the *curandero* Luis de Aguilar affirmed that his knowledge of herbal cures had been imparted to him by the priest Lázaro Sánchez who had encouraged him to search for herbs when he had been his sexton.[10]

Thus, Vásques's appeal to Christian authority to legitimate his cures should not be interpreted simply as a convenient defence. It was an original attempt to reconcile the two religious traditions, the collision of which had plunged many other *curanderos* into confusion and anomie. Because of his total break with his native community, Vásques had succeeded in articulating a new hierarchy which set the two traditions in a logical relationship to each other, not as antagonistic and contradictory systems but as complementary and mutually sustaining parts of a greater supernatural whole. Vásques's answer, in seeking the blessing of the representative of the Christian tradition for indulgence in the rites of the native tradition, was to enact the subordination of the latter to the former. But the subordinate position of the tradition of native healing did not signify its defeat. What was important was the reconstruction of the logic of the native world, the finding of its place in the new universe 'turned upside down', in the famous phrase of the native chronicler Guaman Poma. Vásques's solution enabled him to maintain his dialogue with the native supernatural world, a dialogue he continued to interpret according to indigenous criteria. The Christian priest, although higher in the hierarchy, was manipulated by Vásques in order to reaffirm the validity of his own numinous world. This 'supernatural' reality was lost on the ecclesiastical authorities, blinded as they were by their phantasms of demons and natural causes.

## Notes

1 The trial of Juan Vásques is located in the section *Hechicerías e Idolatrías* of the *Archivo Arzobispal de Lima* (hereinafter AAL Idolatrías). When I consulted it in 1990, it was located in legajo 13 (Causa contra Juan Vásques, Lima, 1710). The account given here is drawn from fols. 1, 24–9, 31–3. The case has inspired one scholarly article (Espinoza 1994: 327–37). I have discussed aspects of this case elsewhere; see Griffiths (1996).

2 In colonial Peru Indians were not subject to the Inquisition (from whose jurisdiction they were formally removed by the Spanish crown in 1571) but to the ordinary ecclesiastical jurisdiction of the archbishoprics and bishoprics. Trials and investigations were conducted under the auspices of the *provisor* (vicar-general) and his officials.

3 It is interesting to compare Vásques's clairvoyant abilities with those of the curing shamans of the Jívaro Indians of the Ecuadorean Amazon. Under the influence of a hallucinogenic drink, these shamans can see into the body of the patient 'as though it were glass' (Harner 1973: 23).

4 Causa contra Juan Vásquez, fol. 32.

5 Causa contra Juan Vásquez, fols. 34–40v.

6 AAL, Idolatrías 11, Causa contra Francisca Huaylas y María de la Cruz, fols. 1, 13, 20, 22 and 26.

7 AAL, Idolatrías 10, Causa contra María de la Cruz, fols. 1, 28, 33 and 36.

8 AAL, Idolatrías 12, Causa de hechicería contra Juana Agustina, fols. 1–11v.

9 For what follows, see fols. 40–2, 44–6, 47–9, 80.

10 AAL, Idolatrías 5, Causa contra Pablo Ato, fol. 3.

## Works cited

Arriaga, P. J. de (1968), *La extirpación de la idolatría del Perú*. In *Crónicas peruanas de interés indígena*, ed. Esteve Barba, Biblioteca de autores españoles, CCIX, Madrid: Atlas.

Espinoza, Javier F. Flores (1994), 'El Capitán Juan Vásquez, indio saludador (Lima, 1710)'. In Gabriela Ramos (ed.), *La venida del Reino. Religión, evangelización y cultura en*

*América, siglos XVI-XX.* Cuadernos para la Historia de la Evangelización en América Latina, Cusco: Centro de Estudios Regionales Andinos 'Bartolomé de Las Casas'.

Griffiths, Nicholas (1996), *The Cross and the Serpent: Religious Repression and Resurgence in Colonial Peru*, Norman and London: University of Oklahoma Press

Guaman Poma de Ayala, Felipe (1980), *El primer nueva corónica y buen gobierno*, ed. J. V. Murra and R. Adorno, 2 vols. Mexico: Siglo Veintiuno.

Harner, M. (1973), *Hallucinogens and shamanism*, New York: Oxford University Press.

Vargas Ugarte, R. (1951-54), *Los Concilios Limenses 1551-1772*, 3 vols., Lima,: Instituto de Investigaciones Históricas.

Villagómez, Pedro de (1919), *Carta pastoral de exhortación e instrucción contra las idolatrías de los indios del arzobispado de Lima*, ed. C. A. Romero and H. H. Urteaga, Colección de libros y documentos referentes a la historia del Perú, XII, Lima: Sanmarté.

Vitoria, F. de (1960), *De la magia*. In *Obras: relecciones teológicas*, T. Urdanoz (ed.), Biblioteca de autores cristianos, CXCVIII. Madrid: Editorial Católica.

# 8
# *El callejón de la soledad*: vectors of cultural hybridity in seventeenth-century Lima[1]

Alejandra B. Osorio

Colonial Lima is often depicted as a segregated city, primarily of Spaniards and their African slaves, with an absence of Indians, and characterized by a Spanish cultural identity spiritually and materially divorced from the 'deep Peru', or *Perú profundo*, of the Andean highlands. The official assignation of neighbourhoods, including the central area around the *Plaza Mayor* for Spaniards and Creoles, the *reducción de Santiago del Cercado* for Indians, and *San Lázaro*, across the Rimac river, for Blacks and mixed-blood *castas*, is cited as material evidence of an effective segregation.[2] Recent demographic and urban studies of colonial Lima, however, are beginning to unravel a different story. Founded in 1535 by Francisco Pizarro primarily as a city for Spaniards, by the seventeenth century Lima was multiethnic and far from segregated. Spanish, Indian, and African populations mixed in the squares, churches, markets, streets, and *callejones*. In 1614 Lima's population was close to 22 000, and by 1700 it had increased to nearly 35 000. Rural–urban migration was significant in this growth and in the new ethnic composition of the city (Charney 1988; Cook 1975; Sánchez-Albornoz 1988; Lowry 1989; Vergara 1997). Men and women from the Andean highlands migrated to coastal cities like Lima, and to highland mining centres like Potosí and Huancavelica, in search of employment and cash to meet tribute obligations, to escape such tribute obligations as the *mita* (corvée labour draft), or simply to seek a better life (Glave 1989; Vergara 1998). In his economic and social analysis of the permanent Indian population of Lima in 1613, Paul Charney (1988) demonstrates the presence of an economically and socially active Indian minority of nearly 2000. Charney suggests that Lima's growing Indian population was well integrated and 'acculturated' given their economic and occupational categories and the spatial distribution of Indian residences within the city limits (Charney 1988: see especially Map 1, 23; Durán 1992)[3] In addition to its Spanish and Indian populations, colonial Lima also held a large African population of approximately 10 300, consisting of some free Blacks and many more slaves from Africa and other Spanish American colonies (Bowser 1974). The studies of Cook (1975) and Charney (1988) reveal that Indians resided alongside Spaniards and Africans in all of Lima's neighbourhoods. Likewise, Charney (1988) and Durán (1992) demonstrate that as early as 1613 persons of different ethnic groups lived in shared residences and rooms all over the city. In short, it seems clear that the so-called segregated neighbourhoods of the capital were never more than shadows of the failed attempt by colonial authorities to implement in Lima an ideally conceived but in this case impossible colonial society of two segregated 'republics', Spanish and Indian, with an auxiliary space for slaves and *castas*.

One consequence of this failure of the colonial state to segregate physically the different ethnic groups of colonial Lima was the development of urban sites which facilitated cultural hybridity. An important feature of colonial Lima's mixed housing arrangements were the *callejones* (sometimes referred to as *callejones de cuartos*), alleys with numerous rooms situated around a common patio, often equipped with a kitchen and chicken coop (Durán 1992: 7). Living quarters in these *callejones limeños* were often overcrowded, holding entire families in small rooms one next to another, making 'private lives' part of the local public domain. The testimonies of women recorded in the trial records of the Extirpation of Idolatry (a quasi-inquisitorial process which acted intermittently in the seventeenth and eighteenth centuries under archiepiscopal authority in order to uncover, try, and punish native deviance from Catholic orthodoxy) reveal *callejón* dwellers sharing many details of their private lives with neighbours, albeit not always willingly. As Flores Galindo and Chocano (1984: 409) suggest in their study of divorce proceedings, tight living conditions and the lack of privacy in the *callejones* allowed witnesses to recount the private affairs of their neighbours in great detail. Such tight living quarters also facilitated the sharing of knowledge of sorcery and healing practices between Andean migrant women and Spanish and African women.[4]

Juana de Mayo, an Indian woman in her fifties, born in Ica (coastal region south of Lima), and famous for her concoctions, good for getting unfaithful lovers to 'turn against their girlfriends' is one case in point.[5] In her trial, Juana declared that she had learned to make her herbal brews from Catana, a Black Creole woman from Panama who used it to get rid of the 'other woman' her own lover was seeing, and, since it had worked, Juana had decided to include it in her own repertoire. Indigenous women, however, were not merely the receptors of other cultural practices. María Magdalena, a *mestiza* (person of mixed Spanish and Indian parentage), ran an herbal bath business to treat harshness or roughness of the skin; she had learned her profession from María de Abalos, an Indian from Surco (rural village east of Lima) who was apparently very successful at curing the women who sought out her remedies.[6]

The multicultural practices of Juana and María, I will argue, were particularly dynamic among poor women of African, Indian and mixed descent, many of whom dwelled at one time or another in Lima's crowded back alleys, or *callejones*. As the urban vectors of an unsanctioned spiritual encounter, Lima's *callejones* were home to an irrepressible process of transculturation[7] that reached far beyond the confines of its solitary quarters. The ongoing process of transculturation of colonial society was very evident in the practices of the women dwellers of these *callejones*. Their physical proximity allowed for a permanent exchange of practices, ideas and behaviours that yielded hybrid urban cultures, albeit with some very Andean features. This paper explores some of the everyday minutiae of this developing cultural hybridity as expressed in the interrogated 'private' activities of poor urban women of various racial and cultural backgrounds. I argue that Lima's unsanctioned cultural hybridity suggests that these poor urban women, many of whom resided in Lima's *callejones* or courtyard alleys, deployed European, African, and Andean knowledge which, thanks in part to their services, were becoming common currency in Lima's colonial culture.

## Re-reading inquisitorial records for culture: methodological considerations

The records of the Extirpation of Idolatry in Peru, most active in the archbishopric of Lima during the seventeenth century (Duviols 1977), pose methodological problems as they raise theoretical questions. For some time now, historians and ethnohistorians have sampled inquisitorial records for 'ethnographic data' on subaltern groups – primarily indigenous women and peasants – traditionally under-represented in official documents. The use of such records as ethnographic sources, however, has been the subject of some recent controversy. Carlo Ginzburg (1989) argued that the Inquisitor could be seen as an anthropologist who gathered ethnographic information much like ethnographers do today,[8] and that their descriptions of beliefs could be useful to historians for reconstructing popular cultural systems, much as ethnographies are used for writing about so-called primitive cultures. Renato Rosaldo (1986) and Edward Muir (1995) on the other hand, criticized this ethnographic approach to inquisitorial trials. For Rosaldo, the use of inquisitorial records as historical evidence by historians such as Emmanuel Le Roy Ladurie – who in *Montaillou* (1975) uses such records to reconstruct the lives and mentalities of fourteenth-century Languedoc peasants – constitute an 'abuse' of ethnographic authority. For Rosaldo, inquisitorial testimonies are not 'direct testimonies' that can or should be used as 'documentary' accounts of events, practices or beliefs, given the conditions (mainly torture) under which they were obtained. For Rosaldo, Ladurie's use of quotation marks to mark the interpolation of the 'evidence' in his historical narrative falls short of accounting for the political production of the text, for it assumes that the document can 'speak' for itself.[9] Edward Muir (1995), on the other hand, questioned the ability of the historian working with inquisitorial trials to reproduce anything beyond a mere account of the trial itself, given 'the constraints of the judicial system and the psychological implications of torture' inscribed in them. For Muir, all inquisitorial trials by definition 'are exceptional events that direct our gaze to the fringes of religious life', perhaps leaving the 'normal' hidden, so that their use inevitably privileges 'lurid details of religious persecution that potentially misrepresents the historical picture' (1995: 182-5). Muir does not explain what 'normal' is, and his concern with a 'misrepresentation' of the historical picture seems to underline a belief in an ultimate 'true' and definitive account of historical events.

While I agree both with Rosaldo and Muir that inquisitorial testimonies are clearly problematic, I do not believe that they are necessarily more problematic than any other source used by historians, given that all sources (oral and written testimonies as well as legal, bureaucratic, statistical and religious documents) are always politically produced, and as such they can never provide 'objective' renditions of any issue. As Ginzburg puts it '[t]here are no neutral texts; even a notarial inventory implies a code which must be deciphered' (1989: 161) in conjunction with other sources. In my view, the historian differs little from the reader of ethnographies, and I would agree with Ginzburg (1989: 156) that the Inquisitor may be viewed as an official ethnographer of sorts, asking the questions and probing for more detail, and thus shaping to great extent the 'subject matter' of the interrogation. In our case it is important to note, however, that Inquisitors rarely wrote down their findings. In colonial Peru scribes were responsible for recording the proceedings of the interrogation, albeit not always *ad verbum*; prescribed legal jargon shaped their discourse (Sabean 1984). It is the scribe's prescribed voices that we hear, to a great degree, when we read these testimonies.

Rosaldo appears to assume that inquisitorial testimonies were always gathered by coercive means, if not under torture, and that the whole 'text' that comprises a single confession or 'testimony' was circumscribed by the questions posed by the interrogator. The issue of power in the production of these testimonies is crucial and notably absent from Ginzburg's analogy, since although punishment and force were ever present in an inquisitorial interrogation, torture is not a 'tool' that modern ethnographers apply in their interviews; informants may simply walk away or refuse to talk. The accused before the Inquisition, on the other hand, had to provide an answer or suffer the consequences. This predicament has prompted some scholars to argue that torture in a certain sense 'created' witchcraft, or at least created 'diabolical witchcraft' (Levack 1987: 13). Nevertheless, in her book on witchcraft and sexuality in seventeenth-century Germany, Lyndal Roper

(1994: 8–9) points out that repression is not simply an imposition of control over the subject, but constitutes an *active* part in the formation of sexual and catholic identities (see also Behar 1987; Foucault 1979, 1990). Thus, in reading these 'confessions' we must account for the possibility that individuals may think and feel 'against the grain', or that accused women were not simply consumers of male discourse, 'providing witchcraft fantasy on order' (Roper 1994: 19–20). Women created narratives, suggests Roper, using available cultural elements that allowed them to make sense of their life experiences. The fact that some elements were presumed to come from the devil himself 'did not rob women of their agency'. For Roper, understanding witchcraft confessions as 'the projection of a male-dominated society', only ignores the creative work of the accused in 'translating her own life experiences into the language of the diabolic' (1994: 20–1).[10] The fantasies woven by 'witches', therefore, although often obtained by torture, constitute for Roper 'condensations of shared cultural preoccupations' (1994: 20).

In the cases I have chosen from the archive on seventeenth-century Lima, there are several points that should be kept in mind. First, I should point out that although there were important institutional differences between the Inquisition and the Extirpation (see Griffiths 1994), the records produced by both reveal some important similarities: both records were produced by systematic interrogations conducted under pressure and intimidation; in both cases the contents are descriptions of deviant (from Counter-Reformation) religious beliefs and practices; historians and ethnohistorians have used them to reconstruct the cultural world of traditionally under-represented groups in official sources. These similarities make the methodological discussion of inquisitional records applicable to a discussion of Extirpation records. In the specific cases of the records of the Extirpation analysed here, most testimonies were indeed extracted under pressure and, in some cases, under torture by an Extirpator (or Visitor-General; see Griffiths 1994: 21). However, many testimonies seem also to have been offered to the Extirpator willingly by people who in many cases ended up being tried themselves as practitioners of witchcraft, but who in other cases were capable of manipulating the institution and its officials for their own purposes. Important also to keep in mind is that the accused as well as witnesses were interrogated, not only by the Extirpator, but by the public attorney or the *Procurador General de Naturales*, and by lower magistrates, in each case providing different renditions of the events in question. These interrogations were indeed 'tailored' by the questions posed by the interrogators,[11] but as Lyndal Roper points out, this is also the case in nearly any conversation. Of course, we must keep in mind that inquisitorial testimonies, like ethnographies, are texts produced for a specific audience. Though they cannot constitute 'true' accounts of a reality, they can be read as finished creations with a political aim (see Clifford 1988). Once we unravel the politics of the multi-layered audience, the language used in the testimonies, and the climate in which they were obtained, and once we incorporate these elements in our critical readings of the texts, I believe, as do Ginzburg and Roper, that these testimonies can be read for insights into the cultural practices, social predicaments, and political and religious fears of both the accused and the interrogators.

## 'Witch hunts'? The cultural dynamics of the Extirpation of Idolatry

Analysis of the various methods and motives used to elicit or proffer testimony allows us to reconsider views of the Extirpation of Idolatries as a 'witch hunt' akin to those which were apparently carried out in northern Europe between the fifteenth and seventeenth centuries. Such analysis also questions the view that colonial Andean culture maintained an immutable 'bone structure' thinly covered by a Christian 'veneer'. Recent studies of the Spanish and Peruvian Inquisition reveal that the 'witch-hunts' and 'witch crazes' never quite happened in the numbers or scope first attributed to them. The absence of a witch craze in Spain was in part due to the fact that Inquisition cases there were tried in ecclesiastical courts and not in civil ones, as in France, where persecutions and burnings were most severe. Another important difference is that the Spanish Inquisition was mainly an urban phenomenon and not a rural one as in northern Europe and Italy (Hsia 1989; Kamen 1985; Levack 1987; Mannarelli 1985; Perry and Cruz 1991; Roper 1994; Sánchez 1991a). Similarly, until recently, studies of religious transformation in Peru, possibly influenced by northern European images of 'witch hunts', have stressed the negative aspects of the Extirpation,[12] often overlooking the transformative or transculturative process that was taking place around it.

When Juana de Mayo informed the Extirpation judge that she had permitted the *mestiza* María de la Cruz to chew coca in her room, she probably did not entertain the possibility that she would end up in jail accused of sorcery.[13] This form of confession or self-accusation was a tactic quite common among indigenous people who hoped to mitigate their 'guilt' and 'punishment' by 'cooperating' with the system (Osorio 1990: 184). Indeed many of the testimonies in the Lima Extirpation trials were reported to be voluntary confessions where no apparent recourse to torture or violence was made. Furthermore, trials were also initiated by women who wished to incriminate other women with whom they had conflictual relationships, usually having to do with sexual and emotional matters.[14] María de la Cruz, an Indian from Huánuco (a highland city east of Lima) , was accused (by the *mestiza* María de Vargas, with whom she had had a long history of conflicts) of being a sorceress and of killing her lover with *maleficios* (evil spells).[15] In Huánuco, María de Vargas had twice lost her lovers to María de la Cruz. María de la Cruz had come to live in Lima, after her community exiled her to Marca (Ancash) for having an illicit affair with one of María de Vargas's lovers. On several occasions the two women had lived together and shared (albeit unwillingly) their men, and, on one such occasion, both Marías ended up pregnant, each having a child by the same man.[16] On her journey from Marca to Lima, María de la Cruz met a man with whom she would live in Lima. This man (no name is given in the testimonies) publicly abused María de la Cruz, both physically and verbally, and when she tried to end the relationship, and expressed a desire to work as a vendor in the local market, he became crazed, prohibiting her from leaving the house.[17] María escaped and sought refuge in several places, going first to the house of her *padrino* or godfather, a man whose surname she did not know (or so she confessed to the Extirpator). After hiding out in different women's rooms (some of whom she apparently did not even know) the paths of these two women crossed again, and when María de la Cruz, battered by her lover, needed a place to hide, María de Vargas suggested that she move into the room next to hers, in the *callejón de la Soledad*.[18] What at first glance looks like an act of sisterly solidarity with a female friend in need of help and protection – as María de Vargas had made it seem – was apparently meant to keep María de la Cruz nearby so that María de Vargas could gather the necessary 'information' she later used to substantiate her accusation before the Extirpator, namely that María de la Cruz was indeed a witch and a sorceress[19]. In many other cases women were reported to have denounced themselves 'to relieve their guilty conscience' because knowing that what they did was punished by the church, they apparently either wanted to prove their good piety, and/or mitigate their punishment, as may have been the case with Juana de Mayo.[20]

Self-incriminations have also been noted by Jorge Klor de Alva (1991) in colonial Mexico. In his essay on the effectiveness of the Mexican Indian Inquisition, Klor de Alva argues that the campaign ultimately failed to convert Mexico's indigenous peoples. Instead, Spanish authorities turned to penitential discipline – promoted by confession and missionaries – to 'colonize' Indian souls, which proved to be a far more effective method than the severe and exemplary punishment of a few Indians by the Holy Office.[21] Following the genealogy proposed by Michael Foucault in *Discipline and Punish* (1979) and *The History of Sexuality* (1990), Klor de Alva sees confessions as an expression of the internalizing of the 'Catholic guilt' characteristic of an advanced state of Catholicism, in other words, as an advanced 'mental discipline' equivalent to a Catholic conscience.[22]

In her recent study of Chancay, Peru (coastal region to the north of Lima), Ana Sánchez (1991b) argues that the Extirpation was a religious project no doubt, but it was also a political 'homogenizing' project that promoted an 'official culture' guided by the ideals and principles of the Counter-Reformation. Kenneth Mills (1994) has shown that the Counter-Reformation religious project of the Extirpation was aimed at relapsed Indians or 'bad Christians' who were thought to have been initially converted in the sixteenth century. By the middle of the seventeenth century, the religious project could entertain political ends: the normative disciplining of a recently invented 'popular culture' now branded as 'uncivilized' and therefore in need of civilizing (see also Pagden 1982). The Counter-Reformation constituted a major epistemological shift on several grounds. First, it was a highly rational movement that sought to transform a disorderly world into a civilized and orderly one by creating new 'civilized' and 'disciplined' subjects through language, mainly through confessions and parish visitations. To achieve this end, the Counter-Reformation church created new (im)moral subjectivities – i.e. the 'fornicator' and the 'sodomite' – at the same time that it sought to eliminate practices considered as uncivilized, and detrimental for this new Catholic society – such as the plethora of patron saints worshipped by European peasants, or the many religious rituals and processions that ended up in 'lewd' acts such as 'fornication' and drunkness (Luria 1991; Nalle 1992; Wright 1982. See also Foucault 1990).

In the case of seventeenth-century Lima, indigenous practices were only one of many cultural identities that the Counter-Reformation church attempted to 'civilize'. This is very clear in the prosecutions carried out in the 1660s by Juan Sarmiento de Vivero, who investigated not only the Indians that were legally under his jurisdiction, but also *mestizo*, Black and Spanish men and women. Sarmiento was clearly interested in eradicating certain cultural practices, such as coca chewing (an Andean practice), but also Iberian practices like using the rope of hanged men to keep the law away.[23] Sarmiento's concern with normalizing cultural practices (as well as religious beliefs) is clear in the language he used to refer to his enterprise.[24] In Peru, this relapsed popular culture implicated revitalized Andean practices and beliefs, but it also targeted non-Andean cultural practices that were attacked with equal fervour on both sides of the Atlantic throughout most of the seventeenth century (see Luria 1991; Nalle 1992). Entertaining the discourses and practices of the Extirpation and the Inquisition as political and normalizing projects (Foucault 1978, 1990) allows us to analyse these institutions not merely as destructive agents, but as generative forces attached to emerging cultures and societies in colonial transformation (see Sawicki 1991).

# Lima's hybrid culture of love magic, sorcery, and healing[25]

Love magic was most often used to entice a man's desire, and the well-known European practice of *ligar* (to 'tie') or *embrujar* (to bewitch) a man was practised in seventeenth-century Lima for the same purpose as it was in Europe (see Sánchez Ortega 1991), that is, for getting a desired man to surrender. The one-eyed *mestiza* Juana Bernarda lived in a rented room, next to the chicken coop, in a *callejón* near Bodegones Street, just off the main plaza. She 'tied' a man for the slave Feliciana Rengifo, who also rented a nearby room, with a spell consisting of the man's hair, a loadstone, silver, and *alagalia* (possibly algalia, a civet bean), wrapped in a piece of cloth from one of his clothing articles. According to Bernarda, the man was '*bien puesto*' (properly set) in the bundle.[26] The *zamba* (person of mixed African and Indian parentage) Josepha de la Encarnación filed suit in 1670 against her ex-lover Carlos de Guevara, for going around claiming that she had him '*embrugiado*' (sic) or bewitched.[27] In her deposition, Josepha accused Carlos of 'faking' being bewitched and insane, as a 'trick' to make his accusations against her credible to the Extirpation judge. She urged the judge to take action against Carlos's accusations, since she claimed they caused her harm and loss of honour. Apparently, Carlos wanted to get even with Josepha for ending their relationship, which she described as 'illicit'. Carlos attributed his love and desire to the effects of a little bundle he had found hidden inside his mattress, and to two coca leaves neatly tied together in a small cloth, arranged like 'a man and a woman', and found on the wall by his bed. The bundle contained one leaf (*higuerilla*), Carlos's hair, a piece of cloth from one of his everyday outfits, dried human faeces, a corn cob, dried quince, a dull pin, and a little snake, all of which was carefully laid out in a piece of paper with dried phlegm or spit.[28] In his testimony, Carlos relates how he tried to leave and forget Josepha by sleeping with other women and seeking potions from different sorceresses. He sought the help of a sorceress from Surco to rid himself of the spell, and when that did not work he sought the remedies of a Spanish sorceress from Chile. In the end nothing worked. He could not remain away from Josepha for very long and every time he saw her again he fell madly under her spell, and assented to her demand that he kiss her behind.[29]

Charges of bewitchment, like Carlos's, were not uncommon. The state of 'being in love,' as well as sexual attraction, was often seen by *limeño* men in a negative light, and was generally attributed to magic spells cast by women. Miguel Cano, one of Juana de Mayo's lovers, had asked her to 'untie' him after their affair ended, because he claimed she had him '*enechisado*' or hexed.[30]

María de la Cruz's lover also accused her of bewitching him, which is why he refused to let her go when she wanted to end the relationship.[31] These men justified their 'blind love' for a woman as the product of an exterior and mysterious force manipulated by the woman who was the object of their desire.

In Lima, women used magic spells – or amulets – and herbal baths to procure the love of a desired man, to rid themselves of the competition, or just for luck and good fortune. The Indian Juana de Mayo, who rented a room on the central street of the *Espíritu Santo*, gave herbal and medicinal baths of mixed European and Andean herbs. She used basil, rue and dill as well as local blue and white corn and the *tapa tapa* medicinal herb to cure a variety of illnesses. The *mestiza* María de la Cruz, a young married woman who had not lived with her husband for several years, had been sick in bed for three years with an (unspecified) illness that had left her '*rota y desnuda*', broken and bare. Juana cured her with a bath made of horse mint, and the *tapa tapa* herb, as well as other herbs that María de la Cruz did not recognize, plus wine, a variety of flowers, apples, and jonquil, which María used to clean her face, arms, thighs and 'private parts'.[32] Juana also gave baths that were guaranteed to bring women success with men. For Aneta, the slave of a nun from the convent of Santa Clara, Juana gave baths of horse mint, peppermint leaves, rue, dill and basil, at the same time that she rubbed Aneta's body with masticated Andean purple and white corn.[33] Aneta had requested the baths because she wanted to sleep with a man, and because she wanted her men to give her money.[34] For good luck, Juana gave Aneta powdered avocado pit mixed with ground *mullu* (a pink sea shell used by the Incas as a form of currency) which Juana put on her neck and face.[35] Juana had used the same powder on the face of Doña Josepha de Araya, a Spanish woman who lived in an upper apartment on Bodegones Street, for luck and good fortune. In compensation Doña Josepha gave Juana a skirt and a shawl.[36] Doña Josepha allegedly went to Juana's house with hurried frequency, to get baths of horse mint, orange leaves, basil and rue, to cure herself of bewitchment.[37] In Spain, spells were concocted of alum and salt, menstrual blood, semen, and pubic hair. In the fabrication of love spells in Lima, Juana de Mayo used a variety of such ingredients, including men's hair, pubic hair, plus Andean ingredients like llama fat, coca, animal-effigy stones, coloured powder, and coloured threads.[38] Juana 'dressed up' a loadstone with pearls, corals, small needles and pins, half a *real*, two white corn kernels, and two blue corn kernels for Doña Josepha, so that she could be loved by men.[39]

Adultery and marital violence were among the most common reasons cited for divorce in seventeenth-century Lima (Flores Galindo and Chocano 1984: 412–15; Lavallé 1986: 449–50). Although in divorce cases these charges were usually brought by women against men, in the Extirpation testimonies women claimed to be using magic to 'appease' their husbands while they carried on extramarital affairs. Juana de Mayo's daughter, María de la Asunción Cano, also known as *La Marota*,[40] had the reputation of 'sleeping around' ('*andar trabiesa con los hombres*'). Her husband Nicolás was privy to her affairs, but never said anything about them thanks to Juana de Mayo's magic. On one occasion when Nicolás found Marota in bed with another man (a young mestizo) he tried to kill them both, but Juana de Mayo sprinkled powdered *mullu* on the 'other man' to protect him from Nicolás's wrath. The magic was so effective that after the incident all three lived together in harmony.[41]

Magic and sorcery were frequently deployed by women who testified before the Extirpation, in most cases to deal with everyday domestic issues, to resolve male/female conflicts, and to tackle social and emotional problems related to illicit sexual relations, adulteries and violence – mostly male on female, although the reverse was not uncommon. Through the practice and consumption of magic and sorcery women attempted to control and sometimes change the world around them. In their attempt to keep men faithful, for example, sorcery was deployed to make partners hate the 'other woman'. Juana prepared a concoction to this end, made up of strong vinegar, salt, hot peppers, unspecified herbs, dog and human excrement, which she boiled and then put in a container which she later crushed on the 'other woman's' door.[42] Magic was also used to prevent and/or stop the physical abuse of partners, as well as to solve domestic conflicts, as in the case of Doña Gerónima, who elicited Juana de Mayo's magic powders to get rid of her husband and in-laws, who had made her life impossible.[43] Juana de Mayo also made amulets to help prevent physical abuse. The little blue bag with *tapa tapa* root, salt, garlic, and a herb (*contrayerba*) that she gave to Ana de

Oserín to wear around her waist would keep her husband from beating her, while some magic powder – to be sprinkled in his food – would make him love her.[44]

Many of the women who used and practised magic and sorcery were either unmarried or widows. The Indian Ana de Oserín, for example, was the widow of Pedro de Oguera, and rented a room from Doña María Contreras, known as *La Manca*, on the street of the *Mármol de Bronce*.[45] She defined herself as a 'good Christian woman', who had married to 'serve God' but had resorted to sorcery in the hopes of ending the physical abuse that her husband had inflicted upon her. After her husband's death Ana saw other men, and when the *mestiza* known as La Camandula found her crying one day because her lover Juan was seeing another woman, Camandula told Ana not to waste her time and energy, urging her to take action. Camandula sent Ana to the nearby port of Callao to gather certain herbs needed to prepare a concoction that would turn Juan into the equivalent of a 'docile puppy'. As Ana ripped the herbs (*hierba del vidrio*) from the soil, she had to repeat that Juan (her lover) was 'a drunk and a pig'.[46] Ana declared to the Extirpator that she never had the courage to use the potions and remedies created by Camandula, rejecting them always at the last minute.[47]

Abortion practices were complementary to love magic, and they were equally transcultural in nature. María de la Cruz, the Indian from Huánuco whom we have already met, was put on trial by the Extirpation's patriarchs, accused of superstition and witchcraft for having in her possession *aguardiente* (strong liquor), wine, coca, a piece of loadstone, and iron shavings. María had become pregnant with a child she did not want, while living with the man she met in her journey from Marca to Lima. Following María de Vargas's accusations against her, María de la Cruz was found by the Extirpation in her room with these ingredients, which she said she had intended to use to cure her morning sickness.[48] María de la Cruz had acquired the ingredients with the help of another Indian woman, Francisca Huailas, to induce miscarriage.[49]

Women everywhere have always practised birth control. Contraceptives as well as abortifacients have been used in the form of suppositories, vaginal douches, and medicinal potions that have changed little throughout the centuries. From ancient times, contraceptives and abortifacients were part of a sophisticated science that reached its highest development – in the form of manuals and treatises describing their use as well as their effects – in Arab medicine in the Islamic world during the Middle Ages (Riddle 1992: ch.12). During the Renaissance much of this knowledge was lost in the West, however, as society moved towards a proto-natalist attitude based on church teachings and ideology. The emphasis of the post-Tridentine church on marriage and sexual intercourse only for procreation meant that contraception and abortion were increasingly seen as detrimental to the moral fabric of society. Thus, by the seventeenth century, much of the information about the properties and uses of herbs for these purposes had disappeared from learned knowledge, being preserved mainly in popular practices (Riddle 1992: 156–7; MacLaren 1990: ch. 5).

In the absence of a well-developed Western medical establishment, popular healing practices were consulted to treat and cure different diseases and illnesses such as *bubas* or syphilis, and to control women's reproductive systems (Quezada 1991). In early modern Europe, many contraceptives and abortifacients were based on sympathetic associations, like the infusions of herbs that did not produce fruits, such as basil. In Hungary, women drank gunpowder dissolved in vinegar because they believed that the fetus would be expelled from the uterus like a bullet. It is also known that European women used beverages made of turpentine, castor oil, quinine, the soaking water of a rusty nail, horseradish tea, ginger tea, ammonia, mustard, gin with iron shavings, magnesium salts, opium, wormwood and rosemary teas as abortifacients (Gordon 1983: 36–8). The loadstone with iron shavings and wine held by the Indian María de la Cruz suggests European origins; the *aguardiente* was probably a local alternative to the use of gin.

We know little about the attitudes of colonial Peruvian society towards abortion. In his suggestive essay on sex and colonialism, Pablo Macera argued that by the end of the eighteenth century abortion had become a form of sexual deviance due to the threat of demographic collapse (1977: 311, 314). If this was also the view held by broad sectors of seventeenth-century society we cannot say, since no detailed studies on the subject have been made.[50] We do know, however, that the post-Tridentine Catholic church was not only opposed to abortion, but also infanticide concealed as accidental suffocation, and the ancient Mediterranean tradition of exposure of unwanted children, or *expósitos*, as well (Wright 1982: 54–5). In seventeenth-century Lima abortion was apparently not illegal, but neither was it condoned. Chroniclers of the period allude to the 'apparent' sterility of the women of Lima, who were often depicted as living licentious life styles without the burdens (and obligations) of bearing children (see Descola 1962; Anónimo 1935). The efficacy of the loadstone as an abortifacient seems to have been well established in seventeenth-century Lima. In María de la Cruz's trial, all male witnesses testified to its efficacy and to its widespread prescription for terminating an unwanted pregnancy or, as they put it, for curing the 'illness' of *mal de madre*. The Spaniard Juan de Ochoa Aranda was emphatic about the effectiveness of the loadstone for curing the *mal de madre*, arguing that he harboured no doubts about its being a 'proven' remedy, since he had seen the women of Huánuco use it and 'be cured by it'.[51] Joseph Mexía, the *Procurador General de los Naturales* or Public Attorney of Indians in the case, also argued that the ingredients found in María de la Cruz's possession – the wine, the loadstone, and the iron shavings – were well known for the cure of her 'condition', thus supporting María's contention that all the ingredients were licit, and therefore should not be taken as evidence for superstition and the practice of witchcraft.[52]

Many of the herbs used as abortifacients like marjoram, thyme, lavender, dill, saffron, and celedonia are emmenagogues (*menstrua provocat*), stimulants of a woman's menstrual period, capable of producing the appearance of an abortion. German women drank teas of lavender, thyme, parsley, marjoram, and oregano leaves; and Tartar, German and French women used the root of the 'worm fern,' also known as the 'prostitute root' (Gordon 1983: 36–8). According to the Spaniard Juan de Ochoa, coca leaves, another ingredient used in Lima to cure the *mal de madre* had, among others, the property of being an emmenagogue since he had seen it used, by Indian as well as Spanish women, 'to induce menstruation in women'.[53]

Coca was not only used in healing practices, but was also an important component of the ritual of invocation, or the sorceress's calling of the devil, or of one of the lesser demons, to obtain instructions or assistance. Invocations were usually part of the love magic ritual of divination (or conjuring) used to acquire secrets. The power and effectiveness of the sorceress depended on her performance of invocations and divinations used to uncover the intentions of the desired man or woman. In Spain, magicians used beans, cards, a sieve, scissors, fire, a rosary, and oranges for their predictions. In Lima, sorceresses used coca leaves and candles. Juana de Mayo, for example, could predict whether a woman's lover was faithful or not by throwing two coca leaves in a dish with water; if the leaves came together, the man was unfaithful, and if they floated apart, her client need not worry.[54] The one-eyed *mestiza* Juana Bernarda made the slave Feliciana Rengifo chew coca so that she could 'hear' the man she desired talk and tell her if and when he was going to leave the other woman he was seeing. The slave Francisca Criolla also had Feliciana chew coca to 'hear' the man's 'voice' tell her he had another lover.[55] Conjurations were also important for getting the desired lover to come to the women and/or leave 'the competition'. In early modern Spain, sorceresses had been known to conjure a man by calling out 'furious you come to me' ('*furioso vienes a mí*'). Francisca Criolla procured Feliciana with a little bundle to put inside her right shoe under the heel and stamp on the floor three times, repeating each time, 'come Lorenzo, come Lorenzo, come Lorenzo', ('*lorenso veni, lorenso veni, lorenso veni*'). Francisca also procured a special water (*agua de fragua*) to throw on the door of the 'other woman' to make her leave Lorenzo. In addition, Francisca spat chewed coca around the hemline of Feliciana's skirt every time she went to Francisca's house, so that Feliciana could win back Lorenzo's love.[56] In Spain, to obtain the love of a suitor one appealed to Santa Marta, to 'wicked' Marta, to Santa Elena, to San Silvestre, and to San Onofre (Sánchez Ortega 1991: 59–61). Sebastiana, a black woman from Quito, also consulted by Feliciana, had her drink wine in the name of Lorenzo and light candles to San Antonio upside down. The woman was able to predict from Feliciana's chewed coca that Lorenzo 'was sure to come to her'.[57] La Camandula could also foretell whether a man was coming back to her client by inspecting chewed coca in her hand. Camandula's powers were apparently transatlantic. She claimed to have made men come back from Spain by saying a prayer to Saint Nicholas.[58]

In Spain conjurations were also made to the sun, the moon, and the stars, the Lame Devil (*el Diablo Cojuelo*), Satan, and Barabbas (Sánchez Ortega 1991: 59). Magic incantations were essential in conjurations, since the sorceress's conviction and force in reciting them was what gave her predictions credibility. When Juana de Mayo conjured coca, in her invocations she alluded to prehispanic figures, calling the '*mama palla linda mia*', adding that in the house of '*cayfas*' lived 'Herod and Pontius Pilate'.[59] Tomasa, a black slave, conjured coca invoking the 'seven' devils, and delineating the physical space of Spanish colonial power by naming the streets adjacent to the main square, where the cathedral, the archbishop's residence, the ecclesiastical chapter, and the public hanging place were all located. For the performance of this ritual Tomasa wore a white cloth over her head 'pretending' to be the *palla* (dancing mistress of the Inca) Chabela, while she sprinkled wine on the coca and curtsied to it. After the conjuring was finished, she put *aguardiente* in a pan on the fire and lit the alcohol so that a flame would shoot upwards.[60] Other women deployed Christian symbols as signs of their powers. Camandula claimed that her powers were derived from a crucifix on her palate. She argued that God had given it to her so that she would always be able to tell people what they needed to know about life. Her powers were such that the Indian woman Ana de Oserín declared that when she looked inside Camandula's mouth she saw the crucifix.[61]

## Some conclusions from the street and the *callejón*: women in colonial culture

Elinor Burkett (1978) suggested that Indian women in colonial Peru were often successful at working the colonial institutions of marriage and domestic service to their own advantage and social betterment, but that they were ultimately manipulated by the criteria and needs of a dominant class of white males, who frustrated their aspirations via the legislation and social practices they prescribed. Irene Silverblatt (1987), on the other hand, argued that rural Indian women rejected Spanish colonialism by making a political decision to revitalize and defend their preconquest culture. It is important to keep in mind that Silverblatt's analysis focused primarily on rural Indian women in the high Andes, while Burkett's is concerned with Indian women in urban Arequipa. In many ways Silverblatt's analysis represents the best work on Andean women within the context of feminist theory in the 1980s and the historiography of resistance, while Burkett's was at the forefront of the historiography of acculturation dominant in the 1970s. This essay, by focusing on the suspect cultural and medicinal practices of marginal women in urban Lima, suggests that cultural exchanges among women of different cultural, racial, and social backgrounds reveal unsuspected processes of transculturation in seventeenth-century Lima.

The indigenous women whose testimonies appear in the trial records analysed in this essay did not flee to the high Andean *puna* (plateau), but migrated instead to the different cities of the viceroyalty, ending up in the capital city of Lima at some point in their journeys. Once in Lima, these women tended to live with other women – and sometimes with men – who were often culturally and racially different. In Lima they shared different cultural practices and beliefs, and in the process transfigured their 'own' cultural practices. Women in seventeenth-century Lima could, under certain circumstances, find themselves 'choosing' among several alternatives to marriage and motherhood. Upper-class women, for example, could enter a convent, or become *beatas* (lay pious women). These Spanish institutions, however, were segregated by race, and usually poor Indian and Black women could enter only as slaves or servants (Lavrín 1986; van Deusen 1994). Poor women, on the other hand, married or unmarried, often entered the labour force as market vendors, sorceresses, small store owners and keepers (*pulperas*), and they often migrated in search of better opportunities (Burkett 1978; Glave 1989; Mannarelli 1985; Silverblatt 1987; Vergara 1997). The women tried by the Extirpation were primarily indigenous, and they worked as healers, midwives, domestic servants, shop vendors of food and alcohol, and in the open markets. Most were unmarried or widows who migrated to Lima alone, in some cases escaping domestic conflicts at home, and in others seeking better fortunes in the city (see also Mannarelli 1985: 143). These women of limited independence could form binding alliances with other women in similar situations,[62] live outside of the 'family' strictly speaking, and in many cases beyond the direct tutelage of a man; some maintained precarious sexual and emotional relationships, few of which were cemented by marriage.[63] Although the colonial church regulated extramarital relationships by declaring the practice of living together (*amancebamiento*) illegal,[64] it remained common practice throughout the colonial period, and for some women it constituted an alternative to Christian marriage. According to their testimonies, these alternative relationships were not free of the 'marital' violence identified by Lavallé (1986), and by Flores Galindo and Chocano (1984) for legally constituted marriages. These relationships were also not free of unexpected (and unwanted) pregnancies. Pregnant women who chose to end their condition, or *mal de madre*, could resort to abortive practices that mixed ancient European and Andean elements. Given the living conditions in the *callejones* these treatments, however, were not always successful nor private. The phenomenon of significant numbers of women living independently was not particular to Lima, however. Ruth Behar (1987) identifies a similar pattern among the women of Mexico City subjected to the Inquisition, a point also observed by Silvia Arrom (1985).[65] But the pattern was not necessarily common to all colonial cities, as the case of the rather smaller city of La Paz on the altiplano of Upper Peru or Bolivia illustrates (Glave 1989; Zulawski 1990).

Although the programme of cultural disciplining promoted by the Counter-Reformation church sought to prohibit the use of 'pagan' elements such as coca, the leaf's use in popular religious rituals and in daily practices on the street was common to all social and racial groups in the city. By the mid-seventeenth century, coca had ceased to be a marker of either an Andean or 'popular' culture; it was now part of Lima's 'local culture',[66] shared by all the social and racial groups in the colonial city. Although the 'witches' and healers of colonial Lima tended to be poor women identified with subaltern groups, their clients included women and men from all of the city's social and racial groups. The multiethnic character of the city's symbolic repertoire was also evident in the minutiae: hybrid arrangements of coca, corn, *mullu* and *huancanquis* or talismans, combined with the use of tobacco, wine, and *aguardiente*; or in divinations, where the ancestral figures of the *Inga* (Inca) and the *palla* were summoned together with God, Saint Martha, Jesus Christ, the devil, Saint Anthony, and Saint Nicholas.

The interior history of Lima's transculturation, and the active role of migrant, urbanized women in the process, reveals a Lima that sits uneasily with historiographical images of a segregated and exclusively Spanish world (see Flores 1991). In the colonial Lima of marginal women, Andean traditions met Iberian and African ones, and the logic behind adopting a new practice as one's own may have been closely related to its efficacy or tactical value in curing or solving an identified social problem.[67] The practices of the indigenous women examined here, and their professed attitudes toward cultural exchange, could be read to support the scenario of 'acculturated' urban indigenous women as described by Burkett for Arequipa. However, these women in Lima appear not to have been so easily manipulated, nor were their practices altogether frustrated by the policies and social discipline dictated by the white male elite which administered the Extirpation campaigns. Some of the women tried by the Extirpation in Lima sought more active solutions to everyday problems than those prescribed by colonial society and the Catholic church for their gender and social group. These women sometimes defied established gender roles, and at other times simply ignored them. Cultural purity and the rejection of 'dominant' patriarchal colonial culture were apparently not issues of great concern to the practitioners or consumers of love magic and sorcery in seventeenth-century Lima. Their cultural practices suggest complex combinations of 'dominant' (i.e. Counter-Reformation Catholic) and 'subaltern' (i.e. Andean, African and Spanish 'popular' practices) elements, revealing that processes of transculturation were at work in colonial Peru, and that marginal women's pivotal role in such processes could be more fluid than either Burkett or Silverblatt have suggested. Transcultural or intercultural practices seem to characterize their at once solitary and marginal, but nevertheless central and generative location in the social and cultural life of colonial Lima.

# NOTES

1    Archival research for this essay was supported by the Helbein Scholarship at New York University, the W. Burghardt Turner Fellowship at SUNY-Stony Brook, and a Fulbright Dissertation Fellowship, and was carried out in 1989–90 and 1995–96 in the Archivo Arzobispal de

Lima (AAL). I wish to thank Mario Ormeño, former director of that archive for his help and courtesy, Melecio Tineo, and the legendary señor Remy for his smiling help; also Kenneth Mills for sharing his good humour (and a few ideas!), Iris Gareis, and Ana Sánchez for her insistence on the importance of the Counter-Reformation. Her views and comments made me reconsider many of my own ideas on the conversion process and 'Andean Catholicism'.

Different versions of this paper were presented to the 1994 Annual Meeting of the American Society for Ethnohistory, held in Tempe, Arizona in November 1991, the I Congreso, 'Mujeres y Género en la Historia del Perú,' held in Lima, Perú in March 1996, and the 1996 Berkshire Conference of Women Historians, held in Chapel Hill, North Carolina in June 1996. I thank participants at those meetings for their comments and suggestions. The New York University Cultural History Seminar provided insightful comments and suggestions in December 1994. I would like to thank Ann Zulawski for reading more drafts of this paper than she probably would like to remember, and for her always generous comments. I owe gratitude as well to Temma Kaplan, Maria Emma Mannarelli, Alejandro Cañeque, Irene Silverblatt, Herman Lebovics, and Nicholas Griffiths. Laura Gutiérrez Arabulú, current director of the Archbishopric Archive, has been of great help in my current research, some of which has seen its way into this paper. And last, but not least, I thank Nicolás Sánchez-Albornoz for encouraging me to follow the paths of these women.

2    For a review article of studies on the early urbanization of Lima and its neighbourhoods, see Panfichi (1995).

3    Several seventeenth-century chroniclers of Lima suggested the multi-ethnic nature of the city, with Indians, Africans and Spaniards living in close proximity to each other. The *Anónimo Judío Portugués*, for example, describes Lima's Indians as 'good scribes, musicians, clothiers and shoemakers' and also depicts an urban situation with different ethnic groups exchanging daily experiences (1935: 48, 63). Guaman Poma also related a city full of 'acculturated' Indians (Guaman Poma de Ayala 1980: 1025/1128[1138]). Other chroniclers such as Josephe and Francisco Mugaburu (1975) ignore Indians altogether in their descriptions of colonial city life.

4    Paul Charney also suggests a sharing of different cultural practices (occupational as well as economic) for male Indians (1988: 9, 11–16). Vergara (1997) makes a similar point in her study of the occupations of Indian women in seventeenth-century Lima.

5    AAL/HI 1668: 7: VI: 46. Citations are from the *Archivo Arzobispal de Lima* (AAL), *Sección Hechicerías e Idolatrías* (HI), and correspond

to the classification current in 1989–90, which has since changed (see Gutiérrez (1992) for new indexation). They correspond to Archive: Section: Year: Bundle: Document: Page.

6   AAL/HI 1668: 7: VI: 46, 28.

7   According to Mary Louise Pratt, 'transculturation' has been used by ethnographers 'to describe how subordinate or marginal groups select and invent from material transmitted to them by a dominant or metropolitan culture' (1992: 6). Transculturation was first coined in the 1940s by Fernando Ortiz, a Cuban sociologist, who proposed the term to replace the 'paired concepts of acculturation and deculturation' used to describe the transference of culture from the metropolis in a reductive fashion (1992: 228, fn. 4).

8   For Ginzburg, both the inquisitor and the ethnographer produced dialogic texts, with an explicit dialogic structure (as in the series of questions and answers that 'punctuate' a trial or the transcript of an interview), or an implicit one, (as in the ethnographic field notes describing a ritual and so on) (1989:159).

9   This format, incidentally, has become an accepted form among historians of the 'New Narrative History', as a method to undermine the authority of the text. See David Samuels' discussion in *Lingua Franca* (1995) of Simon Shama's and John Demo's new historical writing.

10  For a study of the creative transformations undergone by the 'devil', and of the impact of diabolism in Mexican colonial culture, see Cervantes (1994).

11  In the testimonies of the Extirpation of Idolatry trials, the questions posed to the accused during the course of the interrogation were usually tailored around the 'facts' revealed in the previous answers, but also on the facts revealed by those witnesses who wanted to incriminate the accused. As such, many of the Lima cases were initiated by someone who held a grudge against the accused. Thus, the tribunal of the Extirpation of Idolatries seems to have been at once a space for ventilating personal and communal conflicts and a space for church indoctrination. This was also the case in northern European trials, where the Inquisitors relied on the confessions and accusations of neighbours – hence thriving on local conflicts – to locate the witches in the community (Levack 1987: 2, 9 and Roper 1994: 200–6). On the process of constructing sexual, and Catholic, identities through language, see Foucault (1990).

12  See, for examples, Burga (1989), Duviols (1986), MacCormack (1985), and Silverblatt (1987). For a critique, see Estenssoro (1992).

13  AAL/HI 1668 7: VI: 1

14  Brian Levack in his study of the witch-hunt in early modern Europe

argues that women charged with performing *maleficium* were often accused by their neighbours (1987: 9).

15  AAL/HI 1691: 2: XXXII:1.

16  AAL/HI: 1691: 2: XXXII: 13r, 15.

17  AAL/HI 1691: 2: XXXII: 6, 15, 15r, 16, 36, 36r.

18  AAL/HI 1691: 2: XXXII: 13r.

19  AAL 1961: 2: XXXII: 13r, 36r.

20  When sentencing Juana de Mayo, the archbishop of Lima, Pedro de Villágomez, argued that Juana had been a 'good confessant' by coming forward to tell of her sins or guilt (*culpa*) of her own volition. He exorted her to live from then on as a good Christian woman in fear of God, considering also that her time in prison during the duration of the trial had been sufficient punishment (AAL/HI 1668: 7: VI: 63-64).

21  I would suggest that the Inquisition's attempts should not be seen as a 'failure' but rather as one of many different forms used in the conversion process. The move to penitential discipline described by Klor de Alva derived from the Counter-Reformation stress on the importance of individual confession that sought to create new Christian subjects through language, as much as through ritual (and punishment) in the seventeenth century. We should keep in mind as well, that the crown in 1571 prohibited the Inquisition from dealing with Indians, although Klor de Alva finds this an unsatisfactory explanation for the absence of an institutionalized Extirpation in Mexico. Ultimately the slower move to individual confession in Peru and the creation of the Extirpation might have less to do with failures by the church than with political and cultural conjunctures in Peru at the time (Osorio, paper presented to the 'Mesa Verde', Instituto de Estudios Peruanos, 11 April 1996). On confession, see Hsia (1989). On the Counter-Reformation, see Luria (1991), Nalle (1992), and Wright (1982).

22  Ruth Behar (1987) also suggests this in her analysis of the origins of the cases of the Mexican Inquisition, and in her analysis of the language used in the testimonies. This Catholic conscience in seventeenth-century Peruvian Indians has been also suggested by Manuel Burga through an analysis of chaplaincies (1989).

23  See AAL/HI 1669: 7: XIX; also Sánchez 1991a: 39.

24  See especially AAL/HI 1669: 7: XIX: 9.

25  Magic is a power that is activated and controlled by a man or woman. The magician's power is used to produce readily observable, empirical results in the world, and he/she usually acts alone and secretly (Levack 1987: 4–6). In early modern discourse, the practice of harmful black magic was referred to as 'witchcraft', or the performance of harmful deeds by means of some sort of extraordinary, mysterious or su-

pernatural power. This type of magic could include the killing of a
person by piercing a doll made in his/her image, or tying knots in a
piece of leather to cause impotence in a man. These acts were usually
referred to in Latin as *maleficia*, and in English as 'witchcraft'. Sorcery
is the practice of magic by some sort of mechanical process, and is an
acquired skill. It has a broader meaning than *maleficium* because it
can be both harmful and beneficial.

26  AAL/HI 1669: 4: XXXIX: 2, 2r, 3r.
27  AAL/HI 1670: 2: XI: 1.
28  AAL/HI 1670: 2: XI: 1r–3r, 7r, 8.
29  AAL/HI 1670: 2: XI: 7, 7r, 8.
30  AAL/HI 1668: 7: VI: 12.
31  AAL/HI 1691: 2: XXII: 8, 9, 14.
32  AAL/HI 1668: 7: VI: 7, 7r.
33  AAL/HI 1668: 7: VI: 39, 45.
34  AAL/HI 1668: 7: VI: 38r.
35  AAL/HI 1668: 7: VI: 39.
36  AAL/HI 1668: 7: VI: 41.
37  AAL/HI 1668: 7: VI: 6r–7r, 40r.
38  AAL/HI 1668: 7: VI: 11r, 12.
39  AAL/HI 1668: 7: VI: 2r.
40  Marota herself was the product of an adulterous relationship that
    Juana de Mayo had with the Indian barber Miguel Cano (AAL/HI
    1668: 7: VI: 12).
41  AAL/HI 1668: 7: VI: 10, 10r, 11.
42  AAL/HI 1668: 7: VI: 46.
43  AAL/HI 1668: 7: VI: 9.
44  AAL/HI 1668: 7: VI: 45.
45  AAL/HI 1668: 7: VI: 13.
46  AAL/HI 1668: 7: VI: 25r.
47  AAL 1668: 7: VI: 19r, 24, 25r, 26.
48  According to the public attorney, Joseph Mexía, María de la Cruz was
    six months pregnant, and her imprisonment in the ecclesiastical jail
    jeopardized her health (AAL/HI 1691: 2: XXXII: 30).
49  AAL/HI 1691: 2: XXXII: 1, 6.
50  Because Indians paid tribute to the Spanish crown and constituted the
    bulk of the labour force in the viceroyalty, the threat of demographic
    collapse of the Indian population was a crucial concern of the colonial
    state. Since Viceroy Francisco de Toledo's government (1569–81), leg-
    islation had been in place to ensure the preservation and increase of
    the Indian population. Macera's reference to a 'fear' of demographic
    collapse in the eighteenth century might however refer to a possible

fear on the part of the white population about the rising Indian population during that century. This needs to be explored further, particularly the relationship of population trends to the discourses of abortion and sexuality in colonial Peru.

51  AAL/HI 1961: 2: XXXII: 36.
52  AAL/HI 1691: 2: XXXII: 26.
53  AAL/HI 1691: 2: XXXII: 36 y 26.
54  AAL/HI 1668: 7: VI: 8, 13r.
55  AAL/HI 1669: 4: XXXIX: 2-3.
56  AAL/HI 1669: 4: XXXIX: 2r, 3.
57  AAL/HI 1669: 4: XXXIX: 3r, 4, 4r
58  AAL/HI 1668: 7: VI: 27.
59  AAL/HI 1668: 7: VI: 9r.
60  AAL/HI 1668: 7: VI: 18.
61  AAL/HI 1668: 7: VI: 28r, 29.
62  It should be pointed out, however, that while many of these women
    lived alone, their 'circle' of acquaintances included a considerable
    number of people from their places of origin. These women, there-
    fore, did not seem to cut all social ties with the places they migrated
    from, as Glave (1989) finds among the domestic workers of colonial La
    Paz, as does Mannarelli for the non-Indian women tried by the Lima
    Inquisition (1985: 145).
63  According to the *Anónimo Judío Portugués* many women in Lima
    chose to live alone, separated from their husbands, to carry on illicit
    relationships with other men. He also argues that women got divorced
    in order to marry men with a better social and economic position. He
    blames corrupt notaries for making it easy for women to dissolve their
    marriages and, like Poma, sees a lack of moral integrity among the men
    and women of the city, with incest, adultery and illegitimacy being wide-
    spread. He also seems to suggest that not only Indian women were
    involved sexually with Spaniards and Blacks, but also Indian men,
    which is also suggested by Charney (1988; see 1935: 63-4).
64  In the sixteenth century the Council of Trent reinforced the teaching
    of marriage as a sacrament. It decreed that the sacramental ceremony
    in the presence of a priest and witnesses was necessary for a valid
    contract, thus outlawing clandestine marriages as well as common-law
    marriages, which were nevertheless widely practised in many parts of
    Europe up until the seventeenth century (Wright 1982: 54-5). See also
    Hsia (1989), Luria (1991), Nalle (1992), and Seed (1988).
65  This seems also to be the case with healers and sorceresses in early
    modern Spain. See Sánchez Ortega (1991).
66  'Local culture' is a concept used by the anthropologist William Chris-

tian (1981), and refers to cultural practices that are exercised by all social and ethnic groups in a given society and are different from those of the centralized and centralizing church. As such, these 'local' practices cannot be segregated into 'popular' and 'elite' cultures. See also Luria (1991: 8-9).

67 Here I am not arguing for a crude utilitarianism, nor do I mean to imply a rational choice on the part of these women. Rather, the cultural practices that 'survive' or get 'transmitted' seem to 'make sense' or be useful to solve a specific problem to the subjects in question. The space for cultural hybridity in colonial Lima was not limited to these practices, however, as my current research on public civic and religious rituals in seventeenth-century Lima will show.

# Works cited

Anónimo Judío Portugués (seventeenth century) (1935), 'Descripción de Lima'. In Rubén Vargas Ugarte, *Biblioteca Peruana. Manuscritos Peruanos*, Lima: Taller Tipográfico de la Empresa Periodística la Prensa, vol. I: 39-67.

Arrom, Sylvia (1985), *The Women of Mexico City, 1790-1857*, Stanford: Stanford University Press.

Behar, Ruth (1987), 'Sex and Sin, Witchcraft and the Devil in Late-Colonial Mexico', *American Ethnologist* 14(1): 34-54.

Bowser, Frederick (1974), *The African Slave of Colonial Peru, 1524-1650*, Stanford: Stanford University Press.

Burga, Manuel (1989), 'The Triumph of Colonial Christianity in the Central Andes: Guilt, Good Conscience, and Indian Piety'. In Mark D. Szuchman (ed.), *The Middle Period in Latin America. Values and Attitudes in the 17th-19th Centuries*, Boulder & London: Lynne Rienner Publishers.

Burkett, Elinor (1978), 'Indian Women and White Society: The Case of Sixteenth-Century Peru'. In Asunción Lavrín (ed.), *Latin American Women: Historical Perspectives*, Westport C.T.: Greenwood Press.

Cervantes, Fernando (1994), *The Devil in the New World. The Impact of Diabolism in New Spain*, New Haven: Yale University Press.

Charney, Paul (1988), 'El Indio Urbano: un análisis económico y social de la población india de Lima en 1613', *Histórica* XII(1): 5-33.

Christian, William Jr. (1981), *Local Religion in Sixteenth-Century Spain*, Princeton: Princeton University Press.

Clifford, James (1988), *The Predicament of Culture. Twentieth-Century Ethnology, Literature, and Art*, Cambridge, M.A.: Harvard University Press.

Cook, Noble David (1975), 'Les Indies inmigrés à Lima au debut du XVIIe siècle', *Cahiers des Amériques Latines* 13/14.

Descola, Jean (1962), *Daily Life in Colonial Peru, 1710-1820*, London: George Allen and Unwin Ltd.

Durán, María Antonia (1992), 'Lima in 1613: aspectos urbanos'. In *Anuarios de Estudios Americanos* XLIX, Seville: Escuela de Estudios Hispanoamericanos.

Duviols, Pierre (1977), *La destrucción de las religiones andinas*, Mexico: UNAM.

——— (1986), *Cultura Andina y Represión. Procesos y visitas de idolatrías y hechicerías. Cajatambo, siglo XVII*, Cusco: Centro de Estudios Rurales Andinos 'Bartolomé de las Casas'.

Estenssoro Fuchs, Juan Carlos (1992), 'Los bailes de los indios y el proyecto colonial', *Revista Andina* (Cusco) 10(2): 353-404.

Flores Espinoza, Javier F. (1991), 'Hechicería e Idolatría en Lima Colonial (Siglo XVII)'. In Henrique Urbano (ed.), *Poder y Violencia en los Andes*, Cusco: Centros de Estudios Regionales Andinos 'Bartolomé de las Casas'.

Flores Galindo, Alberto and Magdalena Chocano (1984), 'Las Cargas del Sacramento', *Revista Andina* (Cusco) 2(2): 403-23.

Foucault, Michel (1979), *Discipline & Punish. The Birth of the Prison*, New York: Vintage Books.

——— (1990), *The History of Sexuality. An Introduction. Volume I*, New York: Vintage Books.

Glave, Luis Miguel (1989), 'Mujer indígena, trabajo doméstico y cambio social en el siglo XVII (1684)'. In *Trajinantes. Caminos indígenas en la sociedad colonial. Siglos XVI/XVII*, Lima: Instituto de Apoyo Agrario.

Ginzburg, Carlo (1989), 'The Inquisitor as Anthropologist'. In *Clues, Myths, and the Historical Method*, trans. John and Anne C. Tedeschi, Baltimore: The Johns Hopkins University Press.

Gordon, Linda (1983), *Woman's Body, Woman's Right. A Social History of Birth Control in America*, New York: Penguin Books.

Griffiths, Nicholas (1994), '"Inquisition of the Indians?": The Inquisitorial Model and the Repression of Andean Religion in Seventeenth-Century Peru', *Colonial Latin American Historical Review (CLAHR)* 3(1): 19–38.

Guaman Poma de Ayala, Felipe (1980), *Nueva corónica i bven gobierno compvesto por Don Phelipe Gvaman Poma de Aiala*, 3 vols., ed. John Murra, Rolena Adorno and Jorge L. Urioste, Mexico: Siglo Veintiuno XXI and IEP/ Instituto de Estudios Peruanos.

Gutiérrez, Laura (1992), 'Indice de la Sección documental de Hechicerías e Idolatrías del Archivo Arzobispal de Lima'. In Gabriela Ramos and Henrique Urbano (eds), *Catolicismo y Extirpación de Idolatrías. Siglos XVI-XVIII*, Cusco: Centro de Estudios Andinos 'Bartolomé de las Casas'.

Hsia, Ronnie Po-Chia (1989), *Social Discipline in the Reformation. Central Europe 1550-1750*, New York: Routledge.

Kamen, Henry (1985), *Inquisition and Society in the Sixteenth and Seventeenth Centuries*, Bloomington: Indiana University Press.

Klor de Alva, Jorge (1991), 'Colonizing Souls: The Failure of the Indian Inquisition and the Rise of Penitential Discipline'. In Mary E. Perry and Anne J. Cruz (eds), *Cultural Encounters. The Impact of the Inquisition in Spain and the New World*, Berkeley: University of California Press.

Ladurie, Emmanuel Le Roy (1975), *Montaillou, village occitan de 1294 à 1394*, Paris: Gallimard.

Lavallé, Bernard (1986), 'Divorcio y nulidad de matrimonio en Lima (1650–1700). (La desaveniencia conyugal como indicador social)', *Revista Andina* (Cusco) 4(2): 427–64.

Lavrín, Asunción (1986), 'Female Religious'. In Louisa Schell Hoberman and Susan Migden Socolow, (eds), *Cities and Society in Colonial Latin America*, Albuquerque: University of New Mexico Press.

Levack, Brian P. (1987), *The Witch Hunt in Early Modern Europe*, New York: Longman, Inc.

Lowry, Lyn (1989), 'Religiosidad y control social en la colonia: el caso de los indios urbanos de Lima', *Allpanchis* (Cusco) XX(32): 11–42.

Luria, Keith P. (1991), *Territories of Grace. Cultural Change in* the *Seventeenth-Century Diocese of Grenoble*, Berkeley: University of California Press.

MacCormack, Sabine (1985), '"The Heart Has Its Reasons": Predicaments of Missionary Christianity in Early Colonial Peru', *Hispanic American Historical Review* 65(3): 443–66.

Macera, Pablo (1977), 'Sexo y coloniaje'. In *Trabajos de Historia*, vol. 3, Lima: Instituto Nacional de Cultura.

Mannarelli, Maria Emma (1985), 'Inquisición y mujeres: las hechiceras en el Perú durante el siglo XVII', *Revista Andina* (Lima) 3(1): 141–56.

Mills, Kenneth (1994), 'The Limits of Religious Coercion in Mid-Colonial Peru', *Past and Present* 145: 84–121.

Mugaburu, Joseph and Francisco Mugaburu (1975), *Chronicle of Colonial Lima. The Diary of Joseph and Francisco Mugaburu*, translated and edited by Robert Ryal Miller, Oklahoma: University of Oklahoma Press.

Muir, Edward (1995), book review, *The Journal of Modern History* 61: 182–85.

Nalle, Sara Tilghman (1992), *God in La Mancha: Religious Reform and the People of Cuenca, 1500–1650*, Baltimore: The Johns Hopkins University Press.

Osorio, Alejandra (1990), 'Una interpretación sobre la extirpación de idolatrías en el Perú. Otuco, Cajatambo, siglo XVII', *Historia y Cultura* (Lima) 20: 161–99.

(n.d.), 'Poder simbólico y rituales públicos en Lima colonial', Working Paper, forthcoming, Lima: IEP.

Pagden, Anthony (1982), *The Fall of Natural Man. The American Indian and the Origins of Comparative Ethnology*, Cambridge: Cambridge University Press.

Panfichi, Aldo (1995), 'Urbanización temprana de Lima: 1535–1900'. In Aldo Panfichi and Felipe Portocarrero S. (eds), *Mundos Interiores. Lima 1850–1950*, Lima: Universidad del Pacífico.

Perry, Mary Elizabeth and Anne J. Cruz (eds) (1991), *Cultural Encounters. The Impact of the Inquisition in Spain and the New World*, Berkeley: University of California Press.

Pratt, Mary Louise (1992), *Imperial Eyes. Travel Writing and Transculturation*, New York: Routledge.

Quezada, Noemí (1991), 'The Inquisition's Repression of Curanderos'. In Mary E. Perry and Anne J. Cruz (eds), *Cultural*

*Alejandra B. Osorio*

Encounters. The Impact of the Inquisition in Spain and the New World, Berkeley: University of California Press.

Riddle, John M. (1992), *Contraception and Abortion from the Ancient World to the Renaissance*, Cambridge, M.A. and London: Harvard University Press.

Roper, Lyndal (1994), *Oedipus & the Devil. Witchcraft, sexuality and religion in early modern Europe*, New York: Routledge.

Rosaldo, Renato (1986), 'From the Door of His Tent. The Field Worker and the Inquisitor'. In James Clifford and George Marcus (eds), *Writing Culture. The Poetics and Politics of Ethnography*, Berkeley: University of California Press.

Sabean, David Warren (1984), *Power in the Blood: Popular Culture and Village Discourse in Early Modern Germany*, Cambridge: Cambridge University Press.

Samuels, David (1995), 'The Call of Histories. Abandoning Their Charts and Tables, Many Influential Historians are Returning to Narrative. But Can They Write?', *Lingua Franca* May/June.

Sánchez, Ana (1991a) 'Mentalidad popular frente a ideología oficial: El Santo Oficio de Lima y los casos de hechicería (siglo XVII)'. In Henrique Urbano (ed.), *Poder y Violencia en los Andes*. Cusco: Centro de Estudios Regionales Andinos 'Bartolomé de las Casas'.

(1991b), *Amancebados, hechiceros y rebeldes.(Chancay, siglo XVII)*, Lima: Centro de Estudios Regionales Andinos 'Bartolomé de las Casas'..

Sánchez-Albornoz, Nicolás (1988), 'La mita de Lima, magnitud y procedencia', *Histórica* (Lima) XII(2): 193–210.

Sánchez Ortega, María Helena (1991), 'Sorcery and Eroticism in Love Magic'. In Mary E. Perry and Anne J. Cruz (eds), *Cultural Encounters. The Impact of the Inquisition in Spain and the New World*, Berkeley: University of California Press.

Sawicki, Jana (1991), *Disciplining Foucault. Feminism, Power, and the Body*, New York: Routledge.

Seed, Patricia (1988), *To Love, Honor, and Obey in Colonial Mexico: Conflicts Over Marriage Choice, 1574-1821*, Stanford: Stanford University Press.

Silverblatt, Irene (1987), *Moon, Sun, and Witches. Gender Ideologies and Class in Inca and Colonial Peru*, Princeton, N.J.:

Princeton University Press.

van Deusen, Nancy (1994), 'Recogimiento for Women and Girls in Colonial Lima: An Institutional and Cultural Practice', unpublished Ph.D. dissertation, University of Illinois at Urbana.

Vargas Ugarte, Rubén (1935), *Biblioteca Peruana. Manuscritos Peruanos*, Lima: Taller Tipográfico de la Empresa Periodística la Prensa.

Vergara Ormeño, Teresa (1997), 'Migración y trabajo femenino a principios del siglo XVII: el caso de las indias de Lima', *Histórica* (Lima) XXI(1): 135-57.

(1998), 'Tan dulce para España y tan amarga y esprimida para sus naturales', *Dialogos* (Lima), 1, in press.

Wright, A. D. (1982), *The Counter-Reformation. Catholic Europe and the Non-Christian World*, New York: St. Martin's Press.

Zulawski, Ann (1990), 'Social Differentiation, Gender, and Ethnicity: Urban Indian Women in Colonial Bolivia, 1640-1725', *Latin American Research Review* XXV(2): 93-113.

# 9

# Repression and cultural change: the 'Extirpation of Idolatry' in colonial Peru[1]

IRIS GAREIS

## Amerindian religions and the concept of 'idolatry'

From the onset of the Spanish conquest, evangelization in colonial Peru, as elsewhere in Spanish America, was linked to the repression of indigenous religions. In the first decade of the seventeenth century, the so-called 'Extirpation of Idolatry' was established in the archbishopric of Lima in order to eradicate the Andean religions. As suggested by the term 'idolatry' – composed of the word 'idol' which, in this context, means 'false god', and 'latria' signifying 'adoration or worship' – it was assumed that the Amerindians venerated false gods (*Enciclopedia universal* 1925, vol. 28; Metford 1983: 158; *Oxford English Dictionary* 1989, vol. 7). Consequently, the native religions were regarded as false religions that needed to be annihilated by the Spaniards.

In early modern European thought, adoration of 'idols' was considered to be an equivalent of demonolatry; that is, 'adoration of the devil' (*Enciclopedia universal* s.d., vol. 18; *Oxford English Dictionary* 1989, vol. 4). At this time, demonolatry was assumed to be at the core of witchcraft and the origin of the supernatural powers of witches and sorcerers; thus, it was prosecuted as a major crime in several European countries.[2] By establishing a parallel between 'demonolatry' and 'idolatry', the repression of the Amerindian religions could be theoretically justified, since it was assumed that, until the Spaniards arrived, the Americas had been the realm of the devil. 'The father of lies', as the devil was called, deluded the Amerindians, urging them to worship him as a god.[3] At least this was the opinion of several leading missionary theorists and theologians (Ragon 1988: 164ff.). Hence, in Spanish colonial ideology the Andean religions were classified as heresies, which had to be severely punished and completely erased from the minds of the Amerindians.

# The prehistory of the 'Extirpation of Idolatry'

In sixteenth-century Peru, the extirpation of the native religions was also considered a necessary pre-condition for the successful Christianization of the Andeans. Several missionaries, such as the Dominican Francisco de la Cruz, argued that evangelization could only be achieved if the indigenous religions had previously been entirely extirpated. Otherwise, the Dominican predicted that the indigenous priests – apostrophized by the Spaniards as *hechiceros* or 'wizards' – would agitate against evangelization and undo all the success already achieved by the Spanish missionaries. In 1566, Francisco de la Cruz claimed, therefore, in a fervent letter to the Spanish king, that the tribunal of the Inquisition should be installed in Peru and the indigenous population be subject to inquisitorial jurisdiction.[4] In fact Francisco de la Cruz's claim was heard in Spain and with the arrival of the new viceroy of Peru, Francisco de Toledo, in 1569, the 'Tribunal of the Holy Inquisition' was introduced in Peru. The arrival of the Inquisition, however, had fatal consequences for Francisco de la Cruz. Having campaigned for the introduction of this institution, Cruz was to become its first victim (Duviols 1971: 218).

The introduction of the Inquisition to Latin America nevertheless did not immediately change the legal status of the indigenous population, since native Peruvians continued to be exempted from inquisitorial jurisdiction (Gareis 1989: 55, 58). But Francisco de la Cruz had not been the only one to demand that the jurisdiction of the Inquisition should also be extended to the Amerindians. In the 1570s Francisco de Toledo, viceroy of Peru, became the leading figure in the party that advocated the submission of the native Peruvians to the authority of the Inquisition. Over several years he tried to convince the Spanish king to approve his project. Like Francisco de la Cruz, Toledo condemned the activities of the indigenous priests, whom he alleged preached surreptitiously to the Andeans with the intention of recovering their former position in the Andean communities and regaining adherents to the old native religions.[5]

Toledo's efforts to extend inquisitorial jurisdiction over the indigenous population were perhaps not originally motivated by his concern for the Christianization of the Amerindians, but may well have been designed as a means of strengthening the power of the crown. The Spanish Inquisition was one of the pillars of modern absolutism in Spain and could be used as a political tool. One of its purposes was to keep the subjects under religious and ideological control.[6] Throughout the decade-long tenure of his governorship of Peru, Toledo was engaged in forging a powerful absolutist administration and in strengthening royal institutions. The submission of the Amerindians to inquisitorial jurisdiction would have subjected the majority of the Peruvian population to the control of the Inquisition, which was essentially a royal institution. This project thus conveniently coincided with Toledo's efforts to consolidate the power of the crown. In spite of the viceroy's tenacity, he never succeeded in persuading King Philip II of Spain to consent to these plans. At the beginning of the seventeenth century the indigenous population still remained exempt from inquisitorial jurisdiction (Gareis 1989: 58–9).

## The 'Extirpation of Idolatry' as Inquisition for Amerindians

In 1608 the discussion as to whether or not the Amerindians should be subject to the Inquisition was revived by Francisco de Avila. This priest of a Peruvian highland parish claimed that his indigenous parishioners were not Christianized at all but rather went on with their ancient idolatry as if they had never been instructed in the Catholic faith.[7] Over the next few years, Avila's acknowledgement of the limited effect of Christian evangelization of the indigenous people continued to preoccupy colonial Peruvian intellectuals. Some supported Avila's view of the indigenous peoples as only superficially Christianized, secretly continuing to perform their ancient idolatrous rituals; while others persisted in denying that there was any idolatry left in the Andes (Gareis 1989: 68–9, fn. 53, fn. 54).

In time the propagandists of repression were victorious, and the Extirpation of Idolatry was finally institutionalized in the archbishopric of Lima in 1610. Avila was appointed to be the first 'juez visitador de la idolatría', the 'visiting judge of idolatry'. It is worth noting here that Avila was installed as ecclesiastical judge jointly by the archbishop of Lima and the viceroy, by then the Marqués de Montesclaros (Avila [1648] 1918: 76; Duviols 1971: 154). In this particular case the leaders of the ecclesiastical and the civic hierarchy displayed an exceptional harmony. More typical was an uneasy relationship, one flawed by endless quarrels mainly about questions of court etiquette.[8] The fact that the representative of the king and the head of the Peruvian church jointly promoted the Extirpation of Idolatry indicates that both parties had vital interests in this institution: the archbishop wished to maintain his jurisdiction over the indigenous population, a practice that would have been compromised if the Amerindians were subjected to the Inquisition; while the viceroy Marqués de Montesclaros, as well as his successor, the Príncipe de Esquilache, fostered the new institution as a means of controlling the native Peruvians, a means they did not wish to leave to the discretion of the archbishop alone.[9]

Shortly after the installation of Avila as an ecclesiastical judge, other learned priests were appointed as 'visitadores de la idolatría', agents exclusively dedicated to the extirpation of idolatry (Duviols 1971: 154ff., 202ff.; Gareis 1987: 382–3).

## The institutionalized repression of native religions

The institutionalized Extirpation of Idolatry was in fact a substitute for the Inquisition, a kind of 'Inquisition for Amerindians'. Hence, its constituent elements were modelled on the prototype of the Inquisition. The so-called 'visit or visitation of idolatry' was organized in the same way as its inquisitorial counterpart in Spain.[10] This was also the case with the trials against idolaters, the procedures of which were almost identical to inquisitorial procedures, the only difference being that the degree of punishment was less severe in cases against idolaters (Gareis 1993: 288–93). The death penalty was not envisaged for them because the polit-

ical authorities assumed that the Amerindians were still not sufficiently Christianized. Consequently, the Andeans' religious fail-
ings were to be corrected mainly by corporal punishments, such
as lashing. Indigenous priests had to face more severe punishment and were sometimes confined for long periods of deten-
tion as prisoners of the local priest or of a local monastery (Gareis
1987: 378–80, 386).

In 1617, during the government of viceroy Príncipe de Esquilache, a special prison for idolaters was built in Lima. The
'Casa de Santa Cruz', 'the House of the Holy Cross', was in the
custody of the Jesuits who played a prominent role in the early
years of the institution.[11] The convicted Amerindians imprisoned
there were supposed to earn their keep by manufacturing tex-
tiles.[12] In general they had to remain in the prison until they had
demonstrated their conversion to Christianity to the satisfaction
of the authorities. For the majority of the inmates, who were elderly when brought to the prison, this was their last domicile.[13] It
seems, however, that the 'House of the Holy Cross' was not a
secure prison and did not meet the expectations of the authorities. In 1620, soon after its foundation, Father Arriaga, a prominent extirpator of idolatry, complained that many of the prisoners managed to escape.[14] And already in 1639 Antonio de la
Calancha (Lib. III cap. XVIII: 631) stated in his chronicle that
there was nothing left of the prison but the building.[15]

The same building also lodged another institution related to the
overall colonial project of Christianizing and hispanicizing the Peruvian native population. At the time of the prison's construction, a
school for the sons of *curacas* (native headmen), was inaugurated.
Also run by the Jesuits under the special protection of the viceroy
Príncipe de Esquilache, it was a very well-endowed elite school for
Amerindians. Throughout the seventeenth and the eighteenth centuries the native elite, mostly from the coast and neighbouring
highland regions, was trained in the school in order to provide a
link between the indigenous Peruvians and the colonial administration.[16]

The most important activity of the institution of the Extirpation was the 'visit of idolatry', carried out by visitors appointed by
the archbishop of Lima.[17] Though the visitor was an ecclesiastical
judge, he could claim support from the civic institutions for the
prosecution of idolaters and was usually assisted by the local po-

lice authorities. In such a *visita* the ecclesiastical judge would inspect all Amerindian communities of the respective region. He was accompanied by several assistants and a notary or scribe, and in the first half of the seventeenth century he was also accompanied by Jesuits.[18] They were responsible for the spiritual aspects of the *visita*, whereas the visitor general himself was principally engaged in the repression of native religions (Duviols 1971: 202–3). During the time in which the visitor and his assistants were staying in an indigenous community, they had to be supported by the inhabitants.[19] Given the fact that the Spanish assumed that every village harboured idolaters, the visitor general would often remain in a village for a considerable period of time. Long sojourns exacted a heavy economic price from the villagers, and this pressure sometimes yielded suspects (Gareis 1987: 390-2; Mills 1996: 192, 204). Even more distressing than the economic burden must have been the fact that with the arrival of the visitor general an atmosphere of distrust, fear and terror suddenly threatened community life; relationships were likely to break up under the pressure of the visit, especially if hidden tensions already existed between factions of the community.

Take for example the case of Miguel de Menacho, the *curaca* of the Indians of Huamantanga, province of Canta. By June 1696 Menacho decided that the Mercedarians should no longer have access to his Indians as unpaid workers. But the Mercedarians objected and on 29 January 1697 won their case against Menacho.[20] It has to be noted, however, that Menacho may have lost the case due to another lawsuit, which demanded his full attention. In October 1696, shortly after Menacho's refusal to provide the workers to the religious order, he was denounced as an idolater and wizard.[21] The denunciation, it seems, had been launched against Menacho by Juan de Campos, a rival for the office of *curaca*.[22] Campos had tried to replace Menacho as early as July 1695.[23] Due to the gravity of these accusations, Menacho yielded to the Mercedarians' claim and, hence, was not able to pursue the action on behalf of his Indians. At least he was able eventually to rejoice when, in April 1697, he was cleared of the charge of idolatry and reinstated in his office as *curaca*.[24]

The starting point of every visit was the publication of the 'edict against idolatry' that was read out to the Amerindians during holy mass by the visitor general. Roughly speaking, the text invited idolaters to denounce themselves and informers to accuse their fellow villagers. Informers were exempt from punishment and could even be rewarded by temporary exemption from paying tribute.[25] Several days later, after having received anonymous information regarding villagers suspected of idolatry, the ecclesiastical judge would set up his office in the house of the local priest or another dignitary, who was required to collaborate with the visitor general. Then the judge would start to hear testimony and to examine the denounced villagers. After having found some of the suspects guilty, the visitor general would proceed to inspect the places where reportedly native deities were venerated and rituals were usually performed.[26] Images and statues of Andean gods were destroyed, or if this was not possible – for example if an image was carved into a huge stone – then a cross was erected in the same place. Smaller figures, ceremonial garments and so forth were seized, later to be consigned to the flames in a special ceremony. The visit would come to an end with a solemn holy mass, including the absolution of the penitents and the punishment of idolaters. Finally the whole village would move in a procession towards a place where a pyre had been erected to incinerate the religious paraphernalia accumulated during the visit. This ceremony was designed to recall the *autos-da-fe* of the Inquisition and probably made a lasting impression on the Amerindians (Duviols 1971: 222–3; 1986: LXXIV–LXXV). This final *auto-da-fe* must have been terrifying, especially when the Amerindians were compelled to incinerate the mummified bodies of their pagan ancestors, often the remains of parents or near relatives.[27]

The elaborate ceremonial practice of the *auto-da-fe* demonstrates that the Extirpation of Idolatry's principal aim was not merely to punish elderly or stubborn magicians. More important was the desire to extinguish completely the ancient Andean religions by eradicating the native belief systems and by destroying their material expressions: figures of gods, ceremonial costumes, and paraphernalia. Thus, in addition to draining the intellectual resources of the native societies, the Extirpation of Idolatry also resulted in a terrible loss and destruction of cultural goods and artistic artefacts. The ruthless destruction of sacred objects and the incineration of the mummies of the ancestors expressed the contempt in which the indigenous cultures were held by the colonial authorities.

But the visitors themselves were also under great pressure, as the archbishop would not have been satisfied if they had only convicted a few idolaters or destroyed a small number of ceremonial artefacts. In the opinion of the archbishop, evidently, the success of a visitor general of idolatry was measured by the number of convicted individuals and incinerated objects.[28] Consequently, the writings of the visitors reflect these expectations, especially in the first decades after the installation of the Extirpation. The champions of repression were undoubtedly Francisco de Avila, whose complaint of 1608 regarding the hidden paganism of his highland parishioners had initiated the first extirpation campaign, and Fernando de Avendaño, who until the end of his life competed with Avila for political prominence and favours. If at the beginning of the seventeenth century Avila claimed that he had destroyed 800 'ídolos fijos', i.e. immovable shrines such as a rock, and 20 000 smaller idols, then Avendaño, a few years later, boasted of having convicted more than 1000 indigenous priests and incinerated many thousands of idols.[29]

These figures are indeed impressive, especially if one takes into account other visitor generals' writings that enumerate large amounts of destroyed cultural goods.[30] On the basis of these figures, one could assume that the persecution of native religious leaders, in combination with such a ruthless destruction of material goods, caused fundamental changes in Andean societies.

## The Extirpation of Idolatry as a factor of cultural change

Not surprisingly, therefore, several modern scholars regard the institutionalized Extirpation of Idolatry as a major factor of cultural change in the Andes. As early as 1946 George Kubler (1946: 340, 347, 400–3) expressed the opinion that by 1660 the Christianization of the Amerindian population of the Andes had been entirely completed, and that this was due mainly to the campaigns against idolatry carried out during the seventeenth century. According to Kubler, the disciplinary measures executed by the visitor generals of idolatry were successful and fostered the gradual acculturation of the natives into Spanish colonial society. More recently, Manuel Marzal (1977: 110–4; 1988: 55–61, 184ff., 439–

40) has argued along similar lines, emphasizing the eventual success of the extirpation campaigns in the evangelization of the Andeans.

Other scholars, however, differ widely in their assessment of the Extirpation of Idolatry and its effects. The French ethnohistorian Pierre Duviols (1971: 347-9), for instance, doubts that the Christianization of the Andean population was ever fully realized. He believes instead that the campaigns of extirpation led only to a modification of the Andean religions, which persisted tenaciously in spite of the repression. At best, the repressive measures would have contributed to the development of syncretic religious forms. Curatola (1977/78: 149, 160ff., especially 153-64) came to similar conclusions. Wachtel (1971: 236, 239, 241) drew mainly on evidence from sixteenth-century Peru, but at least for this period did not consider that there had been a fusion of the Spanish and Andean religious systems at all. He maintained that there was a coexistence of parallel belief systems each of which remained almost unaffected by the other. Recently, Nicholas Griffiths (1994b: 261-2) expressed the conviction that the so-called 'spiritual conquest' of the Andeans has been overestimated and that it failed to bring about the Christianization of the Amerindian peoples.

In short, one group of scholars ascribes a high degree of efficiency to the institutionalized Extirpation of Idolatry, whereas others deny it had major consequences at all. In view of these divergent interpretations, the question necessarily must be posed: how was it possible to arrive at such differing conclusions? An answer might be suggested if we consider the documentation which has been used. In older works, especially, emphasis was laid on published sources and on official writings, such as the records of the visits of idolatry (generally drafted by the visitors in order to be rewarded for their services). Not surprisingly, the ecclesiastical judges and other prominent figures of the institutionalized extirpation emphasized their successes: they stressed the large number of absolved idolaters and of destroyed ceremonial objects.[31] But they did not discuss the actual consequences of the destruction. Therefore, these historical sources can tell us, at best, only something about the history of repression but they provide almost nothing about the reaction of the native population.[32] Consequently, interpreters of the Extirpation of Idolatry have often turned to probability and conjecture in accounting for the outcome of the repression.

In the present context, such conjecture may be misleading, as the example of a mid sixteenth-century account by an Augustinian friar from northern Peru shows.[33] In this text the author reported that the Augustinian friars destroyed the figure of an important pre-Columbian deity; thereby, the friars believed, the veneration of this god would also be extinguished. Shortly afterwards an Andean woman happened to find a stone in the field, which subsequently was identified by a diviner as a son of the god whose representation had been destroyed. Thereafter, the sons of this deity proliferated at an incredible rate, until the adoration of the seemingly eradicated god was introduced even into remote regions where it possibly had not been worshipped in former times.

There is evidence that the same phenomenon of proliferation of deities following the destruction of their shrines also took place in the adjacent north Peruvian province of Cajatambo. In the early seventeenth century, shrines were discovered in many villages in which goddesses were venerated. They were thought to be 'daughters' of one statue representing a deity which had been destroyed by a missionary long ago (Gareis 1987: 212, fn. 2). In 1620, during a campaign to extirpate idolatry in the same Peruvian highland province, the visitor general Fernando de Avendaño destroyed several representations of local gods. Thirty years later, when Bernardo de Noboa, another visitor general, came to the region, he stated that instead of the five figures of Andean gods destroyed by Avendaño he found ten representations in the same place (Duviols 1986: 11, 15, 121).

This means that the repressive measures taken against the indigenous religions did not always extinguish them, but sometimes led to processes of cultural change, which differed completely from the expectations of those who had initiated the repression.

# The impact of the Extirpation of Idolatry on two Andean regions

As the foregoing examples have shown, to find out about the processes of cultural change that took place as a consequence of religious repression, it is necessary to review the available information thoroughly by drawing on different kinds of historical sources. Furthermore, the history of repression must be studied in each region separately, thereby avoiding mingling of data from areas with different historical backgrounds, each with distinctive local variations. With respect to religious repression, two Peruvian regions are particularly informative: the colonial provinces of Huarochirí in the central highlands, and Cajatambo in the northern highlands.

As mentioned above, Huarochirí was the place where 'idolatry' was first detected by Francisco de Avila. In later writings Avila stated that he had been informed of the persistence of native religions by some of his parishioners. Avila astutely used these denunciations and finally managed to induce many villagers to accuse themselves as idolaters and to surrender their religious paraphernalia. When a native priestess died suddenly, an event which Avila ascribed to heavenly intervention, his parishioners hurried to surrender 200 ceremonial objects within a few hours (Avila 1918 [1648]: 63–4, 67–71). Avila's comprehensive account of these events and of the ensuing visit of idolatry make it look as if the indigenous religions were completely eradicated in the province of Huarochirí.

Almost fifty years after Avila's extirpation campaign, in 1660, Sarmiento de Vivero came to Huarochirí to conduct another visit of idolatry.[34] In contrast to Avila, who – as was mentioned before – in the early years as a visitor general of idolatry destroyed 18 000 smaller and 2000 fixed 'idols', Sarmiento was far less successful in detecting idolatries.[35] In a visit that lasted for more than five months, he found only thirty-two little drums, thirty ceremonial goblets (*kero*), seventeen ceremonial garments, two medicine bundles, a few silver trumpets and some mummies. Whereas Avila apprehended several important indigenous priests, most of the thirty-two individuals convicted by Sarmiento were healers and diviners whose activities were mostly confined to the private sphere.[36]

The difference between the results of the two visits might be interpreted as the success of the Extirpation of Idolatry in Huarochirí. However, Sarmiento himself stated that even in this region where the adherents of the native religions had been persecuted during repeated visits of idolatry, the Andean religions had not been completely eradicated.[37] Several of the shrines devastated by Avila in 1610 were, fifty years later, still worshipped by the Andeans. When Sarmiento visited the shrines of the supposedly eradicated gods he found traces of sacrifices everywhere.[38] The persistence of the native religions and the fact that Sarmiento met with fierce resistance from the majority of the local authorities suggest that the poor results of Sarmiento's visit may be due to the refined strategies of the native population, which had learned how to hide their actual beliefs and religious practices in order to survive the extirpation policy.[39]

The institutionalized extirpation campaigns weakened the indigenous religions of Huarochirí nevertheless. In particular, the great religious ceremonies celebrated in pre-Columbian times in honour of the local deities could no longer be performed. These ceremonies had been in former times at the core of ethnic solidarity, since all the villages gathered for the celebration and were united in worshipping the most important deities of the region. These great public ceremonies not only offered an excellent opportunity to strengthen the ties within the ethnic group, but they also enabled the renewal of the bonds between humans and gods. When as a consequence of the repression these public festivities disappeared, the solidarity of the ethnic group could no longer be sustained. The fact that indigenous religious activities could only be carried out secretly and in privacy soon dispossessed the native religions of their former social functions.

As in Huarochirí, so too in the north Peruvian province of Cajatambo, several visits of idolatry were carried out during the seventeenth century. The first one took place from 1617 to 1622 and a second great extirpation campaign was conducted from 1656 to 1663 by Bernardo de Noboa (Duviols 1986).

In the same way as in Huarochirí, the destruction of the Andean shrines in Cajatambo did not eradicate the veneration of the deities. As mentioned before, the destruction of some of the religious centres by the extirpators even increased the number of adherents through initiating new cults in minor local shrines for the spiritual offspring of the deity, imagined as 'sons' or 'daughters' of the god or goddess. Although this strategy ensured the continuity of the Andean cults in Cajatambo, it led nevertheless to their modification (Gareis 1991b). It must also be noted that the incineration of the most important deities of the region afflicted the inhabitants of Cajatambo so much that they expressed their sorrows in their prayers to these native deities (Duviols 1986: 11; Gareis 1991a: 249–50).

A characteristic trait of the native religions in Cajatambo seems to have been the adoration of the mummies of ancestors. They were called *mallqui* and it was assumed that they had an influence on the fertility of crops (Duviols 1986: 63ff, 72–3, 87, 90, 92, 100). During the visits of idolatry, therefore, the villagers and the visitor general engaged in a fierce struggle for the mummified bodies of the ancestors.

The records of the second visit to Cajatambo by Bernardo de Noboa show that in many cases the indigenous population had succeeded in hiding their ancestors' mummies when in 1620 the first visitor general, Fernando de Avendaño, had been hunting idolaters in the region. In one village, for instance, 2000 mummified bodies were saved by collecting money to bribe Avendaño's assistant (Duviols 1986: 53, 80). Another case reported by Noboa notes that shortly before the visitor general Felipe de Medina came to the Andean community, the villagers buried the mummies in the churchyard, as he required. When Medina ordered the graves to be opened, he found the bodies. He then left the community, pleased with what he had seen and what he believed to be proof of a successful evangelization. Immediately after the visitor general's departure, the villagers restored the mummies to their shrines, where they were found twenty years later by Bernardo de Noboa (Duviols 1986: 14).

The documentation of the visits of Huarochirí and Cajatambo indicates a different historical development in these regions. Towards 1660, the indigenous religions of Huarochirí seem to have been only a poor copy of what they had been in pre-Columbian times. They still persisted but in a hidden, shadow-like existence, whereas the native religions of Cajatambo manifested a greater vitality, especially with regard to the ceremonial life of the community.

# Conclusions

As the brief comparison of the impact caused by the Extirpation of Idolatry in two different Andean regions suggests, the repression was less successful in Cajatambo than in Huarochirí. In the latter province, public ceremonial life, once so important in the constitution of the ethnic group, seemed to have been almost extinguished by the second half of the seventeenth century. In contrast, the great public rituals were still collectively performed in Cajatambo. One of the reasons to account for this variation may be the comparatively short distance of Huarochirí from the capital of colonial Peru, while the inhabitants of the more distant province of Cajatambo, it seems, were under less pressure from colonial control.

Notwithstanding the fact that the Extirpation of Idolatry did not succeed in either region in exterminating the indigenous religions, it nevertheless was partially successful in Huarochirí. There, public religious life was seriously threatened by the repression and eventually passed to a shadowy, underground existence. Religious practice shifted from the collective performance of great festivities to the private sphere, and the persistent veneration of the local deities was confined to the nuclear sociopolitical units (*ayllus*). The break-up of the great regional cults in the province of Huarochirí deprived the indigenous religion of serving an important social function, which consisted in reaffirming the cohesion of the ethnic group by the collective adoration of the regional deities.[40] Thus, the persecution weakened the native religions on the sociopolitical level.

In addition, it may be supposed that the changed conditions of worshipping native numina also fostered religious syncretism. To avoid persecution as idolaters, the practitioners of indigenous cults had to act in complete secrecy. As a widespread strategy for the continued practice of native religions while evading repression, the figures of Andean gods were hidden in the statues of Catholic saints (Arriaga [1621] 1968: cap. VIII: 223; Gareis 1987: 395-7). At first, this procedure enabled the Andeans to worship their own deities safely while visiting the church. In the course of time, however, such a religious practice might well have induced processes of transformation, which eventually resulted in the emergence of syncretistic beliefs. It is quite reasonable to assume that the adoration of a native deity, whose representation was enclosed in the figure of a Catholic saint, would have gradually led to a fusion of the two entities in the indigenous belief systems. This accounts for the great importance Catholic saints achieved in native religiosity. St. James, for example, became almost synonymous with the old Andean thunder god, as his characteristic traits merged with those of the pre-Columbian thunder deity. This saint is still venerated today by the native population of the Andes, at least in part because he is believed to command natural phenomena like thunder and lightning.[41]

At present it is premature to draw any general conclusions concerning the impact of the Extirpation of Idolatry. Yet it is intriguing to recognize that this powerful machine of extirpation failed to achieve its aim of eradicating the Andean religions, even in a region so near the capital of Peru as Huarochirí. It seems reasonable to assume, therefore, that there were even greater difficulties in eradicating the native religions in more distant regions of the Andes. Moreover, not all the measures employed by the extirpators were efficient, because the indigenous population could not be moulded at will by the extirpators. Contrary to the self-congratulatory tone of the writings of the extirpators, they did not generally succeed in imposing Catholicism on the Andeans as the sole religion. It is therefore necessary to complement the more official texts with other documents, such as records from trials, diaries of the extirpation visits, and so forth. A review of a variety of historical sources makes it clear that the image of the native population as the passive, child-like populace postulated by the colonial authorities cannot be sustained. On the contrary, Andean societies proved to be historical agents in their own right as they continued to develop new strategies in order to resist the repression, and responded in quite different ways to the extirpation policy.[42]

All this indicates that the institutionalized Extirpation of Idolatry did not correspond to the expectations of the colonial authorities. In so far as the Extirpation of Idolatry had been designed to serve as an almost perfect means of controlling the indigenous population, the institution must be considered a failure. Yet, it should be taken into account that the Extirpation had not been the only institution dedicated to the disciplining and hispanicization of the native population. Together with other parallel endeavours to colonialize the Amerindians, the effects of the extirpation campaigns may well have proved more effective. In fact, the Extirpation of Idolatry in some cases initiated processes of cultural change as a reaction to the repressive measures. However, on the whole, the impact of the Extirpation of Idolatry was far less impressive than has been assumed, and it certainly did not succeed in transforming the Andean societies into disciplined and submissive subjects of the colonial authorities.

# Notes

1    This article is based on a lecture delivered at the Department of Sociology, University of Essex, Colchester. I would like to thank colleagues at Colchester, especially Dr Andrew Canessa, for the opportunity to discuss my work. I am indebted to Dr Robin Skeates, School of World Art Studies and Museology, University of East Anglia, Norwich, and to Dr Lisa DeLeonardis, Center for Advanced Study in the Visual Arts, National Gallery of Art, Washington, for reading the manuscript and for their comments.

2    In Castile, witchcraft and sorcery came to be regarded as heresy by the end of the fourteenth century. This opinion persisted throughout the sixteenth and seventeenth centuries, when witchcraft and sorcery were generally considered a crime involving heretical practices (Kamen 1987: 238-40). The relationship between witchcraft or sorcery and demonolatry was established by numerous treatises from the late fifteenth through the seventeenth centuries, as for example in the book by Nicolas Remy (1530-1612) entitled 'Daemonolatreiae...', first published in 1595 (Bibliotheca Lamiarvm 1994: 164-5).

3    *Relación de la religión* ([c. 1560] 1992: 17). All translations in this article are those of the author.

4    Francisco de la Cruz to the Spanish King, Lima, 25 January 1566 <AGI, Audiencia de Lima (subsequently quoted as 'Lima'): 313>.

5    The viceroy insisted on this subject in his official correspondence to the king, as for example in the following letters: Cusco, 25 March 1571, AGI, Lima 28 A, n. 49, lib. II: 29, 42-42v; Cusco, 24 September 1572 <AGI, Lima 28 B, lib. IV (at present No. 2): 345v>; La Plata, 3 June 1573 <AGI, Lima 29, lib. I: 134-134v>; La Plata, 20 March 1574 <AGI, Lima 29, lib. I: 44>. With respect to this particular topic see also 'Libro de la visita general...' (1924: 174, 179-81), and Gareis (1987: 380-2; 1989: 57-9).

6    On the Spanish Inquisition as an instrument of social control, see Bennassar (1979: 373ff., 389ff.) and Escandell Bonet (1987: 665-7, 669-72).

7    Francisco de Avila to the king, Los Reyes <i.e. Lima> 30 April 1610 <AGI, Lima 325: 1>; Avila [1648] 1918: 63-4. On the background of Avila's appeal to the colonial authorities, see Duviols (1971: 149-50,

*Iris Gareis*

174–5) and Acosta (1979: 5, 10ff.; 1987: 571ff., especially 584–5).

8   Pérez Cantó (1984a: 983; 1984b: 1137–8) reports that the reason for disputes between the viceroy, the archbishop, and the officials of the Inquisition was often related to their respective areas of authority and competence. Thus, a political decision like the further exemption of the Amerindians from the Inquisition and the installation of the institution of the Extirpation of Idolatry could well have been influenced by the current relations of the colonial authorities with each other.

9   The great importance ascribed to the new institution by the colonial authorities is reflected in the correspondence of the subsequent viceroys and the archbishop with the king. All of them emphasized their own leading role in institutionalizing the 'Extirpation of Idolatry' (The Marqués de Montesclaros to the king, Callao 30 March 1610 <AGI, Lima 35, n. 35, lib. III: 119v>; Príncipe de Esquilache (1615–20), 'Despachos que el Exmo. Señor Príncipe de Esquilache . . . embió a S. M. en los años 1615, 616, 617, 618, 619 y 620.' <BN/M Mss. 2351, Lima 27 March 1619: 392r>, and the archbishop of Lima to the king, Lima 9 March 1617 <AGI, Lima 301>).

10  See Duviols (1971: 221–4; 1986: LXXIIIff.); Gareis (1989: 62ff.; 1990: 625); Griffiths (1994a: 19–22). On the visits of the Inquisition in Spain, see Bennassar (1979: 58ff.).

11  The archbishop to the king, Lima 9 March 1617 <AGI, Lima 301>; the viceroy to the king, Callao 5 March 1614 <AGI, Lima 36, n. 20, lib. VII: 38–38v>. The building was finished in April 1618 (The archbishop to the king, Lima 8 April 1618 <AGI, Lima 301: 1>). For further details on the establishment of this institution see Gareis (1987: 386–9; 1989: 60–2).

12  'Acuerdo que se hizo para ver la forma que convenía tomar para el sustento de la gente que está en las casas que se fundaron en el Cercado', 2 April 1619 <AGI, Lima 38, n. 2, lib. IV: 388–391v, 388v, 389v–390>.

13  Arriaga [1621] 1968: cap. XVIII: 260–1; the archbishop to the king, Lima 15 April 1619 <AGI, Lima 301: 1; id. to the king, Lima 6 April 1621 <AGI, Lima 301: 1v>: 'los juezes/ que de la ydolatria acauan de venir ahora/ an traido algunos yndios dogmatistas y/ saçerdotes que se an puesto en la carçel perpetua/ del Çercado que mientras los tales viuieren/ no se acauara'.

14  Pablo Joseph de Arriaga, Memorial presentado al V. Principe de Esquilache, 1620, in: Copia de títulos de Alonso Osorio, 1640 <AGI, Lima 331>.

15  Only a few years earlier, in 1621, Arriaga [1621] (1968: cap. XVIII, 260) had reported that forty prisoners were under arrest in the 'House

of the Holy Cross'.

16  Esquilache, Despachos 1615-20: 323v (see note 9); Joan de Frías Herrán <the provincial of the Jesuits> to the king, Cusco 9 February 1621 <AGI, Lima 328>; Extracto de los Instrumentos de Fundación, Lima 31 August 1776 <AHN, Jesuitas, Leg. 127, N° 38-39>. On the institutional history of the school, see Cárdenas Ayaipoma (1975/76).

17  In 1621, the first manual for extirpators by the Jesuit Joseph de Arriaga (1968: cap. XIII-XVII, 243-59) was published. Arriaga set out detailed instructions for a model *visita*. Summaries and additional information are provided by Duviols (1971: 203ff.) and Gareis (1987: 382-93).

18  After 1651 the Jesuits declined to take further part in the visits of extirpation, as the archbishop of Lima repeatedly complained in his letters to the king: Lima 20 August 1651; 16 August 1652; 28 August 1654 <AGI, Lima 303>; Lima 10 August 1658 <AGI, Lima 59: 3>.

19  'Acuerdo que se hizo', 1619: 390v, see note 12; Arriaga ([1621] 1968: cap. XIV, 246); the viceroy to the king, Lima 19 April 1618 <AGI, Lima 38, n. 1, lib. III: 140v-141. See also Arriaga's 'Memorial' and the subsequent order (1 June 1620) of the viceroy Francisco de Borja, Príncipe de Esquilache, (Romero 1923: 77), as well as Borja, 10 April 1621 (1953: 222).

20  'Autos seguidos por Fr. Simón Alvarez de Acuña, Procurador general de Corte de la Provincia mercedaria del Perú, contra don Miguel Menacho, Cacique principal y Gobernador del pueblo de Huamantanga en la provincia de Canta, sobre que le enterase el número de indios de mita, que por provisiones reales correspondían a las estancias denominadas Guasca, Pucpus y Cuio, que eran propias de la orden: fs. 12 (in reality fs. 18) <AGN, Derecho Indígena Leg. 11 C. 117: 1, 18>.

21  'Causa criminal que se sigue contra don Miguel Menacho y don Juan de Guzmán caciques principales del repartimiento de Guamantanga.' Huamantanga 1696: 56 <Archivo Arzobispal de Lima, Idolatrías y Hechicerías (hereinafter IH) 2:XXXIII: 4vff.>. All documents from the section 'Idolatrías y Hechicerías' of the archives of the Archbishopric of Lima are quoted according to the catalogue by Huertas Vallejos (1981).

22  'Causa criminal...': 1r.

23  'Por las preguntas siguientes se examinen los testigos que fueren presentados por parte de Dn. Juan de Campos Vilcatapayo, Principal del pueblo de San Pedro de Quipán del repartimiento de Huamantanga, provincia de Canta en los autos que sigue con D. Juan de Humán y D. n Miguel Menacho sobre el cacicazgo de dicho repartimiento.' Lima 3

August 1695: 2 <BN/P, B 1400>.

24   'Causa criminal. . .': 53v–54. There are many other examples of how denunciations of idolatry were used to get rid of personal enemies or to eliminate political rivals. For more references see Gareis (1993: 285, fn. 12), Griffiths (1994a: 24–6), and Millones (1978; 1979; 1987).

25   In 1617, a judicial decree by the archbishop of Lima (Romero 1923: 75) assured that those who informed against idolaters would be exempt from paying tribute for two years. These tributes had to be paid by the individuals who were found guilty of idolatry. For comparisons between the 'edict against idolatry' and other similar texts, see Duviols (1971: 222, fn. 122); and on the negative effects of the denunciations on the social life in the Amerindian communities, see Gareis (1989: 63; 1993: 284–5).

26   For a detailed examination of the trials against idolaters and a critique of this source material, see my articles (Gareis 1989: 64–6; 1993).

27   Duviols (1986: LXXV). Even today, it is striking to read a quotation related to the incineration of mummies from the report of an extirpator (Duviols 1971: 209): 'Le gouverneur en exercice était justement le descendant de ceux qu'on allait brûler; nous l'avons persuadé de mettre lui-même le feu à son père, à sa mère, à ses aieux. Quoiqu'il y répugnât, il fit un effort.' 'The *curaca* was precisely a descendant of those [mummies] which were to be burned; we persuaded him to set fire to his father, to his mother, and to his ancestors. Though he was reluctant to do so, he made an effort.' (My translation from the French quotation).

28   These expectations are clearly expressed in a letter the archbishop of Lima sent in 1652 to the king. He complained of a recent visit of idolatry, in which far fewer superstitions and idolaters were detected than he had expected (Lima 16 August 1652 <AGI, Lima 303: 1v>).

29   Francisco de Avila, Información de servicios 1607–1613 <AGI, Lima 326>, s. fol., quotation in f. 1; Fernando de Avendaño, Información de servicios 1619–1620 <AGI, Lima 327>, s. fol., quotation in f. 2v.

30   It has been pointed out that during the first years of extirpation alone 28 893 individuals were absolved from the charge of idolatry, whereas 1618 Andeans were condemned as indigenous priests. Additionally the extirpators detected 1769 'principal' shrines, 7288 'dioses penates' (family shrines) and 1365 mummies ('Relación de los medios que se an puesto para la extirpación de la ydolatria', s. d., 1619 <AGI, Lima 38, n. 2, lib. IV: 392–397>). This document was published almost simultaneously by Duviols (1967) and Pease (1968).

31   Caro Baroja (1974: 217–18) has pointed out that the judges of the Spanish Inquisition likewise inflated the numbers of convicted witches

and wizards when submitting their accounts.

32    Contreras and Henningsen (1986: 122–3) draw attention to other possible traps inherent in the historical documentation. They claim that it would be misleading, for example, to ascribe the decline of inquisitorial trials in Spain after 1614 exclusively to the success of a sixteenth-century evangelization campaign.

33    *Relación de la religión* [c. 1560] (1992). For the following discussion, see Gareis (1987: 210–12; 1991b: 116–18).

34    For the period of time between these two visits, the record of only one trial against an idolater can be located: 'Causa criminal contra Isabel Guanay hermana de Juan Aucañaupa cacique de Huarochirí, por hechicera.' Huarochirí 1642: 5, at present there are only Fs. 2 <AAL, IH Leg. 2 Exp. VIII>.

35    According to his 'Petición para nueva ynformaçion de nuevos méritos...' <AGI, Lima 326: 27>, it seems that Avila located the majority of these idols in the province of Huarochirí.

36    'Fallo sobre varias personas', Huarochirí 1660. Fs. 6 <AAL, IH Leg. 2 Exp. XVI: 1–3v, 4–5v>.

37    There had been another visit of idolatry in the 1650s. In 1653 or 1654, Diego Barreto was appointed by the archbishop of Lima as visitor general of idolatry for the province of Huarochirí (The archbishop of Lima to the king, Lima 22 July 1657 <AGI, Lima 303>). Unfortunately, no documents of his activities as an extirpator of idolatry have been preserved other than brief details in the correspondence of the archbishop with the king. In a letter dated 29 August 1658, he noted for instance that Barreto had taken away from the Indians many idols and that he had installed a prison in which to confine the 'idolaters-wizards and other pernicious elements' <AGI, Lima 303>.

38    'Memoria que hace una india temerosa de los castigos de dios, sobre actividades de los indios e indias hechiceras.' San Lorenzo de Quinti 1660. Fs. 6 <AAL, IH 3:I: 2, 3v, 5–6>.

39    Several documents refer to the discussion among the Andeans on whether or not they should yield to the visitor general. A lively report of these discussions is to be found in 'Causa criminal por querella del Fiscal de la Visita contra el licenciado Juan Bernabé de la Madris, Melchor Lumbria y doña Francisca Melchora mestiza del pueblo de Huarochirí.' San Lorenzo de Quinti 1660. Fs. 21 <AAL, IH 4:XXXI-II: 1r, 2v, 4, 6, 9, 11–11v>. For more bibliographical references on this subject, see my forthcoming article (Gareis, Extirpación). A discussion of these events is also provided in Mills (1996: 204).

40    The factionalizing effects resulting from Spanish colonization have been also pointed out by Spalding (1984: 299) for the province of

Huarochirí and by Gibson (1964: 403) for the Aztecs of Mexico.

41  For the introduction and importance of the saints in colonial Peru, see Marzal (1988: 184, 203ff.) and Gonzales Martínez (1987: 47ff.).

42  Similarly, Rummel (1986: 52–3) maintained that some scholars of early modern European witch-hunts assigned a far too passive role to those who were affected by the persecution. Thus, they were only seen as objects who suffered history, but not as subjects who lived it. See also Mills (1996) for processes of cultural change ensuing from mid-colonial extirpation campaigns.

## Works cited

AAL         Archivo Arzobispal de Lima.
AGI   Archivo General de Indias, Seville.
AHN         Archivo Histórico Nacional, Madrid.
BN/M        Biblioteca Nacional, Madrid.
BN/P        Biblioteca Nacional del Perú, Lima.

Acosta, A. (1979), 'El pleito de los indios de San Damián (Huarochirí) contra Francisco de Avila 1607', *Historiografía y Bibliografía americanistas* 23: 3–31.

(1987), 'Francisco de Avila'. In Gerald Taylor, *Ritos y tradiciones de Huarochirí. Manuscrito quechua de comienzos del siglo XVII* (Historia Andina 12), Lima: Instituto de Estudios Peruanos and Institut Français d'Etudes Andines.

Arriaga, Joseph de ([1621], 1968), *Extirpación de la idolatría del Perú*, (Biblioteca de autores españoles 209), Madrid: Atlas.

Avila, Francisco de ([1648], 1918), 'Prefación al libro de los sermones, o homilías en la lengua castellana y la índica general quechua, 1648'. In *Colección de libros y documentos referentes a la historia del Perú* XI, Lima: Sanmartí.

Bennassar, Bartolomé (1979), *L'Inquisition Espagnole XV^e-XIX^e siècle*, Paris: Hachette.

*Bibliotheca Lamiarvm. Documenti e immagini della stregoneria dal Medioevo all'Età Moderna* (1994), Biblioteca Universitaria di Pisa, Pisa: Pacini.

Borja, F. de ([1621], 1953), 'Extirpación de idolatrías', *Revista del Archivo Histórico* (Cusco) 4(4): 221–2.

Calancha, Antonio de la ([1638], 1639), *Coronica/ Moralizada/ del orden de/ San Augvstin en el/ Perv, con svcesos/ egen-*

*plares vistos en esta/ monarqvia*, Barcelona: Pedro Lacavallería.

Cardenas Ayaipoma, M. (1975/76), 'El Colegio de Cáciques y el sometimiento ideológico de los residuos de la nobleza aborigen', *Revista del Archivo General de la Nación* (Lima) 4/5: 5-24.

Caro Baroja, Julio (1974), *Inquisición, brujería y criptojudaísmo*, 3rd edn, Barcelona: Editorial Ariel.

Contreras J. and G. Henningsen (1986), 'Forty-four thousand cases of the Spanish Inquisition (1540-1700): Analysis of a Historical Data Bank'. In Gustav Henningsen and John Tedeschi in association with Charles Amiel (eds), *The Inquisition in Early Modern Europe. Studies on Sources and Methods*, Dekalb, Illinois: Northern Illinois University Press.

Curatola, M. (1977/78), 'Aspetti della religione Quechua: tradizione e reinterpretazione', *Culture* (Quadrimestrale di Studi Storico-Culturali) 1(3): 149-66.

Duviols, Pierre (1967), 'La idolatría en cifras: una relación peruana de 1619', *Etudes Latino-Américaines* 3: 87-100.

(1971), *La lutte contre les religions autochtones dans le Pérou colonial. L'extirpation de l'idolâtrie entre 1532 et 1660*, Lima: Institut Français d'Etudes Andines; Paris: Editions Ophyrs.

(1986), *Cultura andina y represión: procesos y visitas de idolatrías y hechicerías, Cajatambo, siglo XVII*, Cusco: Centro de estudios rurales andinos 'Bartolomé de las Casas'.

*Enciclopedia universal ilustrada europeo-americana* (s.d. 1907?-30), 70 vols., Bilbao: Espasa-Calpe.

Escandell Bonet, Bartolomé (1987), 'The Persistence of the Inquisitorial Model of Social Control'. In Angel Alcalá (ed.), *The Spanish Inquisition and the Inquisitorial Mind*, Social Science Monographs, Boulder, Colorado: Columbia University Press.

Gareis, Iris (1987), *Religiöse Spezialisten des zentralen Andengebietes zur Zeit der Inka und während der spanischen Kolonialherrschaft*, Hohenschäftlarn: Klaus Renner.

(1989), 'Extirpación de idolatrías e Inquisición en el virreinato del Perú', *Boletín del Instituto Riva-Agüero* 16: 55-74.

(1990), 'La "idolatría" andina y sus fuentes históricas: reflexiones en torno a *Cultura Andina y Represión* de Pierre Duviols', *Revista de Indias* 50(189): 607-26.

(1991a), 'La metamorfosis de los dioses: cambio cultural en las sociedades andinas', *Anthropologica* (Pontificia Universidad Católica del Perú) 9: 245–75.

(1991b), 'Transformaciones de los oficios religiosos andinos en la época colonial temprana (siglo XVI)'. In Mariusz S. Ziólkowski (ed.), *El culto estatal del imperio inca*, Estudios y Memorias 2, Warsaw: University of Warsaw.

(1993), 'Las religiones andinas en los procesos de idolatrías: hacia una crítica de fuentes'. In Pierre Duviols (ed.), *Religions des Andes et langues indigènes. Équateur – Pérou – Bolivie, avant et après la conquête espagnole*, Actes du Colloque III d'Études Andines, Aix-en-Provence: Publications de L'Université de Provence.

(in press), 'Extirpación de idolatrías e identidad cultural en las sociedades andinas', *Histórica* (Pontificia Universidad Católica del Perú).

Gibson, Charles (1964), *The Aztecs Under Spanish Rule. A History of the Indians of the Valley of Mexico, 1519–1810*, Stanford: Stanford University Press.

Gonzales Martínez, José Luis (1987), *La religión popular en el Perú. Informe y diagnóstico*, Cusco: Instituto de Pastoral Andina.

Griffiths, Nicholas (1994a), '"Inquisition of the Indians?": The Inquisitorial Model and the Repression of Andean Religion in Seventeenth-Century Peru', *Colonial Latin American Historical Review* 3: 19–38.

(1994b), 'Los *hechiceros idólatras* del Perú colonial'. In R. Hitchcock and R. Penny (eds), *Actas del Primer Congreso Anglo-Hispano*, vol.III, Historia, Madrid: Editorial Castalla.

Huertas Vallejos, Lorenzo (1981), *La religión en una sociedad rural andina, siglo XVII*, Ayacucho: Universidad Nacional de San Cristóbal de Huamanga.

Kamen, H. (1987), 'Notes on Witchcraft, Sexuality, and the Inquisition'. In Angel Alcalá (ed.), *The Spanish Inquisition and the Inquisitorial Mind*, Social Science Monographs, Boulder, Colorado: Columbia University Press.

Kubler, G. (1946), 'The Quechua in the Colonial World'. In Julian H. Steward (ed.), *Handbook of South American Indians*, vol 2, (Bureau of American Ethnology, Bulletin 143), Washington, D.C.: Smithsonian Institution.

'Libro de la visita general del Virrey Don Francisco de Toledo, 1570-1575' (1924), ed. C. Romero, *Revista Histórica* VII.

Marzal, Manuel (1977), 'Una hipótesis sobre la aculturación religiosa andina', *Revista de la Universidad Católica* 2: 95-131.

—— (1988), *La transformación religiosa peruana*, 2nd edn, Lima: Pontificia Universidad Católica del Perú.

Metford, J. C. J. (1983), *Dictionary of Christian Lore and Legend*, London: Thames and Hudson.

Millones, L. (1978), 'Religión y poder en los Andes: los curacas idólatras de la Sierra Central', *Etnohistoria y Antropología Andina* (Museo Nacional de Historia, Lima) 1: 253-73.

—— (1979), 'Religion and Power in the Andes: Idolatrous Curacas of the Central Sierra', *Ethnohistory* 26(3): 243-63.

—— (1987), 'Shamanismo y política en el Perú colonial: los curacas de Ayacucho', *Boletín de Antropología Americana* 15: 93-103.

Mills, K. (1996), 'Bad Christians in Colonial Peru', *Colonial Latin American Review* 5(2): 183-218.

*The Oxford English Dictionary* (1989), Prepared by J.A. Simpson & E.S.C. Weiner, 20 vols., Oxford, Clarendon Press.

Pérez Cantó, P. (1984a), 'El Tribunal de Lima en tiempos de Felipe III'. In Joaquín Pérez Villanueva and Bartolomé Escandell Bonet (eds), *Historia de la Inquisición en España y América*, Madrid: Biblioteca de Autores Cristianos; Centro de Estudios Inquisitoriales, vol. 1.

—— (1984b), 'El Tribunal de Lima'. In Joaquín Pérez Villanueva and Bartolomé Escandell Bonet (eds), *Historia de la Inquisición en España y América*, Madrid: Biblioteca de Autores Cristianos, Centro de Estudios Inquisitoriales, vol. 1.

Pease, F. G.Y. (1968), 'El Príncipe de Esquilache y una relación sobre la extirpación de la idolatría', *Cuadernos del Seminario de Historia* 7(9): 81-92.

Ragon, P. (1988), '"Démonolâtrie" et démonologie dans les recherches sur la civilisation mexicaine au XVIe siècle', *Revue d'Histoire Moderne et Contemporaine* 35: 136-81.

*Relación de la religión y ritos del Perú hecha por los padres agustinos* ([c.1560], 1992), ed. Lucila Castro de Trelles, Lima: Pontificia Universidad Católica.

Romero, C. (1923), 'Nota final', *Inca* I(1): 69-78.

Rummel, W. (1986), 'Die "Ausrottung des abscheulichen Hexerey-Lasters". Zur Bedeutung populärer Religiosität in einer dörflichen Hexenverfolgung des 17. Jahrhunderts'. In Wolfgang Schieder (ed.), *Volksreligiosität in der modernen Sozialgeschichte, Geschichte und Gesellschaft*, [Göttingen, Vandenhoeck & Ruprecht], Sonderheft 11: 51–72.

Spalding, Karen (1984), *Huarochirí: An Andean Society Under Inca and Spanish Rule*, Stanford: Stanford University Press.

Wachtel, Nathan (1971), *La vision des vaincus. Les Indiens du Pérou devant la Conquête espagnole 1530–1570*, Paris: Gallimard.

# 10
# 'Chicha in the chalice': spiritual conflict in Spanish American mission culture

LANCE GRAHN

In his recently republished book, *The Mexican Dream, or, The Interrupted Thought of Amerindian Civilizations*, J. M. G. LeClézio declares that Mesoamerican '[d]reams and visions affirmed a relationship between the divinity and man which was absolutely contrary to the strongly hierarchical structures of the Church of the first Christian missionaries' (1993: 142). Likewise, Spaniards also perceived a nearly absolute ideological and cultural gulf between themselves and their American other. So, for them, the conquest of Indoamerica 'was the implementation of a project, conceived at the very beginning of the Renaissance, which aimed to dominate the entire world. Nothing that reflected the past and the glory of the indigenous nations was to survive: the religion, legends, customs, familial or tribal organizations, the arts, the language, and the history – all was to disappear in order to leave room for the new mold Europe planned to impose on them' (LeClézio 1993: 176). 'The silence' thus imposed by the Spanish dream, according to LeClézio,

> was immense, terrifying. It engulfed the Indian world from 1492 to 1550, and reduced it to a void. Those indigenous cultures, living, diverse, heirs to knowledge and myths as ancient as the history of man, in the span of one generation were sentenced and reduced to dust, to ashes.... To carry out such destruction it took the power of all of Europe, of which the conquerors were only the instruments: a power in which religion and morality were as important as military and economic

strength. The European Conquest of the American continent is surely the only example of one culture totally submerging the conquered peoples, to the point of completely replacing their thought, their beliefs, and their soul. (1993: 176)

This assessment of the Spanish conquest correctly captures the intended totality of the enterprise even as it overstates the actual completeness of its efficacy. Similarly, LeClézio properly focuses on the spiritual, cosmological, even theological contest embedded within both the conquest and the subsequent institutionalization of Spanish colonialism, even as he overplays the alleged disappearance of Indian cosmological and belief systems. As both the traditional Eurocentric work of J. Fred Rippy and Robert Ricard and the innovative ethnohistory of Louise Burkhart and Victoria Bricker equally remind us, Indians and Spaniards interacted in the realm of beliefs and faith systems just as they engaged each other militarily, politically, and economically. At the same time, however, late seventeenth- and eighteenth-century Indian rebellions against Roman Catholicism make clear that indigenous antagonism towards European Christianity transcended the conquest era of 1492–1550. Indigenous spirituality not only survived the initial military rush into the Americas; it persisted despite repeated attempts to quash it. In fact, some native American societies simply refused to give up their respective religions. The Amerindian dream was not in all places destroyed or displaced. It also confronted and beat back its Spanish rival.

In part, 'the fluidity of Indian religious constructs' allowed the dream to survive (Mills 1994: 112). Indian spirituality could be flexible, adaptable, and adjustable. It could accomodate a changing reality. It could 'confabulate', to use Ramón Gutiérrez's term, changing on the fringes in such a way as to leave the body of core beliefs intact. Or it could even change in an essential way, if the indigenous dreamers and decision-makers so chose, in order to preserve indigenous autonomy. As Kenneth Mills notes, 'Indians, free from the pressure to conform absolutely, might actively seek the benefits and solace offered by a growing pool of spiritual opportunities' (1994: 115).

At the same time, however, Amerindians could, and did, choose to leave their dream, their cosmos, their belief system relatively unchanged, external secular pressures notwithstanding.

James Saeger, for example, notes in his study of the Paraguayan missions that, while the Guaycuruans 'desired [the] economic security and peace' which the Jesuit missions provided,'many traditional customs survived'. Thus, the Guaycuruans retained a substantial measure of autonomy within institutionalized imperialism. (Saeger 1985: 516). Despite the colonial presence, and sometimes because of it, Indians deemed Spanish Catholicism to be intellectually and emotionally deficient and continued to find cultural strength and godly relevance in their own mythic faiths. Latin American Indians were not concerned with fitting into twentieth-century analytical paradigms of 'the cultural survival school' or the 'resistance school' (Field 1994: 238-9), but they did seek to protect and to maintain their own particular 'worldview and its rituals, social organization, and leadership' as well as to participate in the decision to defend independence or to assimilate. They consequently chose to struggle against those regimes that 'confiscated indigenous territories and resources, legislated against indigenous languages, worldviews, and religious rituals', and hoped to erase their distinctive identities. So, 'the development since the conquest of numerous forms of indigenous struggle – armed conflicts, cultural revitalization, religious movements, repossession of resources, and other manifestations – derive from the characteristics of sociocultural difference that antedate contact' (Field 1994: 238-9). Rebellious millenarianism, of course, exhibited social and political disquiet. Yet, such a defence of self also reflected the intellectual and emotional culture of spirituality and religious beliefs. The consequent *chicha* in the chalice that so distressed Spanish leaders in the late seventeenth and eighteenth centuries signalled theological rebellion just as much as it did political and military insurrection.

Susan Deeds provides an instructive case study of this kind of comprehensive resistance to Spanish colonialism in her examination of seventeenth-century Tepehuan rebellions in Nueva Vizcaya (in northern New Spain). On the one hand, she found them to be 'postconquest responses to the first serious demographic invasions by Spaniards and to the labor demands and social and psychological devastation brought by the intruders.' On the other hand, Jesuit teachings were 'simply incomprehensible', failing the test of practical utility. Tepehuanes even 'came to associate the ringing of church bells with death', indicating that they considered this religious importation to be less effective at regulating social and cosmic balance than their own traditional beliefs. The coincidence of abuse and faith led Indian leaders 'who still had access to native magic and ritual' to reject the Spanish presence, specifically targeting Spanish religion. 'They desecrated supernatural symbols such as crosses, altar ornaments, and church bells' (Deeds 1995: 87).

Similarly, the well known Pueblo Revolt of 1680 illustrated Indian spiritual rebellion. External pressures aside, Pueblo Indians 'viewed their universe as an orderly phenomenon, expressive of a reasonably good fit between perceived reality and practical experience' (Bowden 1981: 39). Even after the advent of Spanish Catholicism, many were

> willing to accept Christianity insofar as it harmonized with their customary understanding of how religion served material and social ends. Others had adopted the externals of the new viewpoint as long as it did not displace their traditional world-view and the activities integral to it. But when the new ethos and its bewildering world-view proved incapable of guaranteeing good harvest and peaceful villages [particularly during the 1670s when drought, disease, and intensified Spanish pressure especially strained Pueblo societal stability], where was the advantage in accepting Spanish ways? (Bowden 1981: 54)

The Pueblo elite, led by Popé, saw no such benefit in further accommodation to Spanish culture, and most specifically to Spanish Catholicism. That summer, Pueblo leaders decided that Christianity was more than 'an unacceptable alternative to the traditional safeguards of Pueblo survival'; it was instead a 'direct threat to their integrated religion and culture'. Priests were the 'real cause of their suffering'. Thus, in a direct and demonstrable renunciation of the validity of Christianity, 'angry warriors burned most churches and obliterated tangible symbols of clerical influence, such as records of baptisms, marriages, and burials, together with all the statuary and altars they could find' (Bowden 1981: 55).

This 'concerted act of a people determined to reject Christian civilization' (Bowden 1981: 55), however, was neither the first nor the last incident in which Indians in northern New Spain conspicuously rejected the validity of Roman Catholicism in their lives. As recently summarized by Andrew Wiget,

> There is no question that [the Pueblo Revolt of 1680] generally was a religiously motivated nativistic movement.... Throughout the pueblos of Nueva Vizcaya, anti-Catholic feeling was so powerful and religious and political power was so intertwined that even after the reconquest, when Catholicism was being reestablished, Indian peoples sometimes killed the converts among them. The most striking instance, of course, was the destruction of the Hopi village of Awatobi in 1706, but an earlier attack by Zunis had occurred against priests and perhaps some Christian Indians when Hawikuh was destroyed in 1632. Desecration of churches was a widespread component of that revolt's agenda (Wiget 1996: 477).

Two other, though lesser-known, Indian groups – the Cunas of the Darién and the Guajiros of Riohacha (in northern New Granada) – similarly demonstrated their agency in and control over spiritual encounters with Europeans. And, in terms of imperial history, the Cuna and Guajiro stances toward Spanish Catholicism posed even greater difficulties for colonial authorities, for these two groups dominated key frontier areas in the new kingdom of New Granada throughout the eighteenth century and maintained active associations with British, Dutch, and French partners. To be sure, the 'geographical and economic marginality' of the frontier – whether it was New Mexico, Riohacha, or the Darién – implied that the Amerindians living there had, a 'relative autonomous position vis-à-vis centralizing forces of state sponsored development'. But, at the same time, this effective distance between Indian and Spaniards on the frontier did 'not imply [the] cultural, psychological or social inadequacy' of the Indians' decisions nor of their subsequent actions (Whitten 1974: 4, 6). Therefore, the Guajiros' and the Cunas' resistance to Roman Catholicism, like that of the Pueblos, was not invalidated by their territorial configuration. Rather, spatial considerations contextualized, even highlighted, their refusal to adopt a religious import. Similarly, Cuna and Guajiro adjustments to certain elements of European imperial culture, such as international diplomacy and commercial animal husbandry, respectively, only accentuated the indigenous rebuff of Spanish religion.

In 1697 or 1698, for example, at least one Cuna headman willingly sought out secular European assistance. Diego requested Spanish help in order to make better use of the gold mines within his chiefly jurisdiction. About a year later, he signed a treaty with the Scotch Council of Caledonia that declared, 'Their [respective] people and dependents ... shall mutually have the liberty of commerce, correspondence, and manuring, possessing and enjoying the lands in the countries and places of their respective obedience in all time hereafter' (Hart 1929: 224-5). Eighty-five years later, the Cuna headmen Bernardo, William Hall, Guaycali, George, Urruchurchu, and Jack signed an almost identical treaty with the viceregal government of New Granada. The Cuna leaders agreed to live among the Spanish settlers as loyal and law-abiding vassals of the Spanish monarch. In return, Antonio Caballero y Góngora (1782–88) pledged to allow the Cunas freedom of travel throughout the isthmus, granted them the right to settle on vacant lands, allowed them to bear arms while planting, harvesting, and hunting, and set stiff penalties for Spanish merchants who cheated Cuna customers (Pérez Ayala 1951: 168-71).

At the same time, one Cuna clan even demonstrated a similar adaptation to European religion. In 1781 most of the residents of the village of Pinogana were 'friendly Indians who [had] become converts' (Davis 1867: 25-6). These conversions may have been bona fide changes of heart. After all, Cuna specialists have also concluded that the concepts of sin, punishment, and guilt in modern Cuna religion likely derived from prolonged cultural contact with European Calvinists (Stout 1947: 99). Or, as some early twentieth-century Cuna nationalists complained, the clan at Pinogana may illustrate that 'some of the Indians liked to take orders from the Spaniards and followed their commands' (Nordenskiöld 1938: 171). In either case, Cuna villagers were making their own decisions according to their own designs, all the while representing a minority cultural position within the larger Cuna world.

The example of Diego's request for Spanish mining expertise and labour is the exception that proves the rule of Cuna–Spanish relations. Cuna headmen generally equated the Spanish search for treasure with the corresponding Spanish objectives of discrediting their traditional religious beliefs and forcing conversion upon them. In that religious assessment, they also found spiritually wanting a Roman Catholic cosmology and ethic on one hand and, on the other, a false religiosity to be openly repudiated. In turn, the Cuna renunciation of Catholicism as preached and practised by the Spanish colonists meant largely a rejection of the Spaniards themselves and of their presence in the region.

The authoritative Cuna history of Cuna–Spanish relations depicts this interpretation with a report of the final confrontation between the headman Igaub and his Spanish antagonists. A Spaniard demanded that Iguab reveal to him the location of several gold mines in the Darién. Igaub responded with a religious story. He told the Spaniard that God formed the world and created the mines of gold, iron, and copper which made the rivers of the region flow yellow, red, and black. Not content with hearing this creation myth, the Spaniard again insisted on directions to the gold mines. Iguab retorted,

> Before your arrival I knew of your people who live in another country, but it never occurred to me to go there and take the country from you. But now you have come to our country to seek us out. But it is on account of the devil that you carry in your heart that you have come here to defraud me. God sent devils down upon the earth like a fierce downpour of rain. These devils entered your body and blasted your heart, and thanks to these demons you came to my country, and your people filled up my land and ousted me from it and robbed me of my valuable possessions. This is the way you approached me for the purpose of cheating me out of my country. (Nordenskiöld 1938: 189)

Angered at the continued rebuff, the Spaniard and his compatriots cut off Iguab's hands, and he bled to death without leading the Spaniards to the mines. The author of the history, Néle Kantule, added this commentary to Igaub's martyrdom: 'I should like to know whether the Spaniards really knew the Bible, for it appears to me that they could not have known the word of God. If they had known it, they would never have treated my ancestors so cruelly' (Nordenskiöld 1938: 193). Although biased, Scottish accounts c. 1700 substantiated this appraisal. They too claimed that Cunas rejected Catholicism because it was 'so cruel' (Stout 1947: 101).

Importantly, Néle Kantule's early twentieth-century expression of Cuna doubts about Catholic sincerity, which was firmly based on Cuna oral tradition, reiterated the same scepticism demonstrated in eighteenth-century Indian militancy. Cuna uprisings in the early eighteenth century indicate that clan leaders had learned some of the catechism taught by an earlier generation of priests, for their attacks on the missions at Cacarica and Tarena in 1719 and at Chapigana in 1727 appear to have been intentionally blasphemous. At each place Cuna raiders 'burned ... its churches, killed its priests, and stole the holy vessels' (Wassén 1940: 102). Like the Tepehuanes' and Pueblos' attacks, these Cuna strikes represented a direct assault on the Spaniards' religion. Clearly the Cuna leaders knew the cultural and religious significance of the Spanish colonists' holy places and accoutrements. Twenty years later, two well-respected Jesuits, Pedro Fabre and Salvador Grande, reaffirmed the relative weakness of Catholicism vis-à-vis Cuna cultural values. Sent to the Darién by Viceroy José Alonso Pizarro (1749–53) to determine the viability of renewing missionary work there, they found little reason to hope for the Cunas' conversion. Upon their return to Bogotá, they painted a bleak picture of Christianity's future in the Darién, simply but firmly apprising the viceroy that evangelization of the Cuna would be only wasted effort (Julián 1951: 248).

Fathers Fabre and Grande correctly linked British and French influence among the Cuna with the futility of Catholic work in eastern Panama. But to leave it at that, as the two Jesuits did, is to depreciate the Cuna rejection of Catholic Christianity on Cuna grounds. It has, in fact, been suggested that the Cunas usually got along well with the English, Scots, and French precisely because the Protestants did not try to convert them. Moreover, the Cunas' experiences with the Spaniards made it easy to believe the Protestants' claim that the Spaniards wished to convert them in order to enslave them. Equally telling, the Catholic missions among the Cunas, such as they were, remained on the geographical fringes of Cuna territory, which points to the marginality of Catholicism vis-à-vis the region's indigenous cultures (Stout 1947:

50–5). The early twentieth-century Jesuit missionary to the San Blas Cuna, Leonardo Gassó, concluded that 'these Indians do not want to belong ... to anybody' (Wassén 1940: 126–7). His comments mirrored the judgement found in an anonymous Scottish letter of 1699: the Cunas' 'love of one's Country and Liberty is ... natural' (Wassén 1940: 128). Until Christianity demonstrated its practical and theological superiority over traditional spirituality and until Christianity could, or would, bolster the Cuna sense of self and better explain the world, most Cunas chose not to change their religion.

Similarly, the Guajiros of Riohacha adopted certain elements of European colonial life, such as cattle, firearms, and trans-Caribbean commerce. They then adapted their mythic spirituality – what LeClézio calls 'dreams' – to these Spanish consequences. Most notably, they incorporated the introduction of foreign fauna and its ramifications into their tales of societal development. A simple but no less powerful myth exemplifies this indigenous connection among cattle from across the sea, clan structure, and wealth.

> Some Uliana Indians [members of the oldest and richest Guajiro clan] lived in Alta Guajira in an area called Sekúalo'u.... They often walked along the beach in search of boards. One day they found some [golden idols] and ... red jasper, which they picked up. Returning to the beach a few days later, they found a cow. It had just given birth to several calves. And that is why today the people of the Uliana clan are rich. Their grandparents found ornaments and cows. (Wilbert and Simoneau 1986: vol. 1, 119)

Some Guajiro clans opted for a Roman Catholic lifestyle in the eighteenth century as well. In the early eighteenth century, Capuchin missionaries reported the conversion of enough Guajiros to maintain high-level administrative support for the Riohacha mission. In 1704, for example, the Council of the Indies ordered two Capuchin friars into the diocese of Santa Marta to continue the work that had begun there among the Guajiros a decade earlier. As in the 1690s, Christianization progressed slowly. But in 1716 Capuchins revived two of the earliest and most important Guajiro missions. Pedro de Muniesa, prefect of the missions of

Maracaibo, Mérida, La Grita, and the Guajiro Indians, re-established the mission village at San Juan de la Cruz, not far from the port town of Riohacha, and his colleague Mariano de Olocau resuscitated the mission of San Nicolás de los Menores on the royal road between Riohacha and Maracaibo.

This missionary effectiveness continued to expand into the 1720s. San Juan de la Cruz grew to include 270 Indians. San Antonio de Orino, not far away, had 375 Indians and a 'fine herd of cattle'. Further up the Guajira coastline, 200 Indians, most of whom continued the traditional Guajiro enterprise of pearl fishing, lived under the direction of priests at the mission of San Agustín de Manaure. San Nicolás de los Menores also had about 200 Indian residents. Closer to Maracaibo, the newest of the Capuchin mission villages, San José del Rincón, housed about 160 Indians. The missions of San Pedro Nolasco, established by the bishop of Santa Marta, Antonio Monroy y Meneses (1716–42) and staffed by seculars, and San Felipe de Palmarito, a settlement of 400 Indians, also operated in the province (Soría, Cartagena, 31 March 1721, Biblioteca Nacional, Madrid, Manuscritos, no. 3570, fols 70–5; and Mena García 1982: 102–4).

Over the next thirty years, the total Capuchin mission population declined by about 15 per cent. In contrast, the number of Indians at San Juan de la Cruz alone increased to nearly 450. Those at San Antonio de Orino, the site of Indian–Spanish hostilities earlier in the century, numbered over 300. By 1759 the six Capuchin mission sites in Riohacha still housed about one thousand Indian wards (Alcácer 1959:140–1). Thus, Catholic Christianity continued to attract a Guajiro minority. The hundreds of mission Indians surely included some Guajiros who genuinely adopted the liturgy and world-view of Capuchin Catholicism in the early eighteenth century. Nonetheless, these mission residents represented only 2 to 3 per cent of the total Guajiro population. Equally important, the numbers also demonstrate that Guajiro Christians were an increasingly localized minority.

Moreover, the missions' linkages with economic activities imply that conversion was superficial. The cattle herd kept by the mission Indians at San Antonio, for example, suggests that they accepted Catholicism for economic, not cosmological, reasons. Three specific examples from 1753 similarly indicate that those Guajiros who adopted mission life did so for what they perceived to be its relatively greater economic security and for the protection of prestige and status which it likely afforded headmen. That year, three Guajiro chiefs requested Catholic missionaries. One chief, Cecilio López de Sierra, already known to local and viceregal authorities as a supporter of Spain, offered to help them reduce (i.e. relocate, convert, and 'civilize') other Guajiro clans, including the placement of missionaries among them, in return for support of his comparatively luxurious lifestyle, his political supremacy over his rivals, specifically the chiefs Coporinche and Masquare, and his greater control over local pearl fishing, brazilwood harvests, and livestock trade. Building on previous contacts between Cecilio and Viceroy Sebastián Eslava (1740–49) and on support for the arrangement among the merchants of Santa Marta, José Xavier de Pestaña y Chumacero, the lieutenant governor of Riohacha, and Cecilio negotiated the deal in the Capuchin mission village of Boronata. At the same time, Coporinche and Masquare sought similar arrangements for Spanish leverage in their own pursuits of prestige and power. Each indicated to Spanish authorities a willingness to treat with them if it would lead to the defeat of his competitor. Like Cecilio's, Coporinche's and Masquare's offers to the provincial government included a provision for the placement of priests among their respective clan members (Tarazona 1984: 41–55).

The decisions and actions of these three headmen highlight the interplay between personal wealth and Christianity in the Guajiro response to Christian missions. Cecilio, Coporinche, and Masquare saw the two as complementary. However, their peers, who outnumbered them at least five to one, if not nine to one, judged them to be contradictory forces. As Robert Lowie describes the economic functions of avuncular inheritance within the Guajiro matrilineal sib, the Guajiros had a well-established sense of personal acquisitiveness which the colonial cattle-complex did not overthrow but, in fact, accentuated.

This comparatively new type of property, along with personal possessions, theoretically passes from matrilineal uncle to sister's son in accordance with the matrilineal system of the people. However, it is only the man's eldest sister's senior son who ranks as legatee. What is more, a man will deliberately strive to thwart the principle by transferring livestock to his own sons during his lifetime, so that actually few, if any, head of cattle remain for the nephew after his uncle's demise (Lowie 1949: 366-7).

Guajiro elites undoubtedly factored into their response to Catholic missionization their perceived ability to promote thereby their status and wealth. If they saw a negative correlation, as most did, conversion carried with it serious liabilities. As Guajiros sought to protect their territory and their sense of self from the uninvited external intrusions of Christianity, they also sought to protect their commercial prerogatives. Although a few Guajiro leaders saw in the missions economic opportunity and judged direct contact with Christianity to be a useful tool, the majority rejected Christianity because it threatened indigenous economic opportunity and the benefits so derived. 'Unpacified' Guajiros knew that subjection to the Spaniards' Christ and church would end that intercourse. Religious motivation went only as far as economic and political self-interest dictated.

The Capuchins themselves admitted that the number of Indian wards hardly displayed missionary success. The priests correctly surmised that the size of the San Juan de la Cruz, San Antonio de Orino, and San Felipe de Palmarito missions did not signal long-term evangelistic prosperity. They realized on their own that the vast majority of Guajiros continued to reject Christianization and hispanization in favour of European contacts and adaptations that would promote and protect their cultural independence and political autonomy. Thus, their missions exhibited only localized and highly personal effectiveness.

Even within that diminished context, the priests proved unable to take full advantage of the opening given them by the chiefs who accepted *reducciones*. They understood that within these villages Indian Christian forms and practices were outward expressions only, that a Christian ethos merely hid a Guajiro worldview, that the Christian 'logos' had never really defeated the Indian 'mythos'. And, despite years of Capuchin presence in the Guajira, Christianity never undercut the dominant mythic metaphors of Guajiro culture. Instead, the Indian refusal of Catholicism represented, for example, the repudiation of the religion's cosmological cult of male dominance. Hispanic *marianismo* notwithstanding, early modern Christianity was a religious system largely based on the heroic attributes and actions of men, primarily designed for men, serviced exclusively on mission frontiers by men, and governed only by men. The maleness of pope, king, Trinity, and priests, and the Christian demand to accept male dominance of heaven and earth as a fundamental tenet could hardly escape the notice of an 'unequivocally matrilineal society' like that of the Guajiros. Family membership and identity, wealth, and political position passed exclusively through the mother's line. While headmen were male, each Guajiro sib over which he exercised authority was nevertheless defined matrilineally (Lowie 1949: 331; and Armstrong and Métraux 1948: 371–5).

Significantly, the eighteenth-century Guajiro dream reflected this feminine societal organization. As explained by John Bierhorst, 'the Guajiro ... preserve a fully developed mythology based on a variant of The Twin Myth'. The male hero, Maleiwa, after taking revenge on the jaguar that killed his mother, discovered fire, saved the world from the great flood, and established human reproduction. The equally central female hero, Pulowi, was the underground mother of game animals. Loath to part with her animal children, she sought destructive vengeance on hunters who killed them. So spiteful was she, in fact, that one version of the Pulowi myth portrayed her as a voracious monster whose companion, the rain spirit, brought her bottles of human blood to drink. As the protector of animals, Pulowi also became associated with domesticated cattle, mules, and horses. Moreoover, Guajiro tales commonly described Pulowi as a 'woman of great riches' who wore jewels on her ankles and chains of gold around her wrists (Bierhorst 1988: 184–6). This dual representation of the female twin that linked the divine, animals, and wealth must have strengthened Guajiro ideological resolve in the confrontation with Catholicism. For Pulowi not only connected traditional mythological beliefs with Spanish innovations and their socioeconomic impact; she also thereby demonstrated the continuing vitality and functionality of pre-Columbian belief systems, even as the material world of the Guajiros was changing in response to European imperialism. The indigenous need to adopt Marian doctrine or an overtly masculine religion and ecclesiology therefore never developed.

Nor were such spiritual realities lost on the Capuchins because the Guajiros made it clear to the priests that they and their call to adjust world-views remained unwelcome. The Capuchin friars legitimately feared Indian attack and their own deaths at Indian hands. This was not a group of evangelists that enthusiastically embraced martyrdom. As a result, the missionaries insisted on armed escorts when they ventured into Guajiro territory (Lodares 1929–31: vol. 2, 364; and Alcácer 1959: 60, 250). In 1721 Father Soría, the Capuchin rector, even requested armed escorts for his brethren from Jorge Villalonga (1719–23), the head of the newly created viceroyalty of New Granada, instead of appealing to local officials.

The pessimism inherent in these requests for military protection grew more overt ten years later. Like the Jesuits in Panama a generation earlier, the Capuchins' assessments of their own work painted another bleak picture of Christianity's influence. In 1730, for example, Father Andrés de Oliva reported that the recent vitality of the missions had entirely evaporated. 'It is impossible to bring forth any fruit (among) these Indians,' he said. 'They have not given rise to even the slightest hope in all the time that so much work has been dedicated with indefatigable zeal to their conversion' (Oliva to the Procurador General de la Religión de Capuchinos, Maracaibo, 10 June 1730, Bibilioteca Nacional, Madrid, Manuscritos, mss. no. 9728, fol. 2; and Lodares 1929–31: vol. 2, 365–6). The order did not abandon the Riohachan mission field, but neither did their fortunes change. In 1754, in the midst of a solid evangelistic decade for the Capuchins, the prefect, Andrés de Oliva, reported: 'The mission is in a deplorable state; as there [are] only five of us, there is almost nothing that we can do among the Guajiros, nor do we serve any purpose except to bear witness to their evil deeds. Fortunately, we will leave their territories to new missionaries, and we will return to Spain' (Alcácer 1959: 138–9). A similar report ten years later was even gloomier. Antonio de Alcoy, prefect of the Capuchin missions in the Guajira in the early 1760s, told his superiors that the missionaries then posted to Riohacha were growing old and disheartened. Their zeal to plant 'in the [Indians'] hearts the sweet seed of the Christian doctrine' had failed to overcome the Guajiros' 'notorious contumacy and natural arrogance'. The Capuchins' only reward for their apostolic self-sacrifice was 'tears of blood'. Because the missionaries could no longer fulfil their evangelistic mandate, Alcoy admitted, the Capuchins under his charge should be replaced (Tarazona 1984: 118-20).

The viceregal government of New Granada joined this chorus of evangelistic defeatism. Sebastián Eslava, who generally supported missionary activity, complained to metropolitan officials about Capuchin ineffectiveness in Riohacha. He too noted that the Guajiros were so independent and so in control of affairs in the Guajira peninsula that travellers in the province, including the missionaries, had to pay Guajiro tolls or take an armed escort (Blanco 1875-78: vol. 1, 62).

This discomfiture within both political and ecclesiastical circles over Capuchin results led Bishop Antonio Monroy y Meneses and Viceroy Eslava to propose jointly the expulsion of the Capuchins from the Riohachan mission field, followed by splitting the friars' territory into two districts administered out of Santa Marta or Riohacha in the west and Maracaibo in the east. That jurisdictional change would place mission governance closer to the field and so hopefully better regulate and promote evangelization on both sides of the peninsula. The vice-prefect of Capuchin missions and Philip V concurred, and the jurisdictional change was made (Blanco 1875-78: vol. 1, 62). Eslava also recommended Jesuits for the Riohachan missions, a suggestion which his successor, José Alonso Pizarro, implemented.

Localized missionary success notwithstanding, Viceroy Pedro Solís (1753-61) demonstrated considerable consternation, if not some panic, over the Guajiros' continued independence in the 1750s. He contracted with the ex-convict and former slave runner Bernardo Ruiz de Noruego to conquer the Guajiros. Accompanied by several priests, Ruiz de Noruego invaded Guajiro territory and bullied the residents of four villages into accepting Christianity and Spanish authority. But that glimmer of hope for colonial officials quickly died when Ruiz de Noruego alienated the men under his command with his bombastic, self-serving, and autocratic attitude. He also failed to subjugate any more Indians, so metropolitan officials turned against him and dismissed him from duty (Restrepo Tirado 1953: vol. 2, 190-3).

Guajiro intransigence towards Capuchin evangelization that had so frustrated both religious and governmental officials throughout the eighteenth century exploded into open rebellion in 1769.

Indian belligerence that year confirmed previous discouragement with mission work in the Guajira and shattered for the time being whatever illusions of success may have remained in Spanish thinking and planning. The hostility flared after the governor of Riohacha, Gerónimo de Mendoza, directed fifty Guajiro men chosen from the missions at Boronata, Rincón, Orino, La Cruz, and Camarones to punish nearby Cocina Indians for their continued obstinacy toward Spanish rule in Riohacha and Santa Marta. The armed mission Indians turned instead against the government and led a general Guajiro revolt against Spaniards and their influence.

Reminiscent of the decidedly anti-Catholic Pueblo revolt of 1680 in New Mexico, the Guajiro uprising targeted missions and missionaries. According to one Spanish survivor, the Capuchin priest Pedro de Altea, the Indian rebels not only burned down the churches at La Cruz, Orino, and Rincón (where the fire destroyed the Capuchin archives) but also 'in the midst of the flames profaned the sacred vessels, drinking from the holy chalices their evil chichas and liquor, which is the drink that they use for their intoxications, and [sharpened] their tools on the altar stones' (Alcácer 1959: 167). These desecrations were not accidental. No doubt the Guajiros knew full well the religious symbolism and significance of the items on which they vented their anger. The Guajiros' abuse of the Christian artifacts furnished clear evidence of their detestation of Catholicism and what it stood for, both ideologically and realistically.

Within weeks Guajiro attackers had destroyed six of the eight Capuchin missions, driven colonists and missionaries from the field, and threatened to overrun the port of Riohacha itself. The 1769 revolt disheartened the Capuchin missionaries. Unlike the 1700 rebellion, this violent and deliberate rejection of their work represented a defeat from which they never fully recovered (Kuethe 1970).

Not surprisingly, secular authorities argued that these events substantiated the futility of religious pacification and necessitated war against the Guajiros. Viceroy Pedro Messía de la Cerda (1761–72) laid the blame for the lack of Spanish progress in the Guajira directly at the Capuchins' feet. He claimed that these friars lacked the necessary 'dedication for a ministry that requires apostle-like zeal so that privations may be suffered without repugnance' (Posada and Ibáñez 1910: 97–8). The viceroy's close associate and confidant, Antonio Moreno y Escandón, even declared that the missionaries not only failed to subdue the Guajiros but, in fact, provoked them to insolence with their own evangelistic weakness and ineffectiveness (Moreno y Escandón 1936: 573–5).

What Spanish administrators continued to overlook or to dismiss was the Guajiros themselves and their persistent spiritual and religious agency. A wavering Capuchin commitment notwithstanding, the Guajiros were still in charge of their own religious fate. Christianity provided them no better explanation of the cosmos than did their own traditional mythology. Even the Guajiros' economic adaptations to European imperialism demonstrated their continuing control over their own lives. They could fully incorporate commercial pastoralism into their culture and society even as they steadfastly refused to accept fully the religion of their trading partners.

By and large, however, Christianity threatened the Guajiros' mythic structure and their cultural independence, both of which most of them refused to concede. Moreover, the 1769 revolt exhibited a deep hatred of Spanish intrusion. And it was an animosity whose roots sank deep into Guajiro self-identity. Eliseo Reclus, the famous chronicler of mid-nineteenth century Colombia, wrote that the Guajiros still hated Catholicism because they saw in it only the 'despised faith of their oppressors, the faith in whose name their ancestors were decapitated [and] reduced to slavery' (Reclus 1947: 97). The goal of Christian acculturation, he concluded, had boomeranged in Riohacha, just as it had in the Darién among the Cunas. The propagation of the Roman Catholic faith had, in general, yielded few converts. Instead, missionization had produced among the Guajiros an aversion for anything Spanish, deepened their own native religion, and promoted their 'love of liberty' (Reclus 1947: 97). In fact, the Spanish failure to dent significantly Guajiro power by the end of the century left 'the city of Riohacha ... at the mercy of the Guajiro Indians. They could, if they wished, easily destroy it' (Reclus 1947: 89).

The embrace of European economic, technological, political, and even religious benefits notwithstanding, Christianity did not, in the main, displace native beliefs and mores in the northern Indian frontiers of New Granada. Intense European contact over a century or more did not persuade most Cuna or Guajiro leaders of the religious efficacy of Christianity. Neither the recog-

271

nized usefulness of European forms of diplomacy nor the accepted profitability and value of Spanish economic forms reached
that threshold of sufficient cultural import that, in turn, would
have overturned the practicality of traditional cosmological ideologies. As Irving Hallowell explains, 'learning new religious beliefs and practices ... had to be motivated' by a sufficiently strong
materialist desire to achieve a new objective more efficiently. 'Man
is essentially a pragmatist, and a belief in the existence of supernatural beings and powers cannot be dissociated from his drives.
The reality of the supernatural realm must meet the test of experience' (Hallowell 1945: 183, 191). Despite the constant potential
of military force to support evangelization, Catholics and Protestants alike failed to overcome Amerindian values, practicality,
independence, and agency in the northern corners of New Granada. Christianity did not demonstrate its superior cultural and
spiritual functionality. Even the singular cases of missionary success appear to be as much the acceptance of Catholic veneers in
order to protect sociopolitical privilege as a genuine shift in spirituality. The friars' small successes are explained in part by Cuna
and Guajiro self-interest. Finally, as Richard Adams has said, 'the
issue of values, no matter how resolved, will at certain points be
central to the analysis of power situations' (Adams 1975: 19). In
the battle over military, political, economic, *and* spiritual power
in the Darién and the Guajira, Indian values won; European religious values lost.

## Works cited

Adams, Richard (1975), *Energy and Structure: A Theory of So-
cial Power*, Austin: University of Texas Press.
Alcácer, Antonio de (1959), *Las misiones capuchinas en el Nuevo
Reino de Granada, hoy Colombia (1648-1820)*, Puente
Común, Colombia: Los Padres Capuchinos.
Armstrong, John M. and Alfred Métraux (1948), 'The Goajiro'.
In Julian H. Steward (ed.), *Handbook of South American
Indians*, vol 4: *The Circum-Caribbean Tribes*, Washington:
USGPO.
Bierhorst, John (1988), *The Mythology of South America*, New
York: William Morrow.
Blanco, José Félix (ed.) (1875-78), *Documentos para la historia*

*de la vida pública del Libertador de Colombia, Perú, y Bo-livia*, 14 vols., Caracas: La Opinión Nacional.

Bowden, Henry Warner (1981), *American Indians and Christian Missions: Studies in Cultural Conflict*, Chicago: University of Chicago Press.

Davis, Charles H. (1867), *Report on Interoceanic Canals between the Atlantic and Pacific Oceans*, Washington: GPO.

Deeds, Susan M. (1995), 'Indigenous Responses to Mission Settlement in Nueva Vizcaya'. In Langer and Jackson (eds), *The New Latin American Mission History*, Lincoln and London: University of Nebraska Press.

Field, Les W. (1994), 'Who are the Indians? Reconceptualizing Indigenous Identity, Resistance, and the Role of Social Science in Latin America', *Latin American Research Review* 29: 237–48.

Hallowell, A. Irving (1945), 'Sociopsychological Aspects of Acculturation'. In Ralph Linton (ed.), *The Science of Man*, New York: Columbia University Press.

Hart, Francis Russell (1929), *The Disaster of Darien: The Story of the Scots Settlement and the Causes of its Failure, 1699–1701*, Boston: Houghton Mifflin.

Julián, Antonio (1951), *La perla de América: Provincia de Santa Marta*, Bogotá: Ministerio de Educación Nacional.

Kuethe, Allan J. (1970), 'The Pacification Campaign on the Riohacha Frontier, 1772–1779', *Hispanic American Historical Review* 50: 467–81.

Langer, Erick, and Robert H. Jackson (eds) (1995), *The New Latin American Mission History,* Lincoln and London: University of Nebraska Press.

LeClézio, J. M. G. (1993), *The Mexican Dream, or, The Interrupted Thought of Amerindian Civilizations*, trans. Teresa Lavendar Fagan, Chicago: University of Chicago Press.

Lodares, Baltasar de (1929–31), *Los franciscanos capuchinos en Venezuela: Documentos referentes a las misiones franciscanas en esta República*, 2nd edn, 2 vols., Caracas: Empresa Gutenberg.

Lowie, Robert H. (1949), 'Social and Political Organization of the Tropical Forest and Marginal Tribes'. In Julian H. Steward (ed.), *Handbook of South American Indians*, vol. 5: *The Comparative Ethnology of South American Indians*, Washington: USGPO.

Mena García, María del Carmen (1982), *Santa Marta durante la Guerra de Sucesión española*, Sevilla: La Escuela de Estudios Hispano-Americanos.

Mills, Kenneth (1994), 'The Limits of Religious Coercion in Mid-colonial Peru', *Past & Present* 145: 84–121.

Moreno y Escandón, Antonio (1936), 'Estado del Virreinato de Santa Fe, Nuevo Reino de Granada, 1772', *Boletín de historia y antigüedades* 23: 547–616.

Nordenskiöld, Erland (1938), *An Historical and Ethnological Survey of the Cuna Indians*, trans. Henry Wassén, Göteborg: Göteborgs Museum.

Pérez Ayala, José Manuel (1951), *Antonio Caballero y Góngora: virrey y arzobispo de Santa Fe, 1723–1796*, Bogotá: Imprenta Municipal.

Posada, E. and P. M. Ibáñez (eds) (1910), *Relaciones de mando: Memorias presentadas por los gobernantes del Nuevo Reino de Granada*, Bogotá: Imprenta Nacional.

Reclus, Eliseo (1947), *Viaje a la Sierra Nevada de Santa Marta*, Bogotá: Ministerio de Educación Nacional.

Restrepo Tirado, Ernesto (1953), *Historia de la Provincia de Santa Marta*, 2 vols., Bogotá: Ministerio de Educación.

Saeger, James Schofield (1985), 'Another View of the Mission as a Frontier Institution: The Guaycuruan Reductions of Santa Fe, 1743–1810', *Hispanic American Historical Review* 65: 493–517.

Stout, David (1947), *San Blas Cuna Acculturation: An Introduction*, New York: Viking Fund.

Tarazona, Josefina Moreno Alberto (ed.) (1984), *Materiales para el estudio de las relaciones inter-étnicas en la Guajira, siglo XVII: Documentos y mapas*, Caracas: Academia Nacional de la Historia.

Wassén, Henry (1940), 'Anonymous Spanish Manuscript from 1739 on the Province Darien: A Contribution to the Colonial History and Ethnography of Panama and Colombia', *Etnologiska Studier* 10: 102–38.

Wiget, Andrew (1996), 'Father Juan Greyrobe: Reconstructing Tradition Histories, and the Reliability and Validity of Uncorroborated Oral Tradition', *Ethnohistory* 43: 459–83.

Wilbert, Johannes and Karin Simoneau (eds) (1986), *Folk Liter-*

ature of the Guajiro Indians, 2 vols., Los Angeles: UCLA Latin American Center Publications.

Whitten, Norman Jr. (1974), *Black Frontiersmen: A South American Case*, New York: John Wiley and Sons.

# Epilogue: the middle ground

Fernando Cervantes

Ten essays on the interaction between Christianity and Amerindian religions can hardly hope to do justice to the complexity of the subject. An important lesson to be drawn from them, however, is the fundamental inadequacy of any analysis of religious interaction which centres upon the notion of conversion, especially if this notion is understood merely as the result of the presentation and acceptance of a doctrine. For any such approach will tend to exaggerate the differences and incompatibilities between Christianity and indigenous religions, overstating their doctrinal and ideological rigidity by seeing them as mutually exclusive alternatives.

All the essays in this collection, in one way or another, call the bluff of this tendency by demonstrating the essentially reciprocal nature of the interaction between Europeans and Amerindians. Equally, they all hint at the existence of an unofficial tradition that allowed, and perhaps even encouraged, the incorporation of indigenous elements into the rituals and ceremonies of Christianity and vice versa. Although it is undeniable that both official Christianity and native religious leaders often deplored and even actively discouraged such developments, it does not follow that the many unofficial manifestations that emerged from the various processes of interaction were in any way marginal, or even heterodox. If their condemnation seems almost axiomatic in the sources, it is because the majority of such documentation is at pains to present the process of Christianization as if it were a single block. The alleged clash between Christianity and 'paganism' is deliberately presented as if it had been fought out in heaven, and the narratives tend to emphasize the almost instantaneous nature of the Christian victory over the native 'gods' or 'demons' (terms often interchanged with careful deliberation), associated with the destruction of a native temple and the establishment of a Christian church. If the otherworldly tone of such narratives is deliberately intended to help the Amerindians accept the inevitability of the brutal displacement of their gods, it also inevitably overlooks those slower and more piecemeal periods of transition and adjustment which the present collection aims to elucidate.

In his analysis of a similar development in European Late Antiquity, Peter Brown has suggested that it is important 'to set the vivid certainties of many Christian texts against a wider background'. The Christianization that mattered most was the 'imaginative Christianisation of the *mundus*' – the world of ordinary experience – a process that entailed the creation of a 'common sense about the actions of the divine and the nature of the universe' which was very different from that held by the 'cognitive majority'. The vigorous flowering of a public culture that both Christians and pagans could share is especially illustrative of this process. European art in Late Antiquity, Brown explains, surprises us by revealing that the parts that we tend to keep in separate compartments – that is, those that belong to the natural and the supernatural spheres – formed a coherent whole. 'The ancient collective representation of the *mundus* gave to ... Christians ... as much as to pagans ... imaginative room for manoeuvre. Its many layers reconciled faith in the One, High God with dogged, indeed reverential, concern for the *saeculum,* that had once been ascribed, more frankly, to the care of the ancient gods' (Brown 1995: x, xi, 4–5, 11–14.)

Brown's observations are paralleled to an almost uncanny degree in this collection of essays. They all make it plain that the symbiotic interplay between Christianity and native religions cannot be adequately gauged through the writings and initiatives of missionaries and clergymen, but that it is essential to go beyond these, to the more sparsely documented contacts of Europeans of widely different backgrounds with indigenous peoples through miscegenation, through immigration and trade, and, especially, through the comparatively unspectacular, often downright suspect, ministrations of itinerant preachers and wonder-workers. The ironical incident recounted here by Murray of the missionary who sought to play the role of the juggler or shaman he was trying to discredit is by no means uncharacteristic. The lure that innumerable missionaries exerted over native peoples was often the direct result of their power as healers, and the way in which their ministrations were requested in much the same way as those of former pagan healers or shamans is a recurring trend. Indeed, it can be detected even among representatives of the official position that had most reason to fear such unholy or sacrilegious mixtures. The indefatigable Jacinto de la Serna, for instance, one of the few 'Extirpators of Idolatry' who flourished in Mexico in the seventeenth century, has left us a particularly apt example of this process. Despite his recurrent insistence that any healing powers of Indians were to be attributed to a demonic compact, he nevertheless described how he himself, in an identical context, once performed a similar healing rite on a servant of his, after failing to find a suitable homely cure, with 'a piece of bone from the saintly and venerable body of Gregorio López' (see the chapter by Pardo in this volume).

This kind of evidence is likely to clash with our preconceptions about what religious conversion should entail. But when we consider that the movement is comparable to the process of Christianization in Europe during the early middle ages, our picture is transformed. It was precisely in this twilight world of the cult of saints and their relics and miracles that the vital transfusion of Christianity with local indigenous religions was most successfully achieved. Much more than the distant bishops and priests, the presence of the missionaries must have impressed the native peoples with the sense of a new power that seemed stronger than the nature spirits of the local religious systems, but not for this reason dramatically different from their world view or religious faith. Like the holy men of Late Antiquity, these missionaries functioned as facilitators of new allegiances and patterns of observance. In a comparatively mundane way they embraced, and gradually reduced to order, a large number of conflicting systems of explanation. To quote Brown again, 'placed between Christian and pagan clients, the holy man aided the emergence of a new distinctive "religious common sense", associated with a more all-embracing and exclusive monotheism'. So although the activities of missionaries are presented in the bulk of our sources as exceptional and dramatic, they were in fact 'nothing more than a highly visible peak in a spiritual landscape that rose gently upwards from the expectations and activities of ordinary Christians'. Thus the early modern missionaries in the American continent, like their predecessors in the early middle ages, became figures of 'genuine supernatural power at a time when the holy was still stretched beyond the narrow confines of the Church' (Brown 1995: 60, 64).

These considerations suggest that the spread of Christianity in the New World should not so much be understood as the result of the teaching and acceptance of a new *doctrine*, as of the manifestation and realization of a new *power*; not so much as the result of a process of assimilation or acculturation, as of one of contradiction and contrast. The missionaries appealed to the native peoples because they were assumed to have access to the holy in its various manifestations, even to the point of being able to embrace and validate a wide range of potentially exclusive explanatory systems. At one level they were capable of identifying so closely with the local cultures that they could not fail to infuse them with the spirit of Christianity. The cult that had been paid to the local spirits of nature was readily transferred to the saints in large areas of the New World; and although there can be no doubt that many local sacred springs and mountains, stones and trees retained the devotion of the people, it is no less clear that they were consecrated to new powers and acquired new associations. More subtly, the missionaries made a strong impact because they represented a scale of values and a way of life that was fundamentally different to that of the old order. The emphasis on the interaction of free wills that the Christian idea of intercession entailed, for instance, brought the notion of mercy into a potentially impersonal cosmos. And with freedom came sin. 'The holy man', writes Brown, 'was not only a favoured courtier of his God: he was a preacher of repentance.' Any dramatic change in the course of ordinary life could be 'held to have registered the most amazing of all discontinuities – the stirring to contrition of the sinful human heart' (Brown 1995: 74-5).

None of the evidence from chronicles or hagiographies or missionary accounts of early modern Europeans in the New World leaves us in any doubt about this most basic of Christian narratives. The message of the missionaries was primarily one of divine judgement and salvation, and it sought expression in the eschatological distinction of the present world and the world to come. As such, it could not fail to make an impact upon the Amerindian world, especially after the effects of conquest had brought poverty and exploitation, illness and death to the forefront as unavoidable facts of daily experience.

This development is especially evident in Spanish America, where an intense asceticism and otherworldliness are among the most striking characteristics of the emerging Christian cultures. These qualities have often been interpreted as a mere imposition of the ascetic way of life of the missionaries, but in reality they responded to a more immediate and essential psychological need. An adequate appreciation of this development, moreover, requires us to dissociate the notions of otherworldliness and asceticism from their modern pietistic connotations of individualism, subjectivism and idealism. For the kind of Christianity that came to characterize most regions of Spanish America was collective, objective, and realist. If it is true that the world to which it aspired was outside history and beyond time, it is no less true that it was firmly believed to be the ultimate end towards which both time and history were moving.

The central place that the Catholic liturgy came to occupy in this process would be impossible to exaggerate; for in the liturgy the church claimed to possess a corporate experience and communion with the eternal world. This was no mere collection of rites and rituals: it was a fully integrated cycle which was inextricably intermingled with the agricultural year and thus readily supplanted the old ritual cycle of sacrifice around which the life of the community had revolved. But additionally, the liturgy provided a clear principle of unity and a means by which Amerindians became attuned to a new view of life and a new concept of history. For all the articles of the Christian faith were historically situated, and consequently the liturgy had over time developed into an historical cycle where the progress of humanity, from creation to redemption, was seen to unfold. Thus the cult of the saints – which presented many similarities with the old sacrificial propitiation of tutelary deities – became inseparable from the Christian liturgy, and the commemoration of the feasts of the saints provided an element of corporate identity and social continuity by which every community found its liturgical representative and patron. Indeed, it is not an exaggeration to suggest that the Christian liturgy became the one context in which the passing of the old ritual order could be explained and raised on to a plane where the cosmos had been brought back to the spiritual source that kept it in being.

At first sight the contrast with the North American case – in particular the developments after the arrival of the Puritans in New England in the great migration of 1630 – could not be more marked. A central Puritan contention, first embodied in the 1572 'Admonition to the [English] Parliament', was that any episcopacy was anti-Christian and that the whole liturgy and order of the English state church should be repudiated. Moreover, it is likely that the Calvinist view of the predestination of the elect would have accustomed the Puritan mind to the idea that the church must form an infinitesimal proportion of humanity. This attitude was in diametrical opposition both to the liturgical character of Catholic Christianity and to the reaction against the traditional Christian ethnocentricity that the new knowledge about the world was provoking among Catholic missionaries, notably the Jesuits. Hence the reasons why both the French and the Spanish Catholic cultures showed a much stronger missionary spirit and a greater understanding of the native peoples than either the English or the Dutch Puritan colonists of the east coast.

As Nicholas Griffiths points out in his introduction, several studies indicate that the Puritans emphasized the contrast between indigenous religions and Christianity by classing the former as devil worship and by adopting an attitude of marked cultural inflexibility which prevented them from infiltrating native societies. Indeed, it must have seemed merely a question of time before the whole of North America west of the Mississippi and north of the Ohio would be either Spanish or French in language and Catholic in religion, and it is revealing that the bulk of developments in British and French America that resemble the process of Christianization in the Hispanic world are the result of Catholic missionary activity. Such was the case of the Algonquian in Maine and the Maritime provinces, where French missionaries deliberately acquired the charismatic status of local shamans, thereby becoming capable of instigating a deeply charismatic Christian movement that did not do violence to local customs and which helps to explain the genuine conversion of this area, still in evidence today. (See Nicholas Griffiths's introduction to this volume.)

It is true that the Protestant colonists were in their way no less concerned with the problem of establishing a Christian society than were their Catholic contemporaries. But whereas in Spanish America the conditions of conquest and settlement served to strengthen the unitary aspects of Catholicism, in the English colonies, by contrast, it was the separatist and individualistic tendencies of Protestantism that became evident. This was in part the result of the English government's deliberate use of the colonies as a safety valve for movements of opposition at home and its consequent encouragement of emigration of religious minorities, first to New England, and later to Maryland, Pennsylvania, and Georgia. It was common for such societies to see the sect or church, and in many cases the individual congregation, as the ultimate cultural unit. Above the congregation, moreover, stood the Bible as the only standard of belief and conduct, which encouraged a moral asceticism well tuned to the strict utilitarianism of a colonial economy fuelled by that ethic of social activity and moral energy which is so characteristic of the Calvinist spirit, whether among the English and Dutch Puritans, the French Huguenots, or the Scottish Presbyterians.

It is tempting to conclude that this Puritan religious culture did not lend itself so well to the degree of interaction at the unofficial level which became characteristic of the Catholic world. But it would be a mistake to regard the several forms of Puritanism – in particular that of the Independents in England and the New England churches – as local variants of a single Calvinist model. For the official doctrine of the New England churches, ever since the great migration to Boston in 1630, was based on the theory of non-Separatist Congregationalism. What stands out in this theory is the explicit attempt to restore something of the traditional view of the dispensation of sacramental grace and the order of a visible church, as against the Calvinist doctrine of divine reprobation and election. In other words, the theory stressed that the foundation of a particular church's existence was the church covenant, and that it was precisely by the church covenant that the believing Christian became a member of the redeemed community, not merely in theory but in actual fact. This involved a belief in the practical law of justification for the saints who participated in the church covenant and who, consequently, enjoyed the same freedom of choice and the same capacity to co-operate with divine grace as the Arminian anti-predestinarians had advocated. It is therefore possible that this ideal of founding a covenant-based community in America, which was a clearly defined purpose of the leaders of the great migrations of 1630, might have left more room for interaction with the native cultures than their strict Puritanism would seem to indicate. Moreover, the colonists were constantly reminded from the Puritan pulpits that they were a people with a mission sent into the wilderness. It is true that this attitude was emphatically intellectual and much more concerned with the battle for reformation that united the colonists with their co-religionists in England than with developing an effective missionary movement. But the attitude survived and was eventually reinforced after the arrival of the Quakers in New England between 1656 and 1662, a movement that represented the opposite pole of English Puritanism and sought expression in the most complete renunciation of anything which could limit the freedom of the working of the Spirit. And although the Quakers initially provoked the intolerance of the Congregationalist regime, in the end they succeeded in defeating the Calvinist theocracy with the support of the English crown (Dawson 1971: 163–231).

Consequently, there may be many more aspects in common between the Puritan and the Catholic experiences that future studies concerned with the interaction at the unofficial level could investigate. But equally, at the opposite end of the spectrum, the inflexible and intolerant traits on the Catholic side are all too obvious. The Extirpation of Idolatries in the Andes and the inquisitorial activities against Indians in Mexico, especially under Diego de Landa, are too well known to merit further attention here. But there was also a Catholic equivalent of Puritanism that became especially conspicuous in the seventeenth-century Jansenist movement of revival, which attained its full development in the protest against the secularizing tendencies of French national culture. The movement was inspired in an exaggerated and rigorist Augustinianism. Both its founders – Jansenius (1585–1638), the Louvain theologian who became bishop of Ypres and author of the famous *Augustinus*, and the Abbé de Saint-Cyran (1581–1643), who first published the *Augustinus* and brought Jansenius's ideas into contact with the French Catholic revival associated with the Arnauld family and the Abbey of Port Royal – conceived it as a movement of moral and spiritual reform based on strict Augustinian principles. These principles emphasized the need for a practice of penance which excluded grave sinners from communion even after repentance and confession – the main issue that brought the Jansenists into a prolonged conflict with the Jesuits. It exerted a powerful influence upon the religious thought and literature of the Grand Siècle, notably in the case of Pascal, Racine, and Boileau, eventually becoming both a sect and a political party which concentrated the middle-class opposition to the Jesuits and the Ultramontanes. In spite of its ultimate defeat, it made a profound impression on French religion and culture, and beyond France its influence can be seen in the moral rigorism of some of the missionary orders that became especially active in the late seventeenth and early eighteenth centuries. The missions of the reformed Franciscans of Propaganda Fide, for instance, often led to movements of violent opposition and reaction like the Pueblo revolt in New Mexico in 1680 and the staunch resistance of the Guajiros of Riohacha and the Cuna of Darién analysed in this volume by Lance Grahn.

Here then is an area that merits future research. The essays in this collection succeed in demonstrating the essentially reciprocal nature of the interaction between Europeans and Amerindians, but they tend to do this in large measure by stressing the different levels of interaction between the various Amerindian religions on the one hand and, on the other, a form of European Christianity which, despite the Catholic–Protestant divide and the various and often conflicting trends within each tradition, is still presented as emphatically doctrinaire. More emphasis is therefore needed on the variations and contrasting emphases within Christianity itself. The official Christianity that emerges from the bulk of the documentation – the Christianity of Diego de Landa and the extirpators in the Andes, of the Puritans in New England, and of the Jansenist missionaries of the seventeenth and eighteenth centuries – is hardly characteristic of the whole of the Christian experience in the New World. Rather, it is the expression of the post-Reformation tendency in Christian thought to draw a much sharper line between the natural and the supernatural spheres, leading to a more emphatic stress on the importance of the question of belief.

As these essays make clear, however, this concern with the extent of belief invariably becomes one of the least rewarding questions that scholars can ask. In a different context, the classical scholar Richard Buxton has suggested that very few people in history would have 'felt the need to work out for themselves ... an explicit reconciliation or hierarchisation of the alternative modes of access to the sacred'. Instead, he continues, they would 'simply have accepted as normal the fact that different ways of imagining the gods were appropriate to different contexts. To ask which constituted their real belief is to miss the point.' (Buxton 1994: 162-3.) The evidence presented in this collection suggests that many of the Christian missionaries to the New World were only too aware of this caveat, and it is to be hoped that future investigations will give the various and often conflicting trends within Christianity at least as much emphasis as that currently given to indigenous religions.

# Works cited

Brown, Peter (1995), *Authority and the Sacred*, Cambridge: Cambridge University Press.

Buxton, R. G. A. (1994), *Imaginary Greece: the contexts of mythology*, Cambridge: Cambridge University Press.

Dawson, Christopher (1971), *The Dividing of Christendom*, London: Sidgwick and Jackson.

# Index

# Index

# Index

*huacas*, 188
Huailas, Francisca, 211
Huamantanga, 235
Huancavelica, 198
Huánuco, 205, 211, 213
Huarochirí, 240, 241, 242, 243, 244, 249 (n. 37)
Huaxtepec, 163, 165
*huehuehtlatolli*, 145
Huguenots, 282
Hungary, 212
Hurons, 5, 8, 9, 10, 11, 12, 16, 52, 53, 56, 58, 59, 65–87 *passim*, 87 (n. 1)
   medicine of, 76, 78, 88 (n. 9)

Ica, 200
icons, 119, 125, 130
iconoclasm, 22
idolatry, 20, 46, 68, 116, 169, 189, 230–1, 240
   Visitors-General of, 189 203, 235, 237, 239, 242
   *see also* Extirpation of Idolatry
idols, 119, 123, 125, 237, 240
I'itoi, 122
Igaub (Cuna headman), 261
Ignatius of Loyola, St, 124
*ihiyotl*, 140, 141
images, 51, 56, 68, 71, 100, 236
Immaculate Conception, 71, 72
   *see also* Virgin Mary
incense, 56, 67
Independents, 282
Indian communities, 43, 232, 235
Indians, 55, 58, 71, 81, 117, 118, 126, 190, 192, 194, 198, 235, 269, 270
   belligerence of, 270
   distrust of Spanish medicine, 169
   exempt from Inquisitorial

   jurisdiction, 196 (n. 2), 231, 232
   inability to 'tell lives', 139
   knowledge of nature, 173
   lacking in 'spiritual dimension', 53
   relations with Spaniards, 117, 118, 125, 126, 130, 151, 256
   relations with angels and demons, 169
   rude intellect of, 165
   spirituality of, 55
   passive and child-like view of, 244
   taught by the devil, 170
indigenous priests, 231
individualism, 151
indulgences, 92
Inquisition, 20, 116, 157, 177, 196 (n. 2), 201, 202, 203, 206, 207, 217, 231, 232, 233, 236
   ethnographic approach to, 201–4
   Mexican, 109
   Mexican Indian, 206, 283
   Peruvian, 204, 231
   Spanish, 204, 232
   *see also autos-da-fe*
intercession, 279
invocation, 213–14
Iroquois, 9, 10, 44, 52, 65–87 *passim*, 87 (n.1), 88 (n. 9)

Jack (Cuna headman), 260
Jacobita, Martín, 157
Jaenen, Cornelius J., 5
James, St, 243
   *see also* Santiago
Jansenism, 283–4, 284
Jansenius, 283
Jehovah, 55
Jerusalem, 105